The Second Sowing

CHANDLER PUBLICATIONS in
Anthropology and Sociology

LEONARD BROOM, *Editor*

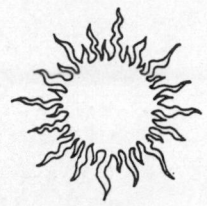

THE SECOND SOWING

Power and Secondary Development in Latin America

Richard Newbold Adams
University of Texas

Chandler Publishing Company
124 Spear Street, San Francisco, California 94105

 **S R A** Science Research Associates, Inc., 259 East Erie Street, Chicago, Illinois 60611
A Subsidiary of IBM   Distributors

for
Betty, Walter, Tani, and Gina

CONTENTS

~~~~~~

FOREWORD

~~~~~~

In 1956, after having lived in Latin America for seven years, I returned to the United States to take up academic responsibilities. At that time I was invited by the Council on Foreign Relations to prepare an essay on the state of Guatemala, as it was there that I had spent most of my time. The final conclusion of that study was that the United States, while much occupied with ways to foment economic development in Guatemala, was effectively without a policy of social change. The ideals of the American Revolution, still to be found in a residual form, turned out to be a matter of some embarrassment in the context of a national policy that consistently aided the growth of foreign capitalists and dealt with the lower social sectors on a charity basis. At that time, I frankly had no suggestions, and so refrained from making any.

In the intervening years, I—presumably among countless others—have tried to find and delineate some meaningful structure in the world of current events, most specifically one that squared with the current knowledge of social science and could provide a sufficient operational base to permit some conclusions concerning our own future behavior. As the events were current, the chief approach was via the social sciences. These fields have many findings that are probably valid but quite inconsequential, as well as many recommendations for action based on very poor theory.

There has been one severe shortcoming to much that has transpired in the social sciences as they have developed in the United States; it is one that was perhaps inevitable, but inevitability makes it no less a shortcoming. The problem is that social science in the past decades has flourished primarily as a way of understanding and predicting useful things in American life. A "useful" thing has to be useful to someone; and the someone in this instance was the upper social sector of America. Applied anthropology, marketing research, operational analysis, the behavioral-science brand of political science, and a great portion of sociology and economics all either directly served this sector or treated of things that were regarded as inconsequential, and as no threat to it. In matters concerning foreign countries, most social-scientific studies followed a generally nationalistic position of assuming that the pattern set by the development of the United States upper social sector was, in its major dimensions, that which was not only good for the peoples of the world, but was that which they would inevitably have to follow.

In defense of my colleagues and myself, I think it fair to say that the ethnocentrism was honest, if misguided. But in preparing the 1957 essay on Guatemala, I was acutely aware that my seven years in Latin America had been merely an eye opener. The job that faced me was to make sense of a series of events that could not readily be explained away either in terms of the political preferences of the developing socialist and communist countries, nor in terms of the presuppositions that lay behind American political and social behavior.

The present study sets forth some ideas on the nature of contemporary Latin America. I have first taken an evolutionary standpoint, which allowed me to view events without being too concerned with either of the world's political extremes. Then I had to find a series of concepts that applied to important factors patently working in a consistent manner wherever observed. I found one such basic concept in power. I then had to analyze what I currently knew of Latin America in terms of this power concept and its ramifications. This analysis led to notions of secondary development and dual sectors and to many of the interpretations found in Part II of this book.

The model constructed here is essentially multilineal and evolutionary. Secondary development is a concept that holds that there is a family of social structures which are necessarily different from those of primary development. The exercise of power, that is, control of the environment, is inherent in natural selection and competitive exclusion.

The manuscript was prepared in time crevices allowed by other responsibilities. The first draft was written during the academic Christmas vacation of 1963; the second draft had to wait until the next Christmas vacation; some rewriting was done in the evenings during the period of research in the summer of 1965 in Guatemala City. Chapters 11, 12, and 13 were finally rewritten during the Christmas vacation of 1966. The Postscript was prepared because of the experiences derived from the 1965 field research in Guatemala, and doubtless reflects concerns that were generated specifically by that experience.

The reader may well ask how one could presume to write a book about *all* of Latin America, when its diversities are so evident and profound. The answer is that this is not a book about *all* of Latin America, but a study of some features that condition much of the behavior that one can observe in Latin America. There is no attempt here to be panoramic, systematic, encyclopedic in coverage of the materials or to generalize to the whole. The data are selected to illustrate certain themes. Similarly, I must avow that I am concerned here with the construction of a model that will help clarify Latin American behavior specifically as it relates to the rest of the world. There is no attempt to test this model; at this point it is too crude and generalized, and its real utility is to be determined by whether it generates productive hypotheses.

My intellectual debt in preparing this volume is great, and it would be impossible as well as interminable to detail it here. The manuscript itself was read all or in part by Daniel Cosío

Villegas, Andrew Gundar Frank, John P. Harrison, Nevin S. Scrimshaw, Jorge Skinner Klee, Leonard Broom, Donald Weismann, Eric Wolf, and my wife, Betty Hannstein Adams. All contributed to increasing its clarity, reducing specific errors of interpretation or fact, and helping me to anticipate some of the critical reactions that I might expect when it is placed before a wider public. To these individuals I am very much indebted; they, however, bear none of the responsibility for the form or content of this book.

The ideas in the first three chapters have already appeared in separate essays, and I wish to acknowledge the permission granted by the Royal Institute of International Affairs, the American Academy of Political and Social Science, and the UNESCO Center for Research in the Social Sciences (Rio de Janeiro) for their permission to reproduce some of the materials that appeared in their publications. The Institute of Latin American Studies of the University of Texas made it possible for me to prepare this manuscript, as well as to pursue study of Latin America; and a grant from the Ford Foundation supported the continuing research in Central America that contributed to some of the recent thinking that went into this book. My debt to these two institutions is current and continuing.

✻ ✻ ✻ ✻

Finally, I would add that the most difficult obstacle to understanding the present world is the shower of knowledge and pseudoknowledge with which one is sodden. I regard the present study as neither an extreme nor a middle-of-the-road effort, but rather one that takes us down a somewhat different highway, hopefully pointing toward some common goals.

R. N. A.

Guatemala City, Guatemala, and Austin, Texas
August and December, 1965

PART I

Processes

Secondary Development and Cultural Evolution

Latin America today is seeking rapid development but showing discouragingly slow progress, is exhibiting rapid population growth but distressingly slow advance in technological ability and general education. It has been customary to see the problem in terms of features that must be attacked directly. Instability of government can be corrected, it is thought by some, through the institution of civil service, by international treaties, or by strengthening of the military. Rapid development, insist others, will occur as it did in the United States, that is, only when there is unrestrained private investment. The problem of the race between education and population growth is answered by a variety of attempts to provide more educational facilities and to transplant technology.

It is reasonable to suppose that most of these efforts will, in the long run, have positive effects. But it is also the case that the features being attacked have been long in the making and that the conditions that support them may continue in spite of direct efforts at change. The plan of this volume is to focus attention on an aspect of human life that has not been examined in the context of development, an aspect that I believe provides an understanding of some of the conditions that resist change. The focus is on power and how it has operated in the cultural evolution of Latin America. This chapter takes up the general nature of cultural evolution and secondary development as they pertain to the recent history of Latin America. There follows a discussion on power, and an analysis of the use of power in contemporary Latin American society. These discussions are placed here because the uses of the concepts are somewhat specialized, and they are central to the argument of the book as a whole.

Although a more detailed discussion of *power* appears in the next chapter, it may be briefly defined here as the control one party (for example, an individual, group, or organization) exercises over the environment of another. It does not refer to the concatenation of influence, favors, and the like, usually included in those discussions of power which derive from Max Weber's usage.

Evolution refers to the process among living organizations wherein new variations are constantly emerging, and natural selection eliminates all but a few. In this sense, evolution includes the various revolutionary processes and does not stand in counterdistinction to them. The innovations of a revolution are always an experiment in something new, and they must face the realities of a competitive environment just as do all other new forms. Evolution is the general framework in which new inventions and processes are seen to face up to the realities of the world in which they exist, and survive or disappear. In the present work, we will look most specifically at social inventions in this light. No matter what their political or ideological heritage, new attempts at social organization are as much a part of the evolutionary process as are new variants of the fruit fly or new modifications on rocket-powered vehicles.

Secondary development denotes a specific phase of cultural evolution that came into prominence during the course of the past century and that is especially evident today in the under-developed areas. It refers to the course development must take when it occurs in an area that was formerly a hinterland of the centers of the industrial revolution. Development in these areas, it is argued, cannot follow the sequence of changes typical of the earlier industrial centers, but must place special dependence upon social inventions for successful adaptation of the society to the increasingly rapid advances in technology. The manner in which secondary development emerged and the role played by power in social development can be best understood if we review briefly the nature of cultural evolution.

PATTERNS OF CULTURAL EVOLUTION

Like all more advanced animals, human beings live in communities. As distinct from other species, however, they invent readily, combine ideas, and produce new things—new ways of utilizing the environment. As a result, different sets of human communities have developed at different rates. No community history can parallel any other; each pattern of growth will vary and display different sets of behavior. These different sets of behavior, the patterns and elements of which distinguish one community from another and identify the peculiar nature of any given set, are referred to as the "culture" of these communities. Cultural evolution, then, refers not to biological change in man, but to the evolution of his behavioral adaptation to the environment.

Since such types of behavior may be learned by almost anyone, a central feature of cultural evolution is that early in human history it was possible for sets of communities to survive because individuals specialized in different tasks. Depending upon the luck of invention, some societies could gradually organize different kinds of specialists so that the real unit of survival of the species became an increasingly complex system. Single communities ceased to be the minimal unit of survival for the species and were replaced by complex combinations of communities. Whenever this change occurred, that particular human society evolved which Julian Steward has called a new level of sociocultural integration.

Each such advance in human living patterns involved important changes. First, innovations permitted some societies to extract a great deal more out of the environment for the same amount of human work. Put in another way, man's control over the environment increased significantly, and the per-capita production of the society similarly increased. In this sense, every major advance in human evolution has increased the power available for man's use.

A second evolutionary change was that the increase in goods derived from the greater control over the environment enabled a great many more people to live in the same habitat. Insofar as nutrition, rather than disease and catastrophe, determined human survival, an increase in production meant that a greater potential population could be supported. Increased power, therefore, meant increased population.

Third, the growth in population posed problems for basic human organization, so that the societies became internally more complex and characterized by permanent residence concentrations. Every human being has other human beings as part of his environment, and as such, they present potential problems of control. Population increase therefore introduces inherent problems of power that must be solved. The evolution of social organization has, in one of its major aspects, been the constant resolving not only of how to exercise power over human populations, but also of how to control those who have the power.

As these problems were solved, neighboring societies could

copy or reinvent these new means of exploiting the environment, of increasing the population, and of controlling the social organization. When two or more of these societies found themselves expanding and in direct conflict, the failure to achieve accommodation meant that one either destroyed or assimilated the other. For expanding societies, a simple coexistence or mutual amalgamation has been possible mainly in open environments. Each of two independent and sovereign societies, growing up with distinctive cultures, usually assumes that its peculiar culture is preferable. So it is that each major advance in cultural evolution has explicitly involved an increase in power in human society. It has, therefore, also implicitly involved for some of the members of the societies a greater chance of conflict. This risk applies inside the society, where reorganization or social invention is necessitated, and applies also between societies, where the relative control of one by the other is usually the issue.

One inherent corollary of this process has been that expanding progressive societies sometimes simply incorporated others, harnessing them as they did other parts of the habitat, limiting their expansion to that which benefited the more powerful society. This development has been referred to as the empire. Students of cultural evolution have found it convenient to distinguish between the state organization and imperial development. A state is formed by the conversion of a series of communities into a larger unit under a ruling body that has established some principle of succession. It is usually a hierarchically segmented organization, composed of a series of pyramidal, unique domains. The empire is an extension of the state and incorporates foreign areas into the structure in a similar manner. Empires, however, have differed in their social methods for binding such conquered areas to the central power. Both states and empires have been founded on agrarian systems, with related mining and workshop specializations. The industrial revolution provided a new role for colonies in that they now became suppliers of a great variety of raw materials for the home industries.

This state-empire distinction is quite useful in the Latin American case, since empires had already started in the New World when the Europeans arrived.

The European conquest of Latin America, disastrous as it was in many ways, was quite in keeping with the general course of evolution that was already under way in the area. Because of this fact—and only because of it—Latin America today has a predominantly mestizo population, a mixture of the Old and New Worlds, whereas north of Mexico we find that the Old World has essentially replaced the New. In the North, the advent of the Europeans produced a major discontinuity. The European colonists were much better equipped and more advanced in culture than were the Indians: They had firearms, the wheel, and writing, as well as varied agriculture; and they had derivative power from the home countries, insecure though it sometimes was. After some adaptation, mainly in agriculture, their superior control over the environment was clearly established.

In Mexico and southward, however, the state of indigenous culture was much higher, and empires had already appeared in two major areas. In both the central Andes and central Mexico, indigenous imperial expansions were cut short by the success of the Spanish conquest. Empires work best when conquered peoples are harnessed. The course of cultural evolution had not reached an imperial stage in North America [1] and the rest of South America; consequently, the peoples of these areas found it difficult to adjust to the new empire suddenly thrust upon them, and in many instances they died or fled. In order to see these events as part of a comprehensible evolutionary process, I shall discuss three different adaptation patterns: the preempire, the empire, and the national-industrial.

---

[1] To the Latin American, the southern boundary of "North" America is the northern border of Mexico rather than the Isthmus of Panama.

Preempire Adaptation Pattern

Prior to the emergence of the indigenous Mexican and Andean empires, the cultures of the New World were already highly varied. The range of cultures included many preagricultural collecting societies, as well as a well-developed variety of cultures based on plant domestication, with minor dependence on animals. Hunting and gathering was basic in southern South America, in scattered marginal areas in the tropical forests and savannahs, and among some riverine bands. It varied from hunting land animals to fishing and river hunting and seed gathering. In many places, such as eastern Brazil, hunting and gathering was combined with farming. Agriculture was more important among most of the forest tribes, and as one approached the Caribbean, it took clear precedence over collecting. In the north of Mexico, the same combination of bases existed, with hunting and gathering dominating in the harsher areas and farming again becoming important in the southwestern and eastern parts of the United States.

Most farming was seasonal, in forest clearings, and usually based on some variation of swidden or "slash-and-burn" cultivation. In some regions, minor states had developed, but in most areas where agriculture dominated, a "chiefdom" was the principal social organization. Where agriculture was weak or lacking, the groups tended to be viable bands, so organized that they could break up if times became hard or join together again when it was their advantage to do so. The degree of development and specialization among the preempire groups reflected both the relative abundance of the habitat and the influence of more developed neighboring groups. The basic limits on population size, density, and settlement patterns were set by the simple technology and by the particular environment. Although some communities had as many as 3,000 inhabitants, most were much smaller. Only in a few exceptionally plentiful areas, or where more effective agricultural techniques were used, did the population density exceed one person per square mile. Trade varied in importance but was especially crucial to the tropical-forest tribes where the specialization of production by community made it necessary even in areas of endemic warfare.

The effect that these peoples had on their environment depended upon the degree of skill they had in gaining a livelihood. The groups subsisting sheerly on hunting and gathering remained small in size, as their hunting technology and concern for survival in the known habitat generally prevented them from growing large enough to exterminate important food sources. Indeed, at this level of development, the habitat served to limit both the growth of the population and also, by extension, the relative power that any single group could bring to bear on an adversary. Among agriculturally based groups, the population was denser. War served to reduce the pressure of neighboring groups, although it was perceived as being motivated by demands for prestige, loot, and captives. Aside from the areas of imperial growth, the most developed areas were in the vicinity of the northern Andes and the Caribbean, where limited irrigation permitted an increase in population density in excess of five people per square mile. A statelike organization, however, was the maximum political entity to develop here. Within it social strata evolved, chiefs differentiated themselves from less powerful individuals, aristocracies appeared, and control through prowess in war and in religious activities marked an increasingly complex internal differentiation.

The geographical range of the power of any single group was usually limited and varied tactically over periods of time. Lack of extensive food storage and low production prohibited permanent coalescence of states or tribes, although federations were formed from time to time. Culturally, however, there were widespread similarities over much of the area. Dependence on manioc as a food staple dominated the tropical lowlands of South America and much of the Caribbean; maize supplemented by beans was central to the Middle American diet; and the Andes depended upon a combination of maize and tubers. Cultural interchange occurred early between Middle America and the Andes, at least in material items, and current studies suggest that later Andean societies may have been structurally similar to tropical-forest farming communities.

Empire Adaptation Pattern

About the time of the birth of Christ and in the centuries following, two areas of the New World were witnessing the emergence of regional states based increasingly on control of irrigation waters. Central and southern Mexico and· the central Andes, both highlands and lowlands, saw the development of ceremonial centers of increasing complexity, of artisanship in metals, and of highly complex weaving, and the gradual growth of state organization through warfare such as has already been described. Unlike the neighboring areas, however, these two areas (collectively called by Gordon Willey "Nuclear America" because of their signal and interrelated position in cultural development) saw the initiation of conquests that brought the lands of their neighboring states and tribes under control. A few hundred years before the advent of Europeans, major areas of Mexico and the Andes were coming under imperial control. As Julian Steward and Louis Faron have put it, "A predatory primitive society may carry out sporadic raids against its neighbors and bring home the loot. More developed states, such as those of the Central Andes, however, insist upon continued and assured access to their neighbors as tribute-paying vassals, or they expand their own political structure and incorporate their neighbors into a multistate empire."

The Incaic and Mexican empires were well established at the time of the appearance of the Europeans. The Incas, especially, had forged an imperial organization that bound together the largest sovereign political entity ever to exist on the west coast of South America. The appearance of the Spaniards in the early sixteenth century was, in a very real sense, merely the appearance of a new conquering empire. And the end of the Spanish empire, three centuries later, found the area breaking up once again into states, although states of an entirely new shape.

In all of the New World, Nuclear America was the only region where the Europeans could effectively harness the local population for imperial exploitation. The lesser states of the northern Andes and southern Middle America rapidly disintegrated. The Indians of southern South America and western North America fought back and were not ultimately conquered until long after the Spanish empire had ceased to flourish in the continental New World. The peoples of the Middle American and Andean empires, however, had been trained to the yoke of civil control under state and imperial developments. Where the people had not been so trained—as was the case everywhere else—their continued response to conquest was war, flight, death, or assimilation into the new culture. As an empire is organized before conquest, so it is likely to remain organized when conquered. The Spaniards, fresh from successful conquest of the Moors, carried the notion to the New World, and easily played the role of conquerors.

We do not know the details of the population expansion under the pre-Columbian indigenous empires, but there is reason to think that the major pre-Columbian population losses were probably similar to those that affected the Old World in the same period. The conquerors and the conquered in America had basically similar technologies; no uncommonly new forms of enforced social disorganization followed conquest, except for organizational schemes of reapportioning the population under the Incas. Long contacts through trade probably counted out epidemics due to previously unknown diseases. Thus, while specific indigenous conquests may have caused significant local and regional population losses, it is unlikely that the entire area of Nuclear America saw systematic decline in the population.

Indigenous states had developed cities; under the empires,

some grew bigger than those of northern Europe. Urbanization, dense rural populations, and highly complex trade devices were all known prior to the Spanish conquest. The empires also were on the road to spreading a common language, Aztec in central Mexico and Quechua in the Incaic Empire. Because of the Incaic bent for organization and the longer tenure of Incaic rule, Quechua dominated the Andean highlands to a degree that Aztec never achieved in central Mexico.

The indigenous empires also met restrictions. The Inca, for all their success in moving north and south in the Andean highland and coastal valleys, were never able to cope with the tropical forest, either as a natural environment or as the territory inhabited by a population to be subjugated to the empire. The Mexicans, for their part, had not been stopped by the natural habitat, but failed instead in organizing an empire that could live in peace as well as in war. They were surrounded by hostile states, and while they enjoyed control as far south as Soconusco, it was through areas of relatively uncontrolled territory. The Mexican empire was apparently ready to be toppled at the arrival of the Spanish. Had the Spanish not arrived, it seems likely that some other Middle American state might have become the major power.

The arrival of the Spanish did not initially introduce a new level of integration. There were important differences, however, between the indigenous and Spanish empires. In the first place, the Spanish homeland was far distant, and it was quite impossible to exercise direct control. The king and his ministers attempted to organize the New World in a manner even more rigorous than the Incaic; but they did so without sufficient knowledge of the environment or people. The Spanish brought with them, as George Foster has pointed out, a "culture of conquest": specific, selected patterns of what in Spain was a much more diversified design. Central to this imported culture was a deep concern for the extraction of wealth. Indian labor was necessary to satisfy both the specific needs of the colonists and the far-reaching demands of the king. For the Iberian in the New World, the Indian's labor was more important than was the Indian's good government. Spanish conquest brought the introduction of new biota, including new diseases that periodically raced through the indigenous populations during the first centuries of the conquest. Once the Indian aristocracy had been eliminated and the surviving peoples superficially converted to Christianity, the Indian population adapted to the new cultural forms. Priests, however, could not protect their new converts against smallpox, influenza, and other maladies to which God and natural selection had granted many Europeans some immunity.

The Europeans who came into the central and southern portions of the New World were familiar with urban living, with the ruling of large populations, and with problems of statecraft and imperialism. Of particular importance was the fact that the Spaniard did not arrive in the New World to find a new way of life and separate himself from alleged social or political evils at home. He came not because he was driven from home but because he was drawn to a relatively more profitable venture. This kind of colonization is to be contrasted in most respects with the colonization of North America, where peoples under pressure at home came to occupy and to work the land. They made deals with the Indians, bought their land, and—through what was in England regarded as legitimate business —took over a new land. When business or survival was threatened, wars and extermination became legitimate.

The Spanish pattern was, if anything, more orderly than the English. Colonists went under imperial control; new crops, animals, tools, town plans, and other innovations were systematically introduced. Everyone who left for the New World was, in some sense, going in the service of the empire, and was expected to add to the royal revenue, irrespective of what the individual motivations may have been. Much has been written on the relative merits of the Spanish and the English modes of taking over the New World. It has been said that the Spaniard enslaved, harnessed, and exploited the Indians, whereas the English, and later the North Americans, first cheated and then exterminated them. The Spaniards, too, were fairly effective in destroying the Indians, although, in great part, the destruction was due to disease as much as to maltreatment. It is probably not an exaggeration to say that the only reason that Indians survived anywhere in the Spanish Empire is that they were so numerous.

If one telescopes the centuries, there is, nevertheless, a magnificent symmetry in the history of the New World. The preindustrial Spaniards, entering the Caribbean, moved both north and south from Central America. From Mexico, they rapidly occupied and set up missions all the way into California. From Panama, they moved south, conquering Peru and moving across the Andes into northern Argentina. And as they were accomplishing their fantastic feats of exploration and travel, the Portuguese were colonizing on the east coast. After the major dimensions of the Iberian effort were clear, the English and French began serious colonization in the north, starting a cultural movement that was ultimately to meet the Spanish penetration in the West and Southwest of the United States. Until the nineteenth century, Spanish occupancy of South America was predominantly in Nuclear America and on the Spanish Main. It was during the great European immigration of the late nineteenth century that the La Plata region saw the influx of colonists that North America had experienced somewhat earlier. But by the time this new contigent of Europeans arrived, the land was occupied not by savage Indians, but by Brazilian, Uruguayan, and Argentinian landowners.

There was, however, an important time differential in these movements. The Spanish and Portuguese settlements were established in the sixteenth century and perpetuated on a preindustrial pattern. By the time that serious immigration was moving into North America in the later seventeenth century,

Northern Europe was already embarked on industrialization, and the migrants moved within a developing industrial area. The nineteenth-century European migration to southern South America came predominantly from southern Europe, and heavily from a proletarian class that was already adapted to playing the lesser role in industrialization. From the outset, therefore, there was a difference in the industrial role of the migrants who populated the different regions.

The Spanish and Portuguese conquests were marked by a drastic reduction of the indigenous population. This varied from their complete extermination in many of the Caribbean isles to their severe decimation on the mainland. Disease (usually in epidemic proportions), migratory and forced labor, and war probably accounted for the major losses. Just how many Indians were lost will probably never be known because of the problems of obtaining accurate demographic figures for the time of the conquest. Recent studies of colonial demography tend to set the figures higher than previously. In Central Mexico, between 1520 and 1700, the population dropped from something over 11,000,000 to 2,000,000 or less; and the Peruvian population dropped from between 3,000,000 and 7,000,000 to approximately 500,000. Specific accounts from other areas, such as northern Colombia, Honduras, and elsewhere report almost total depopulation of areas formerly fully inhabited.

As the seventeenth century drew to a close, Spanish America had suffered the increasingly drastic effects not only of population loss but also of the concomitant gradual economic breakdown that Borah has so aptly characterized as the "century of depression." By the middle of the eighteenth century, in most areas of greatest population loss the surviving populations had reached a point of adjustment. Indian communities were being encouraged to continue production within some degree of protection; reduction in New World production was increasingly recognized as a fact at home.

A new economic and ecological adjustment, based on a combination of European and New World factors, had been developing for a long time. Also apparent was a new biological adjustment, the mestizo, a selected mixture of New and Old World genes that proved increasingly adequate to the biological demands of the environment. The emergence of the mestizo as a biological adaptation has received little attention in the literature, but may be a fact of signal importance in the development of Latin American society. It was paralleled by what can only be interpreted as a highly selective survival of the Indian population. These two kinds of survivors of conquest and depopulation, the mestizo and the Indian, began to multiply in the seventeenth and eighteenth centuries, and did so in terms of a new ecological adjustment. They were the descendents of those who had survived the wars and diseases, the harsh labor, and the dislocation of the colonial period; they were biologically on the increase, and the increase was occurring at the very time that the Old World was becoming incapable of containing them politically and economically.

If the period of empire in Latin America is seen to continue from the rise of the Incaic empire in the fifteenth century to the collapse of the Spanish and Portuguese empires in the nineteenth, it marks one of the major readaptations in human cultural history. This readaptation involved the shift from local states to local empires and finally to a world empire. In the course of these changes, an entirely new and composite race emerged, a race of extraordinarily wide variety. In the eastern areas of the hemisphere, in the Caribbean and in Brazil especially, the racial variety included a heavy component of African Negro; elsewhere, it tended to vary from Indian to white.

The National-Industrial Adaptation Pattern

The collapse of the Spanish empire in the nineteenth century did not find the expanding populations of Middle and South America politically prepared for a new order. Since an empire is essentially composed of states, the discontinuance of the empire produced what one might have logically calculated: a reduction again to states. But this reduction occurred at a time when no competing empire in the classical sense was prepared to take over. Spain fell in consequence of competition in Europe; she was not eliminated by any outside competitor for Spanish America. Had the world at that time been torn between cold-war combatants, it is likely that the results would have been somewhat similar to more recent events in Southeast Asia, Africa, or the Near East. But Europe of the nineteenth century found Latin America of only marginal political interest. With relatively little pressure from the outside to threaten survival, Latin America saw the gradual buildup of the population and the appearance of large numbers of new migrants in Argentina, Chile, Uruguay, and Brazil. The question of development was seen increasingly in terms of the most successful models then available, Northern Europe and North America.

Latin America did not, however, adopt one of the crucial elements of the North American formula for development; it did not industrialize. Instead, the earlier relational pattern of agrarian support for the Old World was continued. Instead of starting factories on a wide scale, the Latin Americans incorporated larger farms. Instead of becoming a participant in industrial development, Latin America became increasingly a hinterland to the industrial revolution. Natural resources in metals, no longer extractable with a preindustrial technology, were not attacked with new techniques. The political and economic weaknesses of the individual countries could not be corrected by conquering a neighbor, despite some bloody but sometimes inconclusive wars. No new empires were building.

In Europe and elsewhere, a new event was taking place. States were taking on the trappings of industrial nations. The industrial revolution was producing, at a new level of production and population, a political evolution that paralleled the earlier rise of the state on a preindustrial level. Latin American states, tardy in industrialization, were also tardy in claiming nationhood. By the latter part of the nineteenth century, however, the direction of the effort was clear: The growing export of raw materials was seen as the way to reproduce the increasingly visible economic successes of North America and Europe. It is apparent, in hindsight, that this choice led Latin America to a position wherein development of a western European pattern was made increasingly difficult. In North America and Europe, industrialization was based in part upon hinterland production of raw materials, and this situation provided the basis for the emergence of the nation. The suppliers of raw materials were denying themselves the possibility of a parallel industrialization and nationhood.

Well into the twentieth century many Latin American states were still concerned with rather preliminary and basic issues of nationhood, such as final agreement on the location of national boundaries, spreading of a common language in the population, and development of an economy in which a large proportion of the population could participate directly.

In 1910, the adaptation of the Latin American states to their environment was still, in many respects, similar to that of 1810, except that the hinterland quality had increased profoundly. Argentina was now a region of huge estates with agrarian tenants; the colonial mines of Peru and Bolivia were being reexplored with newer techniques, and railroads were being opened from the mines to the shipping ports. Efforts at industrialization were still minimal, and available labor was scarce. Important new crops such as coffee and beef became exports to the Old World. But some signs of the future were already evident, though probably not understood. The first slum settlements composed of destitute rural peoples were appearing in Lima. Increasingly, newer commercial enterprises were arriving from North America, and United States foreign policy became, in many instances, indistinguishable from commercial relations. The long-admired northern neighbor had recently eliminated the last vestiges of the Spanish empire from America and was undertaking to send Marines into smaller countries to assure the payment of debts. The Mexican grumblings that were shortly to erupt into the first major successful social revolution of our era were being heard.

During the first half of the twentieth century, and especially following the First World War and the Russian Revolution, Latin American countries began to turn into a battlefield for international competition. Hitler's rise in Germany brought shouts of "*Sieg Heil!*" in Guatemala and Brazil. The Panama Canal became a bastion of the American defense establishment. The international communist movement fomented a revolt in El Salvador in the early 1930's that resulted in the slaughter of thousands of Indians. Latin America was arriving at the point at which the states either had to become nations in their own right or increasingly became pawns of the growing international competition.

Secondary Development

The major reason that Latin America today is developing differently from the western European countries is the relative timing of its expansion and growth. Two kinds of development patterns should be distinguished in the expansion of human societies, the primary and the secondary. Primary development produces technological inventions and discoveries and elaborates social and economic forms to handle the consequences. Western Europe and North America underwent primary development with the advent and course of the industrial revolution. Technology was learned by the industrialized laborers, but only gradually did they develop social devices such as strikes, syndicates, and unions to achieve better conditions of employment and to secure a greater portion of the increasing wealth. The prevalent attitudes of the time placed great value on the free variation necessary for trying out new things to see which would work. Free enterprise became an ideology rather than a method, and specific industrial and commercial success was seen to be possible only with the operation of "natural forces."

As primary development occurred in western Europe and North America, the need for raw materials brought in much of the rest of the world as an adjunct. Africa was increasingly cut up into colonies, and its peoples were exploited for the extraction and production of raw materials for European growth. Latin America emerged from its colonial status as a group of states with relatively few inhabitants and almost no educational system worthy of the name. The whole area thus continued with little industrialization, and its population expanded gradually into the vast, unoccupied interiors.

Latin America passed through most of the nineteenth century with basically minor technological innovations. When industrial growth began in the twentieth century, it did so through secondary development. The major difference between primary and secondary development lies in the fact that the majority of the basic technological devices and economic forms are already invented before they are introduced into the area. Therefore, industrialization in secondary development does not mean the process of laissez faire, trial and error, invention, discovery, and general innovation that permits a society to find a subsequent adjustment, but rather, the importation of the basic processes and the attempt to graft them onto a social structure already specifically organized to carry on a different kind of process. The basic adaptation of Latin America was agrarian, and when industrialization arrived, it had to adjust to the social patterns that had been established under that agrarian past. The result was the harnessing of local labor in a way reminiscent of the early colonial period, and the growth of large landed domains.

When the technical phase of the industrial revolution began, it was impossible for the trial and error of early industrial adaptation to take place. The pattern of agrarian liberalism took over in the technical-industrial process as well, gradually bringing to the fore the major differences between primary and secondary development. Secondary development involved social adaptation to newly introduced, but already elaborated, technical and economic forms and was, therefore, a process primarily of social reorganization and derivatively of technological innovation. Given this difference, there was really no available section of the society to undertake this kind of innovation except the government, and at the beginning of the twentieth century, the most progressive Latin American governments were essentially run by agrarian liberals.

Nineteenth-century Latin American liberalism complemented that of England and other northern countries.[2] Governments were controlled by, or fully allied themselves with, expansive entrepreneurial interests. Commerce, natural-resource and labor exploitation, and colonial expansion were all coherent parts of the picture. In Latin America liberalism specifically meant that the government promoted the success of enterprise and investment, foreign and domestic. The church and unprofitable agrarian holdings seemed to be directly opposed to this effort in economic development.

The Mexican Revolution serves as a historical marker for the beginning of Latin America's secondary adaptation, even though industrial technology preceded it. It was followed rapidly by the Russian Revolution. In the Soviet Union the situation differed significantly in that a huge backward area existed within the same state boundaries as an advanced area. What followed in both Mexico and the Soviet Union was the emergence of the government as the only focal organization in the society that could attempt to restructure the society so that some of the benefits that had begun to spread through the population of the more industrialized world could be realized by the masses of the underdeveloped areas.

---

[2] The liberalism of England was focused on industrialization, whereas the Latin American version obviously took the hinterland focus, and emphasized agriculture and extraction.

A basic characteristic of secondary development is that the government exercises a position of power, allowing it to juggle the factors of development to achieve a social reorganization that will not only permit but also hasten development. Secondary development, for better or worse, involves social engineering and, hopefully, orderly planning. In primary development, social engineering and planning have usually followed well after technological change; until the inventions are made, no one can plan what to do with them and with their consequences. In secondary development, however, a country finds the market full of available technology, and the question becomes one, first, of selecting that which will be most appropriate for the local scene and, second, reorganizing the society so that the new devices may become operative. There is also considerable readaptation of the devices, and this does require a great deal of local innovation. But there is awareness ahead of time that the devices have worked elsewhere, and the central problem becomes one of adaptation.

The geographical line dividing sectors of primary and secondary development are not necessarily congruent with national boundaries. As mentioned above, Russia began a somewhat secondary development entirely within its own boundaries, after having earlier embarked on a primary phase. Today, in the United States, we are witnessing a very similar process in the attempt to bring the old South into the national scene. The particular political rallying cry may differ from country to country, but the basic issue of developing an area that has been an underdeveloped hinterland is common to many parts of the world. Whether the movement goes under the banner of communism (as in Russia), nationalism (as in many areas), or civil rights (as in the United States), the problem is to adapt a more backward section of the society to the realities of a developing industrial world.

So it is that government occupies a place of extraordinary importance in the contemporary evolution of Latin America, a place that is closely comparable to the role of the major industrialists and entrepreneurs of the nineteenth century in North America and in northern Europe. Just as the enterprises of the earlier period exercised freedom of experimentation to determine just how a new machine should work or where a new railroad would prove most profitable, so the governments of Latin America today must experiment and, quite literally, invent the social, political, and administrative devices that are going to work best in furthering their own development. It has always been the case in the industrial process that an entrepreneur may look to his neighbor to see how he might do something better. So it is that the governments of Latin America today look to their neighbors who have already embarked on secondary development to get some ideas and to see how it might be accomplished more easily.

The nature of the process of secondary development has only recently become apparent. It has been obscured by a smoke screen of concern with forms of political organization and worldwide competition for power supremacy. It was not until the second half of the nineteenth century that Japan initiated the steps necessary for secondary development. Mexico, then Russia, followed early in the twentieth century. In Japan it took place under the imperial umbrella. In Russia, the writings of Marx and Lenin provided the ideological base, and the new state benefited from a world tired of war, from industrial beginnings inherited from the czarist regime, and from two decades of relatively undisturbed peace. In Russia, the presence of a segment of northern European primary development meant that a more advanced area already existed. In Mexico, however, industrialization was in its infancy, and the problem of adaptation was much greater. The emergence of the Mexican system, with its gradual strengthening of the government, took an equally long time, but the development was quite different. In both Russia and Mexico, however, an entirely new form of governmental activity had been invented, which took as its necessary field of action development in the broadest sense, including social reorganization.

A cardinal feature of secondary development is the invention of new social devices that are intended to permit the society to adapt better to the demands of expanding populations and industrial technologies. Japan, Mexico, and Russia have all provided models that any underdeveloped country might imitate, just as the economic entrepreneur has borrowed ideas from his competitors. Social inventions are of many types. Some are introduced through subtle pressure, others are demanded of a population with revolutionary zeal. Most of them originally involve only a small segment of the population and become established in a small niche in the social structure. As with many basic inventions, the component parts are almost always available somewhere for their local elaboration, and the sources are more a matter of historical interest than of functional importance. However, in this era when the immediate origins of an innovation mark it with the ideological label of either "communist" or "capitalist," the source of a social invention apparently becomes a matter of high political importance. Consequently, it is perhaps worth reviewing some of the more visible social inventions in use in Latin America today.

A significant South American social movement in the early twentieth century was *Aprismo*. The *APRA* party (*Alianza Popular Revolucionaria Americana*), initially a Peruvian affair, briefly reached out to become a Pan-American issue, then relapsed again into the privacy of Peru. The basic APRA organization was modeled on the cellular structure of the Communist Party. Because of this model, and because of the fact that the movement did have certain socialistic goals, its opponents did not hesitate to use the label of "communist" to damn the movement.

One of the major social devices currently on the increase in

Latin America is the use of guerrilla warfare. It actually has quite a respectable history in Latin America. The most successful recent effort, that of Fidel Castro and Che Guevara in Cuba, was modeled especially on the earlier methods of Augusto Sandino, the Nicaraguan patriot who carried on guerrilla war with the United States Marines and the Nicaraguan Constabulary. It is generally recognized that Sandino's guerrilla tactics, as such, never proved unsuccessful; his career was ended when he was shot while under a flag of truce.

The manner in which some Latin American governments have developed and controlled labor unions is a social invention of considerable importance. Mexico, and Argentina under Juan Perón, utilized the unions as a weapon of the government to bring pressure on other segments of the society. Another kind of organization, adopted as a bilateral arrangement between the United States and various Latin American countries, was the *servicio*. In trying to provide technical assistance during the Second World War, the United States wanted to have North American technicians work directly with Latin Americans in agriculture, public health, housing, and various other areas. The Latins, for their part, also wanted to receive such assistance, but did not want the *gringos* working directly in the governmental ministries, disrupting the customary procedures. The servicio was an organization composed of both Latin nationals and United States technicians that worked parallel to a ministry, but not in it. At their discretion, the Latin Americans could then take the men who had experience in the servicios directly into the ministries. The specific origins of the servicio are not known to the present writer, but it is certainly an instance of a social invention that has answered directly to the demands of secondary development.

Secondary development may also be seen as an attempt to resolve the problem of how to control power so that the forces of the nation can be turned toward development. In this light, the Mexican single-party system—including its relation to the government—is a remarkable invention. This party probably represents more of the interests of more of the people than does either major political party in the United States. Of particular importance is the manner in which it both concentrates and distributes control of the power within Mexico.

In the variety of agencies organized by Latin American governments to promote development, one can clearly see the trial and error of social invention in process. No two development ministries or institutes have chosen the same means. Mexico tries to keep the government well in control of most enterprises, either through ownership or through severe legal controls. Venezuela tries to establish enterprises and then encourage private investors to take over when the original costs have been met. Chile attempts to become a partner with the major enterprises in order to exercise control over them. To these cases may be added the growing role of international organizations, international banks, and the like. A full account of social inventions in Latin America would be little short of being a historical account of recent cultural history of the area. Today, of course, the Latin American countries are borrowing heavily from each other as well as from both major and minor nations of the world. The United States continues to sell its particular way of doing things, and Cuba provides a window to the devices in Russia, China, and Eastern Europe when these devices are not directly available.

Much, then, that we see in operation in Latin America today is an attempt by social inventors to solve the problem of how to accomplish secondary development. Seeing the issue in this way provides support for arguments by Latin Americans that they have to develop their own destiny. The present line of reasoning would hold that not only must they be allowed to do so but that, in fact, this way is the only way in which development will ultimately be effected within sovereign nations. There is no reason to think that the social inventions that accompanied the industrial expansion in North America can serve in the same manner for Latin American development. They would not necessarily serve even if the entire area were politically subverted and became subject to external rule. The current (1965) relations between whites and Negroes in the United States show that otherwise advanced nations are also challenged to produce social inventions to achieve secondary development in those sectors that have been left in the hinterland of the industrial revolution.

Can it be assumed that other countries undergoing secondary development can serve as models? The answer conditionally is "yes," because the problems faced in secondary development will be alike in many ways, and therefore a solution reached in one country may well provide clues for readaptation in another. But certainly not every item invented in one place can be expected to work in another, and it is even less likely that an entire social complex can be so transferred to a different setting. The fact that North American two-party democracy, or the entire Communist Party system, or the totalitarian governmental forms developed in the Old World and in Asia may not be readily exportable does not mean that some of the devices within these systems may not be viable in new settings.

Latin America, along with most of the rest of the world, is trying to catch up technologically in an ongoing process that obviously cannot be thought of as an end point. The question naturally arises as to why the underdeveloped parts of the world are only now entering the industrial revolution. The answer is, in part, because some areas (North America, Europe, and Russia) have now moved beyond the industrial revolution into a new phase of cultural evolution, the so-called "atomic age." The incredible scientific complexity and technological development leaves Latin America and all the other underdeveloped countries even farther behind than they were under their nineteenth-century agrarian mercantile system. This handicap, however, is qualified by the fact that the restrictions on the internal reorganization of underdeveloped countries by the more developed nations are beginning to drop. Colonies have become nations, and politically independent hinterland areas like the Latin American countries are increasingly challenging the controls of the export economy. Furthermore, the social inventions within some secondary-development areas are permitting a selective technological advance aimed at militarily challenging the older atomic powers. So it is that China, in many respects one of the most developed areas in the world before the industrial revolution, has force-fed her social system to achieve technological advances within limited areas.

It may be well now to ask whether it is possible for the Latin American countries to shift from solving the problems of secondary development to taking a technological lead and thereby becoming involved in primary development. The only answer we have is that this shift has in fact been successfully made in two cases: Japan and Russia. It is currently being attempted in Cuba and to some degree in Mexico. But the conditions that must be removed before it can happen are formidable.

If we examine the cases of Japan and Russia, we find that they have three features in common that seem particularly relevant. In the first place, both countries abandoned a social system whose primary power resided in the hands of a set of agrarian, landed interests. The samurai bureaucracy replaced these interests in the nineteenth century in Japan, and the communists replaced them in Russia. Second, there was an extended period of peace during which the Soviet-Russian and Japanese societies elaborated the social inventions necessary to permit an advanced technology to develop. Time was necessary because social inventions, like technological inventions, require trial and error, and some of them may be extremely costly in terms of human life and welfare. A long period of peace is needed to reorganize the society so that it can readily digest the changes demanded if increasingly complex technology is to operate.

Finally, in both cases there was an involvement in a total war in which governments and people were vitally joined in a fight for what they considered to be their own survival. This situation provided an incubator for technical development, for pushing technical advances ahead much more rapidly than would probably be possible under the quieter and less pressured life of peace. These three features do not constitute a theory, but a proposal to shift from secondary to primary development must take them into account.

Among Latin American countries, Mexico has already met the first two of these conditions. She has eliminated the grip of the agrarian oligarchy and has benefited markedly from a long period of peace. I cannot predict whether Mexico will have a total war to permit her to incubate her technology, but it is possible that she is currently trying to find ways to achieve this accelerated development without war. Argentina, a country that has seemed to many to be far advanced technologically, has not fulfilled either of the conditions that Mexico has. While Argentina has weakened the agrarian power holders, she has thus far been unable to replace them with governmental power except for military coups and the effort at social invention under Perón. It is an open question whether Perón—had he not been so pressured by opponents—could have succeeded in mending the economic damage that his regime was causing.

There is a possibility that Chile may be in the process of social invention that will neutralize the agrarian-commercial-industrial control of the country, and that the government is taking control. Brazil is more difficult to analyze because, at the moment, she apparently has exiled or jailed many of her most promising social inventors. Cuba, like Mexico, has succeeded in eliminating the agrarian controls, but is faced with such great pressures and so few resources that it is difficult to see how she can make any real progress in this direction.

In general, however, technological advance in primary-development areas continues to leave the underdeveloped areas behind. The necessary preeminence that the control of social organization has taken in secondary development has led to the use of social organization as a tool, and indeed a weapon, in the competitive struggle for advancement. The most important transformation in world relations in the present age is the emergence of underdeveloped countries to positions of power, almost irrespective of their size and technological potential. The major struggles since World War II have taken place in such countries as Korea, Vietnam, Guatemala, Cuba, the Congo, Hungary, Algeria, and others—some big, some small, but nearly all relatively underdeveloped. It would be a grave mistake to assume that these conflicts reflected a new kind of colonialism by the leading power blocs. The major difference from colonialism is that each area of conflict has its own government (or two governments). For the most part, outside powers can send in arms, but only those physically close enough are likely to join in military alliance and action. Thus, arms and advisors from Russia, China, and United States, and from various other countries pour into Vietnam, the Congo, Laos, or Cuba. In the last analysis, however, it is the local governments that must act, or the battle is not fought.

Thus it is that the lands of secondary development are in a position to extend their governmental action beyond their own borders and to involve themselves in international affairs, to treat directly with the technologically superior areas. It is the task of all such governments to so manipulate the outside powers that they obtain what they need in terms of technical aid, technical advice, arms, and other assistance without giving up their sovereignty. They can do this by tactical manipulation and control of events that are important to the welfare of the larger blocs. Essentially, the relative balance of power among the larger blocs places the smaller nations in a position in which they can manipulate power. And this situation is what is fundamentally new in the evolution of Latin America. The nations of that region, as of other areas of secondary development, are finding power in their hands. This power lies primarily in the control of the social organization, not in technological superiority.

Power

Primary development is characterized by the primacy of technological innovations. Secondary development, however, is distinguished by the central concern with control over social behavior. It is this control, the issue of power, that lies at the core of much that directs and guides the society. Although human motivations form around valued things, making and getting these things depend not only on the presence of enough control over the environment to produce them but more crucially, on sufficient control over people to compete successfully for them. Power, the control over people, is not an unchanging facet of human society. It has grown as a part of advancing cultural evolution, and as it grows, the problems it solves and generates become increasingly complex and ramifying. The concern for power is so paramount in Latin America that an understanding of its operation is indispensable. This chapter is devoted to exploring briefly the nature of power, and the following chapter, to the social structure that it has generated in Latin America.

POWER AS A SOCIAL RELATIONSHIP

The concept of power to be used here has been developed to make explicit certain important variables. Power, in general, refers to *the control that is exercised by a party over the environment;* power in a social relationship, therefore, refers to *the control that one party holds over the environment of another party.* The term "party" here is not used in the sense of "political party," but rather in the sense of "the party of the first part" or "the party of the second part." It may, therefore, refer to any individual, group, or organization.

It is important to see that power exists both in and apart from social relationships. With respect to any given social relationship, other individuals or parties may be considered as parts of the environment. (The term "environment" is used broadly here to include the entire set of features relevant to the control of all parties involved in a social relationship.) Power refers to one aspect of a total relationship, that aspect which concerns the relative control that each party has over the environments of the others. I say "relative control" because the actual control over aspects of an environment is a *tactical* matter. That is, I may have a gun, and you none; but my ownership of the gun gives me no power over you if I have made the tactical blunder of not having it in my possession.

An important quality of power, even if it is rarely reduced to this basis, lies in the fact that the various parties command different amounts of physical force that they can ultimately bring into play. Even though cultures always place some emphasis on activities and values that openly deny the importance of physical force, such beliefs have not materially reduced the tendency of man as an animal to slaughter and torture his fellows in order to convince them of his power. Most relationships are not reduced to physical struggles, however, since it is much easier to make rational decisions based on an estimate of tactical power. Rather than resorting to force, each party to a relationship sizes up the power and tactical controls of the others, and makes a rational decision about his most effective behavior under the circumstances. Each estimates his own tactical control, compares it to that of the others, and decides that he does or does not have the upper hand. By seeing power in social relationships as the rational evaluation of a situation in which an individual decides to do what is best for him, we necessarily imply a common culture.

In defining the exercise of power as the tactical control of the environment of another party, I am not referring to a stockpiling of force, but to the particular condition and manipulation of force to which different parties may have access. Kenneth Boulding, apropos of a comment that there were enough thermonuclear bombs to kill the entire world population, remarked that there were also enough hands to strangle everyone. Clearly, the issue is the tactical application of any such available force, not its mere existence. Power may be exercised when a person points a gun at another, withholds a salary check or a job promotion, places the other in jail, or threatens to withdraw his political support. Anything that threatens the environment of another person provides the basis for the exercise of power.

While an analysis of social power in any situation should contain an understanding of the physical relationships that exist (that is, what specific aspects of the environment can be controlled, how great that control is, and what are the tactical possibilities of mobilizing the control at some point in time when it needs to be exercised), it also requires an understanding of the participants' cultural and cognitive systems. Furthermore, if the parties have very distinct cultures, some understanding is required of the particular ways in which each party perceives the cognitive processes of the other. The elements of an environment and the relative tactical access to them will be variously estimated by different parties, and the indicators of power behavior vary greatly from one society to another. For the threat of power to be effectively exercised, the parties must have common understanding: they must, to some degree, share the same culture. Their ideas must be similar enough so that the power holder can predict the rational response of the other party. If one individual threatens another with a gun, the power that the first has over the second is that he may take his life. For the threat to be effective, however, the two parties must both know (or believe) that the gun is loaded and that it can, in fact, kill a person; and they must further agree that a person will value his life sufficiently to do as he is bid rather than choose death as an alternative. If a sorcerer says that he will change me into a frog if I fail to do what he wishes, we simply are not sharing enough culture for his threat to be effective: becoming a frog is not a serious alternative for me.

The fact that power claims may be forced into a direct check with reality is crucial to power wielding and affords the opportunity to learn. A person who continually threatens but is unable to make good on the threat can ultimately be ignored. Experience provides an irregular test of the validity of the way power is perceived. If no test is given, cognitive patterns may diverge widely from an external description of the same event.

Two further features of the present concept of power are important to its understanding. First, power is assumed to exist as an aspect of all social relationships. That is, whenever human beings set up a relationship, for whatever reason, there is an inherent relative control of the environment of each party by the other. Quite obviously, it is equally important to recognize that the power aspect of a relationship may not be manifest. It may be latent because of a lack of knowledge that it exists or that it could be mobilized; or it may be unused because of a rational decision to leave it unused.

Second, power in a social relationship is always reciprocal. That is to say, wherever there is a social relationship, there is always power available to *both* parties. Even a prisoner in a dungeon holds some threat to the environment of his jailer. Should the prisoner escape or should he die at an inappropriate time or under inappropriate circumstances, his jailer would be in trouble. Obviously, the differential of power between the jailer and prisoner is enormous; but the magnitude of the differential must not obscure the fact that a differential does exist, rather than total control by one and utter absence of control by the other. Were it possible to demonstrate that the prisoner had no power of threat over his jailer, that he was, as it were, forgotten, then it would have to be argued that the social relationship had ceased to exist, and with it the power aspect.

THE EVOLUTION OF POWER

An advantage of the above concept of power is that it enables us to describe, and thereby better to understand the nature of the development of power through the course of the evolution of culture, and to see how it has operated in the process of the development of increasingly complex forms of social and political organization. Essentially, what happens to power during cultural advance is that as technological ability to control the environment increases—with increased skills, new inventions, and the discovery of new resources—the amount of available power grows. Since power is defined in terms of control over the environment, the increase in this control enlarges the amount of power available. When this increase occurs, a disproportionate and differential control develops so that some individuals or sectors of the society have greater control than others.

Among very primitive human groups, the major mode of subsistence is hunting and gathering, with perhaps a little agriculture. The tools are few, both in variety and number, and constant migration is often necessary to obtain sufficient food. Under these circumstances, the relative difference of power exercised by the members of the group varies with the prowess and skills of the individual and the immediate circumstances in which he finds himself. No individual will long abuse what little margin of power he may have, since he may need the help of others at a later time. In short, the minor control that primitive societies exercise over their environment means that very little power is available to them. Their technology does not permit large production or storage of foods, so power in the sense of control over the environment cannot be accumulated.

If a group such as the above is compared with a more advanced agricultural tribe—one that harvests crops regularly and need not move to follow food sources, hence can live in permanent villages and erect houses of some complexity—then it is obvious that the agriculturalist has superior control over the environment, and that he thereby has a good deal more power than does the hunter and gatherer. Crops, such as the manioc that is almost ubiquitous throughout the Amazonian and Orinoco lowlands, can be dried and stored for a considerable period, thus making time available for doing various things. Quite literally, more power exists in such a society. Under these circumstances, particularly ambitious individuals may attempt to concentrate this power within their control. Control over other men becomes an issue and is effected through the organization of the group into networks and segments, with individuals allocating certain rights of decision making to a few for whom particular respect is held.

In broad terms, some individuals obtain a disproportionate control through gaining the obedience of other individuals. Such a group acquires an organizational structure very different from that of one with little or no power. Power permits new activities: wars for trophies may become popular and habitual; time is increasingly spent on fancy work in wood, baskets, or feathers; and individuals are singled out for special qualities which are entirely cultural and seem to have little physical basis. Witches, curers, and diviners become more important. In a very real sense, groups that achieve this kind of organization become somewhat corporate; they turn the control of power inward to some degree and invest it in some agent (collective or individual) of the group.

Internal political organization was born in such groups. In a social sense, politics could not exist in the most primitive of human groups because there was not enough power to manipulate. So long as "government" consisted of allocating authority on the basis of skill rather than power, as was the case in hunting-and-gathering bands and in incipient agricultural societies, there could be no political system based on anything other than the personal abilities of the individuals involved. However, when the advance of culture brought additional controls over the environment, it simultaneously brought increased controls over men. Politics emerged as a part of human society when the amount of power available became sufficient to be differentially allocated among the members of the society. Organized politics required the presence of enough power to necessitate an organization to control it.

The presence of power, then, depends ultimately on a technological base that provides production, which, in turn, signals control over the environment. As technological innovations take effect and more of the environment is brought under control, more time is available for doing other things. One of the most important of these "other things" to emerge is the attempt to control other people. While somewhat oversimplified, it is not incorrect to say that at this point Parkinson's First Law begins to operate. Increased control provides more time; time becomes a burden for some people, and they invent something to do with it. Once invented, of course, the activity is cultural; value is placed upon it and it becomes an important thing in itself. The culture and society adjust to incorporate the new activity and both, thereby, become more complex.

The sequence of human motivations that appear with the increment of new wealth seems to manifest constant features. Studies from two divergent societies at two quite different cultural levels have suggested many similarities. Charles Erasmus studied what Mayo Indians of northern Mexico did as their society underwent secondary development, and Richard Salisbury studied a situation in which steel tools were introduced into a neolithic New Guinea tribe. Erasmus and Salisbury found that before the change both peoples had developed methods of exchange and of accommodation to the needs of the neighbors and the community. The introduction of new wealth brought first a need to obtain symbols indicative of the power, and then a desire for luxuries. Only later did interest turn to investment, development, and increased production. The same phenomenon may be seen when an underdeveloped country suddenly has access to a large grant or loan. The first concern is for control of the newly available power, for the acquisition of luxuries, and for graft; only later is there concern for development.

The situation today is one in which the Western powers have long since developed an overwhelming amount of power that is wrapped up in military equipment, an enormous production establishment, and a level of consumption that is, in the case of the United States, of an order different from that found anywhere in the less-developed parts of the world. The total amount of power available has now reached such proportions in military terms that it seems safe to predict that either of two major nations can now eliminate most of the human race, and that within another decade a number of other nations will perhaps be capable of the same feat. Mutual destruction is, however, hardly an effective tactic, and destruction of a minor nation accomplishes nothing. Evolution has brought human organization to a point where power—control over the environment of another party—is self-neutralizing between the major powers. This standoff, of course, is not new. The relationship that now holds between the major nations is quite similar to that between stone-age individuals. Each has about the same power; hence it is to the benefit of each not to exercise it against the other. However, in areas of secondary development, where much of the power resides in control of social organizations, it is the organizing of the people—obtaining their affiliation and thereby controlling them as a part of the environment—that makes the manipulation of power a matter of specifically governmental concern. Both within countries and outside them, governments find themselves competing for and balancing power. To understand this process, it is necessary to see something of the structure of power.

THE STRUCTURE OF POWER

The Power Domain

Although cultures vary in the way power is perceived and handled, there are features common to power structure in general. A basic concept is that of the power domain. A *power domain* exists when one party has greater control over the environment of a second than the second has over the environment of the first. Since the inferior party in a power relationship always has some power too, the superior's desire to control the inferior means, implicitly, that a failure to control him is a threat to the superior. Thus, a power domain is a polar social relationship. The power of a superior becomes absolute in a relationship only when the inferior has ceased to be a social object; and if this occurs, it may be argued that the relationship has ceased to exist. It is the reciprocal quality of a power domain that establishes it, even if the parties involved may not be happy with the situation. Both Russia and the United States hold a superior-domain position with respect to Cuba. Relatively speaking, in one case, Cuba likes it; in the other, it does not. However, the qualities of the power relationship in a domain are such that Cuba can try to use either power against the other.

There are some basic kinds of relationships that develop between and within domains. Between domains the relationships involve equals; within domains, they involve unequals. The relationship between a superordinate and a subordinate power in a domain involves the inferior's recognition that the superior has limited the inferior's range of alternative actions. The superior can make binding decisions concerning the inferior, whereas the latter may only suggest, request, or beg. The superior has the discretion as to when to change the inferior's possible alternatives.

Two kinds of power sources can be distinguished in these relationships. If the superior has the control in his own hands and does not need to turn to another party for aid, then he holds *independent power* and exercises an *independent domain.* If the superior depends upon another party, however, he is exercising *derivative power* and has a *derivative domain;* he stands, in short, within the domain of the third party upon whom he depends for power.

The nineteenth-century hacienda system of Mexico and the Andes and the *estancia* and *fundo* systems of southern South America provide examples of independent power domains. Each hacienda or estancia was essentially in control of the population that was dependent upon it. There was no other authority or source of power to which the *colono,* or tenant, could turn, because the landlords had complete rights of exclusion. It may be argued that they obtained these rights from the government, and legally that was so. But in fact, they exercised these rights without help from, or recourse to, the government.

There are three different circumstances under which relations between equals occur, and they have quite different effects on the power behavior of the parties involved. They are: two inferiors within a larger domain; two independent domains with no particular area of overlapping interest; and two independent domains with an area of overlapping interest.

The presence of two inferiors within a single domain is illustrated by the relationship between two colonos, or two tenants, on a nineteenth-century *latifundio,* a landed estate. Each could receive what he needed only from the *patrón,* who could use one colono to threaten the other; that is, each was available to the patrón to use as he wished. When the issues were of no interest to the patrón, the colonos were in a situation of two equals, neither of whom had any more power than the other. Within a single domain, each inferior under these circumstances has derivative power that he may exercise against the other, providing the superior grants it. Some Latin American governments have used this method to control the internal development of their countries. It has been used by Mexico with considerable success in situations in which both business and industrial enterprise, on the one hand, and labor, on the other, were subordinate to governmental control, and the government could therefore push one or the other, depending upon the direction in which it wished affairs to move. In this relationship of inferiors within the domain of a superior, an important aspect is that one inferior may be induced by hopes of immediate gain to exercise derivative power against the other, thereby destroying any tendencies toward reciprocity between the two inferiors. When disputes and disagreements arise, they must be taken to the superior for resolution, thus enhancing his control.

Relations between two independent domains with no overlapping interests may almost be said, by definition, not to exist. They are important, however, because of what an inferior within one domain may do when the presence of another is known. Latin American national borders are very convenient for individuals who have broken the law in one country. Where extradition agreements do not exist, a bandit may skip from one sovereign state to another to avoid capture. Even more important is the fact that the right of exile is so recognized in the case of political refugees. The quality of the relationship between independent equals is essentially similar to the one described earlier for members of primitive bands within which no power is wielded; each member has approximately an equal possibility of making his neighbor uncomfortable, but equally needs him in time of stress. Each party observes the rights of the others to insure respect of his own. These relationships are characterized by reciprocities, by attempts to use influence and persuasion. Power activities in these situations consist mainly of correcting or punishing someone who has offended the group as a whole, and this is done principally by ganging up on the offender, sometimes collectively, sometimes through an individual agent representing the group. Such power activities occur in most preagricultural societies, and, indeed, in any group in which the power differential between any two members continues to be insignificant over extended periods.

When two independent domains have an area of common interest in which each controls part of the environment of a third, there exists a basis for conflict. As opposed to the situation in which a single independent power has unique control over inferiors, which we might call a *unitary domain,* the situation in which two or more independents control a third inferior is a *multiple domain.* Whether or not conflict occurs under these circumstances depends upon whether the two superiors find any conflict of interest. Certainly, the church and state in Latin America have experienced both kinds of situations. Under these circumstances the inferior may play one superior off against the other, thus extracting benefits from both, a situation that many underdeveloped countries find themselves in with respect to the world power blocs. It should be noted that it makes no difference under these circumstances, as in the Cuba case cited earlier, whether the powers involved are friendly or not.

A further characteristic of power structures is that domains appear in groups. Although there is no space to explore this characteristic here, it appears that it is for practical purposes impossible to have a single independent domain for any length of time. If one domain actually became independent and superior over all others, it would dissolve into a number of competing domains. A domain can be independent only in a community of independents. Part of the explanation surely lies in the problems inherent in competitive exclusion; part also lies in the nature of the organization of the power controllers in the superior set.

Changes in Power Domains

Power domains, obviously, are subject to change. There has been relatively little systematic research on this subject as yet, so the following observations must be regarded as preliminary. In principle, a domain may be said to have changed when one or more of the following things occur: (1) a party is added or removed; (2) two parties are incorporated as one; (3) one party splits into two or more parties; and (4) the relative control of a party over the environment changes.

The first kind of change is illustrated by the advent of a guerrilla force into the political arena. The economic and political power that the United States formerly exercised over Cuba was changed by the addition of Russia and China as parties to the domain. In this instance, Cuba left the unitary domain of the United States and came under the multiple domains of the United States, Russia, and China. The virtual abandonment of sections of Central America by the United Fruit Company is an example of the removal of a party. A more obvious case is the elimination of political leaders, such as the overthrow of Juan Perón from Argentina, Fulgencio Batista from Cuba, and João Goulart in Brazil.

The incorporation of two parties into one is, of course, in part merely the loss of one party. The resultant usually represents a broader area of control than either party had formerly. The merger of Fidel Castro with the communists provided each with a new measure of power. Incorporation usually involves the dominance of one of the parties by the other. In military coups, it is essentially the case that the military incorporates the government as a part of itself for a given period and dominates its various branches.

When a military government steps aside, decorporation or

splitting occurs, whereby two separate parties are once again created. More common cases are the splitting of political parties, a phenomenon that is related to the rather common allegiance of partisans to individuals and ideas, rather than to the parties themselves.

The most difficult kind of change to evaluate is that which involves a change in the control that a party exercises over the environment. An implicit belief in the power of an individual, for example a political leader, may obscure the fact that he is weak. Yet the time comes when a challenge dislodges him. The downfall of Batista is an excellent example. The Latin American military is enhancing its power through an increase in armament and through expansion of its sphere of action. Control is often a matter of organization; the amount of power that a party exercises may be enhanced through improved organizational changes. The proliferation of commercial, industrial, and upper-sector agrarian interests in Guatemala in the years following 1954 provided a case where the organization of the economic entrepreneurs gave them increasing power.

Besides these basic kinds of change, there is one particularly central pattern of change that has occurred with great frequency in Latin America as a way of altering the relative position, or even presence, of members of power domains. This change involves precipitating unbalance in a multiple domain. The multiple domain, it will be remembered, exists when two or more independents exercise control over a single inferior. This situation may be unbalanced by the insertion of a new party between one of the independents and the inferior in order to contest the second independent's control. If the contest succeeds, the second independent is eliminated and the first establishes unitary domain; if the contest fails, presumably the second independent has not lost all because he can maintain that he was not directly involved.

This situation was illustrated when Guatemala, under J. J.

Arévalo and Jacobo Arbenz, encouraged a variety of organizations, such as labor unions, agrarian committees, and mass organizations, to contest the power held by the landowners and foreign companies. The government set up an authority to judge these disputes; when the landowners submitted to this authority, they came under the power domain of the government to a degree that they had not been before. Similarly, when the United States wished to contest the Arbenz government, it supported Carlos Castillo Armas as the intermediate party to carry out the contest. The most obvious case of this kind of activity today is the support of guerrillas in various countries. Cuba cannot expect much success in an openly declared war on other Latin American countries, but it can train and support guerrillas who act as the intermediate powers that contest the operating governments. If some of these guerrilla forces fail, it is no great loss to Cuba; but if they win, it is clearly Cuba's victory.

This kind of change may also occur in reverse; that is, a unitary domain may be converted into a multiple domain. After Castro's victory over Batista, when Castro was still effectively under the economic control of the United States, this type of multiple domain was briefly in effect. To escape this situation, Cuba placed itself in the position of also being inferior to Russia, thereby receiving the benefit of derivative power from Russia to help contest the pressures of the United States.

The role of power in the current affairs of Latin America is obviously important, but it is probably the least systematically analyzed phase of the developments in that area. It is a thesis of this study that much of what is occurring in Latin America can be understood if we have an understanding of the place of the Latin American countries in the ongoing evolution of culture, and specifically, of the role played by power in that evolution. The growth in importance of Latin American governments is not due merely to an increase of available power within each of the countries, but also to the continuing increase of derived power from international and foreign sources. Basic to this power increase is the growing control of the environment that marks our epoch.

Dual Sectors

An imperial economic and political pattern necessarily produces a society divided between the rulers and the ruled. The Spanish empire was no exception. Colonial economic production relegated Latin America and the greater part of its population to a mercantilistic hinterland, and the continued presence of the Crown government marked off those of royal and aristocratic affiliation from the rest. The decline and breakup of the empire in the eighteenth and nineteenth centuries did not destroy this distinction, but the "ruling" class evolved into local landowners and those involved in the export trade. The society continued to reflect in its basic value system a cultural dichotomy that continues today.

The current importance of these cultural sectors has been somewhat obscured in recent works about Latin America. Both North and Latin Americans have turned their attention to what has been thought to be the appearance of a significant "middle class," "middle mass," or "middle sector." Evidence for this emergent segment of the society has been found in differentiation in occupations, in the increasingly large proportion of the population in a middle-income bracket, and the obvious dominance in the governments of individuals from other than an oligarchic elite. North American social scientists have, I believe, been a little hasty in concluding that these features signaled the appearance throughout Latin America of a class comparable to the middle class of Euro-American industrialism. In southern South America the actual migration of nineteenth-century Europeans has contributed to the development of a middle class of the classic variety. Elsewhere, however, the values of the upper cultural sector have been taken over by the growing middle-income group; they have not developed an ideology or class consciousness of their own.

Structural Parallels between Sectors

The two sectors have both distinctive value systems and different bases for social mobility. They do, however, manifest some parallel structural features. The lower sector has wealth as its goal, and the recognized means to obtain it is work. The upper sector has a variety of prestige symbols as its goal, and the means of achieving them lie in the manipulation of power. But there is continuity between the two sectors, since wealth is one of the prestige symbols in the upper sector and may be said to be the principal prestige symbol leading to mobility in the lower sector.

Two major structural parallels can be seen between the upper and the lower sectors. The lower reaches of each sector are characterized by individuals who are mainly concerned with survival within that sector system. At the bottom of the work sector are the destitute and the unskilled laborers who are principally concerned with staying alive; at the bottom of the prestige sector are what Andrew Whiteford has called the "Middle Middle Class," a group that struggles to avoid returning or falling into the work sector. Although there are important individual exceptions, both lower levels are characterized by fairly little motivation to accept innovations, a conservatism born of the need for survival.

The upper reaches of each sector contain individuals who have entered that area by virtue of successful accumulation of wealth. The successful small entrepreneur who continues to do manual labor himself while employing additional labor and investing some of his capital stands at the head of the work sector. The financially successful "new rich" occupy part of the upper portion of the prestige sector. In both cases the upper sections also include individuals who inherited the materials necessary to occupy those positions and who had the abilities to keep themselves in them. In the upper sector, the old upper class, the "aristocracy," occupies the highest prestige positions and will continue to do so as long as it has any basis of power. At the top of the lower sector there are similar survivors of the older era: the individual craftsman with a workshop or the peasant of reasonable wealth who employs a few workers but is quite uninterested in competing for the prestige symbols of the upper sector.

Since many delineations of social strata have depended on occupation, the dividing line between the two sectors has been confused. This confusion is illustrated in the allocation of the entrepreneur who rises from the lower sector but continues to work manually himself and pays little or no attention to the basic value system of the upper sector. A case in point concerns the allocation of skilled labor. In completely independent studies from different disciplinary backgrounds, Andrew White-ford, an anthropologist, and Melvin Tumin and Arnold Feld-man, sociologists, decided to allocate it to the middle stratum. Whiteford did it because his informants so classified many skilled occupations; Tumin and Feldman did it because "skilled workers enjoy relatively high incomes and prestige, due mostly to the scarcity of such workers in proportion to the high demand for their services. Further, their work, dress and attitudes toward work resemble the white-collar more than blue-collar echelons."

These kinds of distinguishing features are essentially ethnographic, are not descriptive of social structure, and provide little insight into social development. Under these circumstances, ethnic groups and social strata are essentially the same kinds of concepts. They are descriptions of styles of life or of the subjective allocation of the members of society. Social stratification has always been an unsatisfactory way to cut up a society for general theoretical purposes, although such subjective estimations are invaluable sources of insight. And the variations in form used by Tumin and Feldman are most difficult to handle in any comparative instance.

The problem faced by Whiteford and Tumin and Feldman, as well as by other analysts, is well expressed by Whiteford's recognition that a distinct discontinuity separated this "Lower Middle Class" from the rest of the middle sector: "The cultural discontinuity which existed between the Middle Middle Class and the Lower Middle Class was obviously a reflection of the traditional Spanish disdain for hand labor." The people in the lower sectors work; if one is to be mobile in the upper reaches of the society, he has to stop working. The individual who rises in the work sector through the ingenious accumulation of wealth will not automatically be able to move into the prestige sector. Mobility into the upper sector requires control of a series of prestige symbols. These symbols require some wealth, but wealth alone is not enough. Correct use of language, dress, mannerisms, and indeed an upper-stratum culture is difficult to acquire unless one grows up in or near the upper stratum. Many specific symbols are so obscured that only the initiated can know what should be learned.

The notion of dual cultural sectors is hardly a new one, but the literature on Latin America has seldom been clear as to the relationship between these sectors and the class and stratification systems which can also be distinguished. The nineteenth-century export mercantilism and economic liberalism did little to alter a class system that dated back to, and before, the conquest. The growth of the mestizo population did increase the size of an economic middle sector, a population that Eric Wolf has so aptly characterized as the "power seekers." This middle sector, however, by its very nature retained a strong orientation towards the values of the upper class. As a result, the appearance of a middle socioeconomic stratum did not mean the appearance of a middle class.

Moreover, the fact that there are two distinctive value sectors and that there is still much evidence of a two-class system does not mean that the sectors and classes are congruent. Although unquestionably related in origins, the value sectors have, in a sense, been displaced so that the people holding the values are not necessarily those associated with the appropriate class. The Latin American upper sector contains many of the owners and controllers of means of production, but not all, since some belong to the work sector. Working for subsistence is a major characteristic of the lower sector, for it is the only way one can obtain wealth. A problem also lies in the allocation of white-collar workers. Dahrendorf gives what is probably a reasonable neo-Marxian view by allocating them to the lower class, since they are completely without control or ownership and live off wages. In the present analysis, however, they are unquestionably part of the upper sector. It is by means of this placement that we can see the structural similarities in the two sectors, and see the continuity of prestige as the criterion in the upper, and the continuity of work as the criterion in the lower.

THE LOWER SECTOR

Despite their several structural parallels, the upper and lower sectors also have specific structural differences that hold over a wide area of Latin America. Much literature on the lower sector in Latin America clearly distinguishes the rural from the urban components. Not only have observed differences been emphasized, but most specific studies have focused on one or the other component. Studies of the past fifteen years, however, have revealed important continuities. Oscar Lewis challenged the simplistic, contrastive, folk-urban dichotomy of Robert Redfield and the entire tradition on which it was based. Lewis succeeded in pointing out some of the structure common to both urban and rural components of the society and in indicating that the convenient sociological dichotomy has been vastly overworked.

The picture that now emerges, supported by much additional scholarship, focuses on the increasing rural-urban migration of the past half century and permits us to distinguish three rather different kinds of cultural adjustments: (1) people raised in a rural environment, living in that environment; (2) people raised in a rural environment, living in an urban environment; and (3) people raised and living in an urban environment. Comparatively speaking, the migrants generally undergo considerable tension when entering the urban environment, and the adjustment period is eased through maintenance of strong rural bonds. The longer the migrants stay in the city, the more they take on its culture. According to Gino Germani, fewer children are born, legal marriage becomes preferred over free unions, the husband's salary increasingly provides the economic base, the domestic unit becomes more stable, urban voluntary associations are joined, more friendships develop outside the kin network, movies and newspapers play an increasing role, and children are more likely to be in school.

Kin bonds provide a major continuity spanning both rural and urban areas. Germani's examples, in which so many changes were associated with length of urban residence, did not show any very significant change in kinship bonds. The reason has been expressed by Arnold Strickon as follows:

What is necessary for survival within such a context is access to the subordinate roles which can provide at least some de-

gree of physical security in a world over which the criollo has
no control. Lacking in effective industrial answers to his problems, e.g., unions or cooperatives, he depends upon his kindred
to provide the necessary "insurance." By increasing the number
of his kinsmen, he increases the probability that at least one
of them will be in a position to be of service to him in time of
need. The wide lateral extension of kin terminology reflects this
need.

A similar importance is attached to kinship in another geographical extreme of Latin America, in the Texas Mexican population; there individuals are able to list the names and addresses of as many as 500 relatives, and, insofar as has been
determined, the specific utility of this knowledge has to do
with the help these relatives may render if one has to seek work.
Current evidence suggests, then, that the formation of an urban proletariat does not require cutting off rural relatives and
rural values. Since this continuity was not the anticipated result, we must ask ourselves why such strong kinship ties continue to survive in the face of urbanization. One possible answer may be found in contrasting the United States experience
with that of Latin America. In the United States, labor tended
to move to cities in response to a call from the cities rather than
because of agrarian pressures. The fact that many rural Latin
Americans migrate to cities because of agrarian insufficiency
rather than industrial attraction means that the effects of the
adjustment to industry may not be as strongly felt as in the
United States. This relates to Albert O. Hirschman's observation on the reason for dualistic economic development. Industrialization in Latin America, he argued, cannot readily begin
in the areas where handicrafts and cheap labor can easily
compete. If rational investment is the mode, there will continue
to be a large area of production that can be industrialized only
slowly and at later points in time. This analysis ignores the
continued importance of small-scale urban production and

service enterprises that keep many immigrants in a life style close to that of their rural counterparts. The urban work situation is similar to that of the towns, and the social organization surrounding it is supported by the same factors that supported it in the more rural setting. The same kinds of devices that provided insurance for survival in the rural area continue to operate. "The *vecindad*," writes Oscar Lewis of Mexican rural-urban migrants' settlements, "acts as a shock absorber for the rural migrants to the city because of the similarity between its culture and that of rural communities. Indeed, we find no sharp differences in family structure, diet, dress and belief systems of the vecindad tenants, according to their rural-urban origins."

Internal structural continuity seems clearly evident as regards spatial relations in the lower sector. It is important to recognize that there is also internal coherence in other dimensions of the system. Earlier we suggested that the principal basis for recognizing internal vertical structure, that is, ranking or stratification within the lower sector, was wealth. Wealth occupies this rather special position in lower-sector structure not because it is the only basis for prestige, but because it is the only basis for cumulative prestige. Prestige in the lower sector may depend upon wealth, and will depend on it whenever it is necessary to expend time and wealth in maintaining prestige. In Meso-American and Andean Indian communities, the men who are recognized as community leaders must have enough wealth to take time off to handle community matters. Beyond this requirement, however, lower-sector prestige always involves personal qualities that cannot be had by wealth or power. Quickness of mind, ability in certain tasks, selfishness or lack of it, honorableness in relations are features that cannot be inherited, accumulated, or shared. Therefore, prestige in the lower sector is not something that permits social mobility in the sense that this term is generally used. Mobility can only be had by the accumulation of wealth, since that permits a person to do things which are clearly beyond the capacity of his fellows, and it can be shared by the entire family of the individual.

The central position of work in mobility hinges on the fact that it is the only means regularly available to lower-sector individuals to obtain wealth. Buried treasure, the lottery, and other devices both legendary and real might catapult an individual into a position of wealth but cannot be depended upon by the rational upward-mobile individual. The value of work in the lower sector revolves around the role it is perceived to play in an individual's aspirations. It ranges from high value to disparagement. While these aspirations vary superficially from one place to another, the pattern is in fact highly consistent. The central issue is whether the amount of wealth that one can accumulate within the going system is sufficient to achieve any of the valued symbols visible within the total system. In most instances it is not.

Whiteford quotes an apparently energetic but puzzled entrepreneur from Queretaro, Mexico, on the subject of one of his dairy-farm employees:

I have a dairy farm and I have Indian workers in charge of it. I told them, "For every liter more of milk I will raise your wages one-fourth of a centavo." They said, "Oh, sí, señor, sí señor," and smiled. What happened? Nothing. I know they could have raised the milk production, but they weren't interested. . . . Some of the Indians are skillful, and some of them are good workers, but they have no ambition.

One needs to know little of Mexican dairy economies to recognize that the proposed rate would require an astronomical increase in milk production to produce any significant increase in wealth for the Indian. No special sociological insight is necessary to see why extra work is not popular. Since wages are judged in terms of the lower sector and prices of most valued items are set by the upper sector, it is only under unusual circumstances that work will permit the accumulation of sufficient wealth to obtain the values that are purchasable.

If we look at cases in which work has been highly valued, as among Guatemalan Indian village dwellers, it is clear that the gains available are significant within the somewhat closed value system of those villages. Achievement in the Indian cultural system is possible through exercising important community positions. Gaining these positions requires some wealth and demonstrated ability, but the amount of wealth necessary is achievable. Under these circumstances, work is valued.

This discussion of vertical structure makes no initial distinction between what might be called "ethnic groups" and those that compose the general "civil population." The reason should now be obvious. Although sedentary agricultural Indians and other such distinctive cultural entities have sometimes violently divergent visible cultures, an understanding of their behavior within the system as a whole and an understanding of the system itself requires that we assume that centuries of interaction have provided a common structure and that this common structure will be reflected in behavior.

THE UPPER SECTOR

The upper sector comprises the entire set of upper strata and most of the middle strata ordinarily distinguished in sociological analyses and in the common view of the contemporary Latin American. In Whiteford's analysis of Popayán and Queretaro, it would include everything from his "Middle Class" upwards. All the people included within this range have a common mobility structure, since both the goals and the means for their achievement are the same. The importance of wealth to this sector lies in the fact that it provides the means for obtaining and maintaining the symbols that demonstrate the upper-sector status of individuals. So it is that the income of a white-collar worker may well be less than that of a lower-sector entrepreneur, but that wealth is used to obtain certain household appliances and equipment, clothes, brand cigarettes, and other material items that are presumed to signal an individual's upper-sector membership. The *empleado* takes great pains not to be confused with the manual laborer.

The structural continuity of rural and urban components exists through the direct linkage of a rural "local upper class" with the so-called "middle stratum." The urban middle stratum includes bureaucratic and white-collar employees, businessmen, and probably most professional people. Government, business, and industry are operated through their activities, and it is generally to their advantage that these institutions be maintained. Consequently, their interests are best met when salaries and profits flow with regularity. The provincial or local upper class (including as it does the local "importers" and "exporters") also benefits from this kind of stability. Rural and urban elements are cemented by kinship here as in the lower sector.

The upper sector is distinctive in having other means besides wealth for mobility within the sector. When Eric Wolf characterized the emergent mestizo population of the past century and a half as "the power seekers," he identified—and correctly, I believe—power as the crucial feature of the upper sector. Power seeking is not limited just to the mestizos in the upper sector. Power is a process that exists as a part of many relationships, and anyone who fails to keep the process going may suddenly find himself without it. Wolf's characterization should, therefore, be extended to the entire upper sector. It would not be too exaggerated to say that the entire internal structure of the upper sector may be seen as a series of relationships established and altered by virtue of a constant concern for gaining, retaining, and using power.

This upper-sector structure has been little analyzed, although Anthony Leeds has made a valuable sortie in his brief study of career patterns in Brazil. The reasons for our ignorance are multiple. In the first place, most sociologists and social anthropologists have tended to examine systems only when they were aware of the boundaries of those systems. Thus we have studies of communities, kin groups, social classes or strata, even whole societies. Since the concept of a middle class is dominant in the ideology of Western social science, it has been assumed that the structure relating the middle and upper classes is less important than the dividing line between them.

In the second place, as a field exercise, an adequate exploration of the upper sector of the society requires rapport at a financial and stylistic level that is beyond the ability of middle-income sociologists and anthropologists. The sociologist who gains the knowledge and ability to enter the higher areas of the upper sector would be tempted to stay there rather than pursue sociological studies. Entrance into the higher parts of the upper sector by marriage inevitably places the student in the awkward position of betraying his kin if he studies them. Fortunately or unfortunately, the student of modern society cannot behave with the ethnographic irresponsibility that marks the work of a few anthropologists who, when they write up their materials, assume their reports will never be read by the members of the society under study. A reporter on the upper class will have his work thoroughly criticized and perhaps shredded by his subjects.

Third, there are surprisingly few concepts in sociology for dealing with power-based upper-sector mobility. Most middle-level sociological concepts have developed in the Euro-American tradition in which this kind of mobility has not been considered a dominant characteristic. This ethnocentric bias (that has, incidentally, diffused to the Latin Americas themselves since much of their training has been in European hands) is related to the fact that the very strangeness of the phenomenon of power-based mobility has led interpreters to regard it as inexplicable or antirational. The power-motivated behavior is seen to exist in the interstices of a structure that is thought to be immature or underdeveloped. In short, what might better be regarded as central features of the upper sector of Latin American society have been characterized as irregularities that the Latins will someday outgrow.

The activities generated by the concern with power are multiple and complex. Since there is a wide variety of bases for power, the effective power seeker is one who not only uses effectively the particular bases that he has at hand, but also extends his activities over a wide range of such bases. By way of example—and also to indicate the kind of role that wealth plays—it is not enough to have control over the incomes of a set of individuals; one must also be able to call on a wide network of kinsmen and *compadres,* have many acquaintances through associations with sports clubs, political groups, or former fellow students, and have established the pattern of many small reciprocal obligations. The exercise of power in Latin America (and presumably, in principle, elsewhere) does not depend on the total amount of such contacts and controls, but on the ability to mobilize what is necessary for tactical advantage at a given point in time. Not only do individuals move up within the upper sector, but they also move down. An inability to maintain the symbols of higher status within the prestige sector inevitably results in downward mobility. With the changing bases of power (to be discussed later), it becomes increasingly important to maintain a wide series of contacts. Flexibility in organization is crucial, and consequently a major kind of organization is a set of somewhat shifting, interlocking cliques.

Leeds, in his exploration of the career aspect of this kind of structure in Brazil, holds that this structure is peculiar to what he regards as a transition from a "static agrarian" society to an "expansive industrial" society. I do not think that the major features of this kind of power structure are necessarily transitional phenomena, nor must we anticipate that Latin American society will eventually shift over to a structure more like that of Anglo-American culture. The nature of demographic expansion, economic development, expansive nationalism, and international power manipulations is such that this kind of structure may well endure indefinitely.

Among the many things that we do not know about the upper sector is the nature of the complex articulations within it. Whiteford sees the upper class as composed of sets of preferred interaction, with each set, in turn, being part of a larger set of sets. The manner of the development of the di Tella industrial operations in Argentina suggests that such a general model would also serve there. Leeds describes the Brazilian *panelinha* as a ". . . closed, completely informal primary group, held together in common interest by personal ties and including a roster of all key socio-politico-economic positions."

One feature of the upper sector upon which many observers agree is that kin ties play an important role in industrial, commercial, and governmental operations. "As industrial families proliferate, so do enterprises," writes W. Paul Strassmann. He goes on to present his belief that "family-centeredness has been typical of early industrialization everywhere" and that "as in countries outside Latin America, restrictive family control has weakened in many large enterprises." Although predictions continue to be made that familial interests will decline as industrialization advances in Latin America, we find indications that such interest continues to be a central feature of the society. Discussions of mobility always include marriage into the upper strata as an important alternative device. Restrictions on maximum land ownership in Mexico are reported to have led to the strengthening of kin bonds in order to hold together large land areas under multiple individual ownership. It is probably true that flexible industrialization can proceed more rapidly without binding kin ties, but whether true or not, it does not follow that this will be the way chosen by the Latin Americans to ease their industrial problems.

The individual who operates in the upper sector today manifests psychological characteristics that are entirely congruent with the structural situation as it has been here observed. Raymond Vernon's summary of the character of Mexican businessmen indicates that they fall little short of the "economic man" incarnate, a model that can hardly be unique to one period of history or one cultural tradition. The entrepreneur in Latin America well illustrates the generalized description given by Kerr and his colleagues: "They do not advance on the wings of a rigid ideology; rather they tend to be pragmatic. They favor a structure of economic and political rules which best permit them to pursue their gains . . ."

It is important to remember that the structure of the upper sector is such that it has, in a sense, its own built-in labor force which shares its ideology and its prestige system, but shares only in the most restricted way the prestige symbols that indicate high status. The white-collar worker may find himself at odds with the existent powers; nevertheless, his way of life is a basic attempt to survive within the upper-sector system. He survives in the system without power, the primary means available for mobility.

The upper sector of Latin America, containing the elites and most of the so-called "middle classes," still constitutes the home of the rulers of the society. This classification holds true whether we are speaking of Cuba under its highly divergent regime or of the rest of the Latin American countries. When it is said that the middle classes have taken over the ruling positions in Latin America, the statement should be considered in the framework of the interrelation between the various parts of the upper sector. For it is the changing structure of power relations that exist around these diverse components of the upper sector that, in the present view, accounts for the structural changes that have generally been seen in terms of class or strata systems.

INTERDEPENDENCE OF SECTORS

The development of Latin America as an essentially agrarian-export area among competitive world powers has led to the emergence of similar relations in many places. These relations may be discussed in terms of occupational statuses, although it is the set of relations contingent upon the status, and not the individual himself, that is the issue. Thus a given individual may be an expansionist banker, but it is his behavior in playing this role that concerns us, and not all the other features of his conduct and role in society.

Among the positions of special importance are the military, mechanized agrarian capitalists, internal merchants, industrialists, expansionist bankers, the resurgent Catholic clergy, university-trained technicians, students, and guerrilla revolutionaries. All share the common interest of gaining and utilizing power, but all use different instruments and base their efforts on somewhat different elements of control.

The military, with their unique combination of organization and weaponry, find themselves in a position of being able to take over a government at almost any time they wish. The military has seldom been able to police its own activities so as to eliminate what inevitably develops into abuses that antagonize the rest of the country. The military's position on power, then, tends to be a jealous guarding and augmenting of prerogatives within the framework of a civilian government. There is no political ideology peculiar to the military, but there is a tendency for younger officers to see their civilian support as including the lower sector, and for the older officers to assume that their support lies almost wholly within the upper sector. This break, however, is far from universal, and it is often an older officer with younger colleagues who actually takes control of the government at a given time, thus bridging the gap between the more traditional power wielders and the newer power seekers.

The export-based agrarian capitalist who flourished as the basic liberal element of the nineteenth century has been complemented by a newer brand of agrarian capitalist whose interests turn more on internal markets and whose activities increasingly require mechanization. The progressive labor laws that appear on many books in Latin America, while often evaded, nevertheless have made it increasingly advisable for the entrepreneur to reduce direct labor costs as much as possible and thereby reduce the possible control the government can exercise through labor. The importance of internal markets has grown with the expansion of urban populations and middle-income groups. As rural populations have grown, the relative amount of subsistence-agriculture land has decreased, and along with it the relative dependence of countrymen on their own production. This growing demand for agricultural products has included both food staples and raw materials for industry. The new agrarian capitalists differ somewhat from the older export-oriented group. They have a concern for the wider population because that population comprises their market. It is to their advantage both to promote wealth in the lower sector and to encourage mobility from the lower to the upper sector. The first widens the market, and the second increases the variety of desired products. This trend bespeaks no newly discovered morality but merely a rational vision of how to promote entrepreneurial success. In contrast to the older agrarian exporter who saw the lower sector as a labor source, the new internal producer sees the lower sector as both labor source and market.

An essentially similar attitude is found among the merchants and industrialists. Their relations with the lower sector have an additional quality that varies with their specific businesses. Industrial goods and wider ranges of commercial products require not only a wealthier lower sector but also its adoption of the tastes and prestige prejudices of the upper sector. It is to the advantage of the industrialist and commercialist to change the emphasis on wealth in the lower-sector prestige system to a desire for the wider variety of prestige symbols that characterize the upper sector. The widening of the industrial market thereby entails fundamental cultural changes in the population.

The need for credit to develop production and the internal market has led to the emergence of an entrepreneurial banking philosophy. Older banking policy tended to restrict credit to a clientele defined by family background and elite social status. With the expansion of the upper sector, banks have changed their policies to provide credit to people who in earlier years would have been excluded by virtue of their lack of social standing. In most instances this has been done through establishing new banks rather than by miraculously transforming the policies of older establishments.

The expanding internal market and the emergence of the new entrepreneurs has been accompanied by a growing nationalism. The export capitalist's focus of interest could never be wholly local, even if his mannerisms marked him as provincial. The newer capitalists have a direct and vested interest in the nation since not only their products but also their markets are located there. They collectively manifest concern over foreign competition that makes the marketing of national products more difficult. While their economic policy places them squarely on the side of world capitalists, they are equally squarely in competition with those capitalists and are active in pressing their governments into economic protectionist policies; in some instances they even decry the overcapitalizing that may be available from foreign sources.

Of quite a different order has been the change evident in the manners and activities of the Catholic clergy. The decline of the Spanish empire in the New World increasingly placed the church in a position wherein it had to support itself. Nineteenth-century liberalism hit the church especially hard in some countries, both in terms of financial support and quality of the clergy.

The new papal policies of this century have recently had marked consequences in Latin America. Priests are becoming more progressive socially, and high church officials have openly spoken of the evils of social suppression inherent in the conservative governments and the social sectors that control them. What might be regarded as a new orthodoxy—if contrasted with the practices of the colonial period—has extended the role of the clergy to one of missionizing an already Catholic population. Unlike the new capitalists, however, the new clergy has been heavily composed of foreigners, and the ideologies being introduced are still competing with older, more conservative tendencies still present in the church. The progressive policies reflect a change in the policies of the world church, and do not always coincide with the vested interests of the local clergy. Thus, the clergy tends to be less nationalistic, except where it is recruited out of the local population. The church is concerned with expanding and consolidating its position, and to do this, it is trying to identify its interests with both the upper and lower sectors of society.

Besides the new agrarian, industrial, and commercial capitalists who represent a new series of viewpoints within the upper sector, of equal importance are certain power seekers who face quite different obstacles in their efforts to gain power. Three instances will illustrate this variation: students, economists, and revolutionaries.

The students of specific concern here are those at the major national universities. For the most part, students at private (usually Catholic) universities already have their foot firmly on the ladder of success, and their futures are reasonably secure. The national universities, however, provide the only access to higher education for students from the lower sector or from less successful families of the upper sector. They enter in considerable numbers, spend 70 per cent of their time in supporting themselves, and most of the rest of the time in classes, study, and debate. An enormous number never complete their studies. Within each student population are a few who have determined that one way to power is through leadership in student activities, specifically political activities. In these activities they tend to concern themselves with national as well as student problems. These efforts have, from time to time, an effect on the national scene. The most important interventions have been those that challenged the activities of governments. Given the traditional picture in Latin America, these interventions usually were directed against governments that supported capitalists.

Students generally identify themselves with the lower sector politically and try to act as representatives of that sector. They are heard, whereas the real members of that sector often are not. The students illustrate well many problems inherent in the aspirations of the upper sector. The overwhelming majority of those who eventually graduate must be satisfied with mere scraps of upper-sector prestige. The challenges and objections they made as students are readily put aside. As in any case of learning, the repeated failure of student efforts is unrewarding and eventually leads the individual to seek some other kind of behavior.

One of the more important products of the national universities over the past few decades has been the graduate of the faculty of economics. The growing role of government in development and in the control and direction of problems of growth has increased the demand for trained economists. Unlike lawyers, whose numbers usually exceed their market, there are not enough economists to fill the demand. The study of economics offers the student, nurtured in an attitude of protest, a professional situation where he does not need to drop his old complaints. Most faculties of economics have long since been heavily influenced by concerns for social justice, and most have leaned towards Marxian theories for concepts to resolve economic problems. This leaning has given a flavor of socialism to the products of many economics faculties and has served to introduce into the governments—often in positions of increasing importance—individuals who have not been directly dependent on a capitalistic enterprise for their support.

Just as the student who emerges from the university follows a course quite different from that often visible among those he leaves behind, so the economist seldom goes into professional work as a rank Marxian theorist. However, since the theoretical training is usually heavily social in content—if not actually political—rather than strictly economic, the economist is one professional who carries on at least some of the concerns and issues that characterized his student days. He challenges the economics of export capitalism and demands that a different set of answers be achieved. Perhaps more than that of any other professional group, the economists' efforts to get power are providing a basis for change within the organization of Latin American society.

For years, a few of each generation of students have continued to follow some of the more extreme allegiances that stirred them during their university days. The standard response of the governments has been to exile these rebellious individuals and to allow their return after they have been tamed by age and unsuccess outside their own country. Most return to sink into a middle-class oblivion, to reflect cynically on the realities of their Latin social order. It has always been the custom in Latin America to accept the exiles of a neighboring country, to allow them life, but usually to inhibit their political activity. The advent of Fidel Castro in Cuba has proved to be a turning point for the activities of the present generation of student extremists. Having a base for and a direct channel to socialist doctrine and training, the contemporary exile need not drift about in the world; he has a place where he can further the processes that he found attractive as a student. The emergence of revolutionary guerrilla groups in Latin America has been made possible not only by training and provision of individuals from the outside but also by the recruitment and support that is available from the university student. As a student, the individual may be a little more effective in strikes and demonstrations than the nonstudent. But as a guerrilla sympathizer, he can provide both information and services to the guerrillas that would be impossible otherwise. So it is that the active revolutionaries who may be hidden in the forests and cities of Latin America have in the students a strong propaganda voice that speaks in public forums and also a center for recruitment in the core of the upper sector of the society. Through their guerrilla contacts, the students have found another channel into the larger society and a more active and challenging way of expressing their need and striving for power.

NEW POWER BASES

The past half century has seen the emergence of a number of new bases of power. Various elements of the upper sector have utilized these new bases, creating a larger number and greater variety of competitive power seekers. Those members of the lower sector who have been involved in this change have thus moved into the upper sector. The new power bases include the following: new wealth from profit-oriented agrarian enterprises; financial support and governmental action from foreign governments; new wealth from industrial enterprises; control of "paper pushing" and intermediate decision making implicit in the increased complexity of governmental and business expansion; weapons, usually supplied from different foreign sources; organized labor; organized agrarian leagues; mass political organizations; and others. These power bases may be added to the list of other more traditional ones such as the market in specific goods, especially staples; latifundios; church social organizations; local municipal or communal organizations; and the influence of regional *caciques* (political bosses). Each of the power bases provides the opportunity for not one but many individuals or groups to exercise power. It is not one latifundio, but many; not merely one kind of agrarian enterprise, but diverse ones in coffee, sugar, or cotton; not just one industry, but steel, textiles, or plastics; not just the Catholic Church, but a variety of Catholic orders and Protestant sects; not just arms for the military, but arms for the revolutionaries too.

It is misleading to think that only a middle class is involved in this apparent power fragmentation; the entire upper sector is involved. New means to power have proliferated the varieties and modes of power. The multiplication of control areas has made analysis in terms of strata almost impossible because the product has been the continuing emergence of a series of fluctuating, sometimes corporate vertical structures. The prestige system similarly does not fall readily into strata but rather into a complex set of interrelated cliques, each manifesting slightly more or less prestige at any given moment.

The continued existence of the dual sectors in Latin America is directly traceable to the operation of and concern for power. Differential access to and exercise of power provides the backbone for the class system. The recognition of the importance of utilization of power is the mark of the upper cultural sector. Apart from those areas such as southern South America where there is good evidence for a real middle class, the major challenge to the dual system seems to rest with the governments. Their role in secondary development carries with it a natural corollary of concern for a balance of power among the various segments of the society. Their efforts to exercise such control, at the time of this writing, seemed most evident in the party system in Mexico, and in periodic resort to military force elsewhere.

PART II

Aspects and Components

Technology
and
the Land

The methods man uses to extract and mold the riches of his natural habitat into the things he needs set limits on all his efforts at cultural advance. The recent history of Latin America illustrates a wide range of cultural development. The continent still holds bands of hunters and gatherers and also boasts advanced and complex petroleum and iron-extraction facilities. Contrasting phases of human history and cultural evolution stand side by side; the obvious discrepancy of such extremes is not only recognized by the people involved, but must also be included in any attempt to explain their behavior.

A popular way of looking at these variations is to see them as different layers of history. Some years ago, a symposium on Middle American cultural history delineated technologies derived from prehistoric Middle America, medieval Europe, and the industrial revolution. Evidence of the nuclear age is also present. This kind of analysis chooses the historic origin of various traits and classifies them in accordance with their historical order of appearance. For purposes of economic analysis, Hirschman has telescoped these stages and considers only the extremes that now dominate the continent, ". . . the coexistence and cohabitation of modern industry and of preindustrial, sometimes neolithic, techniques." Hirschman points out that simply because the techniques, and entire sets of habits and life styles that are contingent thereupon, are differently derived does not mean that they do not currently operate in a perfectly comprehensible and rational economic context:

. . . there are a number of sectors in which the appearance of advanced industrial methods is seriously handicapped by the possibility of competition from independent, small-scale producers. Examples that come to mind are the manufacture of furniture, shoes, apparel, bricks, ceramics, cigars (as opposed to cigarettes), baskets (holding back the development of modern forms of wrapping, bagging, and packaging), some metalworking as well as large parts of the food-processing and construction. Most services, in particular retailing, are also in this category. In truck and bus transportation, the dual wage situation and the relatively small size of the needed capital investment make for organization along traditional small-business lines preferable to modern large-scale operations, and consequently the service provided retains a distinctly preindustrial flavor in spite of the modern equipment used.

Where distinctive complexes of tools and methods of older eras survive in Latin America, they also mark the survival of other aspects of those eras. Rational though they may be, these now antiquated life ways necessarily survive in those areas where development has been the slowest, and continue to signal the extreme economic inferiority of that portion of the population. Even though sectors of Latin America are striving, and in some instances with admirable success, to improve the technology and the effective use of the resources over which they have dominion, the irregularity of this success may be better understood if we examine some of the workings of the more primitive technologies that still characterize much of the region.

PRIMITIVE TECHNOLOGIES

To see the changes and the processes whereby the primitive technologies effect the social process, we can examine three aspects of the technology: the power sources; machinery and skills of operation; and the social organization of labor.

If there is any single index for the general advance of a society, it is some measure of the capacity of that society to harness energy. At the time of the Spanish conquest, the advanced civilizations of both the New and Old Worlds had succeeded in harnessing and controlling waterpower for purposes of irrigation, but waterpower for turning machinery was still primitive. The incoming Iberians had a marked advantage in having domesticated animals for carrying cargo, pulling plows and wheeled vehicles, turning primitive mills, and providing transportation. The Meso-American and Andean civilizations domesticated animals mainly as sources of food. Only the llamas of the Andes worked as beasts of burden. The Europeans also had gunpowder, a concentration of power for which the aboriginal civilizations had no tactical match. But underlying these sources of power—as also those provided by the tools described below—was the major source of power in both worlds, man himself. To the Spaniard, the key to exploiting the new colonies lay in the availability of Indian labor. Without that labor, the Spaniard could extract no more wealth from the world than did the French, Dutch, and English colonists to the north.

Throughout the colonial period down through the nineteenth

century, these sources of power continued to be the basis for Latin American life. Very few of the mechanical gains of the industrial revolution were imported. Most of Latin America was related economically to Europe, in the same way that the old South in the United States was related to the North. It provided basic resources, extracted predominantly by human labor. The conquest had introduced cattle, donkeys, and horses; their laboring offspring, the ox and mule, also became crucial power sources, especially to large enterprises. Apart from their economic value, the very ownership of these animals served as a mark of social distinction. The horse was restricted to the Spaniards' use, and today, mules are often found only on relatively large enterprises. Except for their use in plowing, oxen were mainly of value in transport and travel. Waterpower was harnessed principally through the waterwheel, but this source of power did not replace the human female as the carrier of water and grinder of cereals. Great stones for crushing and grinding minerals were obviously of interest only to large enterprises. Thus, water and wind power, while known, were not widely harnessed.

Into the twentieth century—until the arrival of steam, petroleum, and hydroelectric power—the human being, supplemented with draft animals, continued to be the major power source for all efforts, whether in small peasant agriculture or in extensive latifundios producing sugar, cacao, or other crops for export. As might be expected, the basic machines and tools were those used by individuals, usually alone, but occasionally in groups. Still crucial to the agricultural economy of Latin America are the following handtools: the machete (the bush or cane knife), the hoe, the digging stick, the ax, and—more rarely—the sickle, scythe, saw, and a variety of specialized tools for particular products. Among the last are implements of indigenous origin used for indigenous crops, such as for the bitter manioc of the tropical lowlands.

With the ox came the plow, the *trapiche* (sugar mill), and

the wheeled vehicle. The fact that oxen were the most expensive kind of cattle (that is, they did not reproduce themselves) made them generally available only to the wealthiest, whether at the peasant or the latifundio level. Much of Latin America, however, is mountainous, and the lack of level fields and wide roads continues to make hand agriculture and the use of single beasts of burden important even today. In Nicaragua, the same cultivator may use oxen and plow on his level lands and then take up the digging stick and machete to plant his hilly lands. For the most part, however, the farmer who can afford much level land, and therefore oxen and plows, will either put his marginal lands out for rent or sharecropping or plant them in coffee or some other cash crop for which the terrain is appropriate.

A comparison of hoe and plow agricultures was made by Oscar Lewis in the Mexican community of Tepoztlán. He concluded that the exclusively hand agriculture of the hoe produced more per unit of land area, but that the input of human energy was relatively greater. The issue is, therefore, not the amount of yield but the ratio of human activity to output. On this basis, the availability of plow and oxen obviously frees the individual of considerable labor. One of the ecological aspects of this situation is that in a great many niches of Latin America the hand agriculturalist has been forced into marginal lands for which there is no better technology than the digging stick and the machete. A study of one area of Venezuela illustrates how the relative size of the land holding being cultivated varied quite closely with the mechanized modes of cultivation.

Tools used in working the land	*Size of exploitation (in hectares)*		
	0–9.9	*10–99.9*	*100 or more*
Tractor	9	7	10
Yoke of oxen	46	17	0
Hand tools	142	27	2

What I have said about the sources of power and the degree of complexity of machinery also holds for the processing of local raw material and the local hand fabrication of goods. In the colonial period and the nineteenth century, the artisan, craftsman, and the workshop were restricted to limited amounts of power and primarily to handtools. Except where water wheels were introduced, hand skills were the principal base of production. Specialties each had their own tools—forges for copper and iron workers, lasts for shoemakers, looms for weavers, and so on —but always it was the human being who forged the metal, sewed the shoe, and wove the cloth.

The major differentiating feature among the various complexes of production, fabrication, and processing of goods before the twentieth century had little to do with tools and skills, but rather, with the social organization of their use. With human labor and fixed technology, the only way to vary production significantly is either through more abundant resources (richer mines, more fertile lands, more irrigation water, and the like) or through more units of production, that is, more men. What distinguishes the hacienda from the peasant organization over all of Latin America is that the former involves a centralized control of the human power sources whereas the latter does not. In the hacienda, the field workers, the artisans, and the administration were all dependent upon the process of producing the goods and maintaining the establishment. In the peasant community, the family was much more frequently the unit of production. Only in a few areas was there community production. Not only did the realities of Spanish colonial rule sometimes severely reduce community production, but much republican policy was dead set against it. The independent peasant and the rural laborer on the hacienda worked with essentially the same technology. The benefit of the greater yield that the hacienda may have permitted through better organization of labor and resources was naturally channeled off into the profits of the owners. The hacienda laborer may or may not have had a somewhat better life than the peasant under these circumstances, depending upon the relative wealth of the local peasants, the local traditions of treatment of labor, and the goodness of heart of the hacendado. Today there is little question that among the most poverty-stricken of peoples are those to be found on the surviving backward haciendas in Meso-America and the Andes.

The industrial revolution entered Latin America late and has been slow in diffusing specific technology to the rural as well as to the urban areas. In the countryside, its major effect has been on the gradual reorganization of the large-scale enterprises. Most machinery is expensive and constructed for large-scale production. Few peasants, no matter what their crop, can afford to operate any but hand-powered machinery, and the regional lack of electric sources and the cost of petroleum products often prohibit any other kind. It is among the larger holders, the more wealthy, that the necessary capital for new machinery is to be found. It is they who can afford the capital investment to set up an electric plant, who can afford a few years of no return so that they may later benefit; and, obviously, it is only they who command large enough extensions of land to make investment in a new technology worth the effort.

Although the use of nonhuman energy, mechanization, and scientific knowledge is available to a limited few, not even all to whom it is available have cared to exploit the possibilities of increased production. The fact that the social organization and control exercised over rural labor differentiates the hacienda and latifundio systems from peasant endeavors has not made the systems any easier to change. They were never geared to high production with low labor input, and many problems stand in the way of so converting them. Since the kinds of relations involved and the entire way of thought of all the participants, laborer and owner alike, have not held greater productivity to be a criterion of performance, all aspects of technology—the tools, the motor skills, the ways of thought and kinds of knowledge, and the quality and kind of social relations implicit—must change if the new direction is to be taken.

Whether or not they take advantage of newer technology, it is those who control the large extensions of land who have unique access to that technology. The peasant can seldom afford it or risk it, nor does he in practical fact have cultural access to it. The individuals who introduce the new technology, therefore, are those who combine the control of the land with motivation to gain through increased production. Occasionally it is the older landowner; but more often it is the younger entrepreneur, sometimes the foreigner, who enters the field to establish rational enterprises from the paraphernalia of the older hacienda system. Some of these enterprises are devised as long-term operations, such as the corporate enterprises in bananas or sugar. Increasingly, a rather different kind of enterprise, speculative agriculture, has been making its appearance. Annual crops, especially cotton, can be planted and harvested on a rented piece of land over the period of years that the market seems to hold. When the market breaks, the entrepreneur has either foreseen it and already abandoned the fields, or he breaks with it and starts seeking capital for some other venture. These operations are marked by heavy investment in new technology. In warmer tropical regions, insecticides, fertilizers, and machinery are applied in quantity and most often on credit. The speculator is irresponsible about the welfare both of the habitat and of labor.

Whether the application of new technology is made by the older landowners or the newer entrepreneurs, consistent factors of control over land and over fluid capital or credit are necessary. The first of these controls essentially underlies the social organizational differences that distinguish the peasant from the hacendado, and, when combined with the second, permits innovation. In its entirety, this control system depends upon many things, some of which will concern us later in the discussion of government and power in general.

LAND OWNERSHIP

The ultimate authority for dominion over the land has, since independence, been held by the state. In practice, however, poor communication and transportation have permitted local men to hold positions of power in which they can exercise their own interests. Either the state has been too weak to protect offended parties effectively or it has delegated its powers to the local authorities. As a result, the term "private property" in much of Latin American history has taken on a very different meaning, depending upon the locus and kind of real power that could back it up.

There are two intermediate entities that modify the rights that the small landholders may expect to exercise: the large landholders and communities. Classically, in the Andean highlands in parts of Meso-America, the more powerful local individuals have succeeded in dispossessing large numbers of small landholders through foreclosure on debts, manipulation of legal devices, greater influence with authorities, and sometimes through sheer exercise of force. In some cases, these powerful landholders have been former small landholders who raised themselves by this means. Local political action and support from friends produced one or several competing strong men in a region, from whom smaller landholders eventually had to seek protection. Such was the case in areas of Brazil well into the twentieth century, and the same pattern continues in many other areas. Local regions became essentially dominated by, and the rights of individuals therein dependent upon, the interests of the strongest proprietors in the region. Elsewhere, the large holdings were originally granted by the crown or government and then extended by the gradual takeover of the neighboring lands or communities (particularly the case in the Andes) or of individual landholders who could exercise no effective defense.

The power of the community in Latin America has varied between the exercise of what may be likened to eminent domain over lands in its area to merely being the locus of an authority derived from the state. Three different forms of collectively held lands are commonly to be found: municipal, communal, and coowned. Municipal lands are those which belong to the municipal government, a government which is part of the national hierarchy of governing bodies. Municipal lands are usually wooded or grazing lands; in some cases, they are good for agriculture and are rented out to individuals. They are controlled by the governing body, and this body, in turn, receives its authority from the national government. In the abortive agrarian reform in the early 1950's in Guatemala, municipal lands were the first to be expropriated.

Communal lands are those that belong to a social entity that recognizes itself as having some corporate concern over the area in question. Such a community is usually a town or village, sometimes a municipal capital. But the lands in question are not controlled by the municipal government; rather, they pertain to an organization that at some point in time declared itself the proprietor of the land. Thus a community may begin with a set of communal lands, and when an outsider moves into the town or village, he is excluded from membership in the collective ownership. This type of ownership differs basically from municipal land rights, since in the latter any resident who is a national citizen usually has the right to rent municipal land, the authority of the municipality being derived from the state. Depending upon the code drawn up by the governors of communal lands, however, nonmembers of the community may be entirely excluded, or they may be allowed to use the lands only under restricted circumstances. Most community lands in the Andes are of the latter type. In many cases, the title to the lands derives from crown grants or viceregal allocations; in others, they are lands that were purchased by the community in the nineteenth or twentieth centuries.

The Mexican *ejidos* illustrate a special case of communal

lands that were set up following the revolution. Even though they were old in form, the fact that they were directly controlled by the government was entirely new. In this sense, Mexican ejidos are different from most other community lands, since they are often not formed around already existing communities, and their tenure is especially protected by the national government.

The coownership of land is similar to communal ownership except that it usually starts through the banding together of a small group of individuals who take title to a property as coowners. As with community lands, inheritance involves only the heirs of the original owners, and new individuals who may move into the area are excluded. Following the breakdown of haciendas that has occurred in some regions over the past one hundred years, various properties of this kind have been established. Sometimes it is the laborers on a hacienda who band together and purchase the hacienda from its previous owners.

Communal, ejidal, and coowned lands all suffer from increasing population. In many instances, and potentially in all of them, the heirs become so numerous that the original lands cannot support them. Over the years, in these, as well as in many municipal lands the practice often develops that the individuals assigned the plots have continuing right to them. Reapportionment is a difficult procedure and may not, in fact, take place until the last member of a family dies or leaves town. As the individuals with rights increase in number, the pressures on the system become apparent, and those who hold land stiffen their defense to retain their rights. Under these circumstances, community and coowned lands lose all semblance of serving their original purpose and in fact tend to be handled like private property but with the right of repossession still held by the community.

Everywhere in Latin America the state claims ultimate rights to the lands. In many countries there are vast extensions of potentially productive land still held as national land, onto which anyone has the theoretical right to move and stake a claim. For specific historical reasons that vary from place to place, formalizing such a claim may require legal action that is difficult or impossible for a poor man to undertake; as a result, over the years much of this land has been staked out by entrepreneurs who have ready access to the legal process, even though extensive areas that have been claimed go unused.

When the European migrants poured into southern South America in the last century, they found most of Argentina and Uruguay already owned, although not used. Similarly, the frontiersman in Brazil today will often discover that old claims make it all but impossible to enter otherwise unused lands. Many areas do, however, remain in the hands of the nation, and colonization movements are being attempted in many countries. Usually, these lands are farthest removed from currently occupied areas. An extreme situation with respect to national land usufruct occurs in Panama, where most of the land is still retained by the nation. Unlike other countries where small landholders or renters account for most of the agrarian population, the largest number of Panamanian farmers are officially regarded as squatters. Simple legal requirements for using the land can be handled locally, but they require that the individual not plant permanent crops. As a result, the basic pattern of slash-and-burn agriculture is institutionalized and reinforced through national legal restrictions.

Exploitation of Natural Resources

In many countries, the handling of national lands poses a crucial question. It is in these lands that major agricultural production areas might still be expected to develop; but there is pressure from the ever-expanding agrarian population that lacks the capital and technological abilities to undertake highly productive enterprises. This conflict illustrates the basic issues and problems in the development of technology and resources in Latin America. Resources of considerable richness exist; their exploitation increasingly demands a technology that can answer not only the needs of the growing population but that can produce capital to provide for serious economic development. The population that is pressing for the land is the very population that is technologically least equipped to develop it. And the sector with the capital and access to new technology still has such control in most places that it often feels little or no commitment to development. Decisions in resource use are made in terms of limited but quite rational interests. The layers of history, the "dualistic development," continue to expand, each providing a significant sector of the environment for the other, each being unable to survive without the other, and each pressing for its own survival.

Whether agrarian reforms can satisfactorily provide solutions to these complex questions is far more difficult to know than agricultural and production issues would suggest. For the central question is: Who will control, who will have the right and authority and the power to back up the decisions as to what choice of production factors is most advisable in a given place at a given time? The solution to this problem necessitates social invention in almost every Latin American country, a goal toward which significant sectors of the Latin American populations are working. In addition, there is a very real technological problem still facing many of the countries.

The technology of direct exploitation of the habitat that diffused into Latin America from the leading industrial nations was, in many instances, developed to handle problems peculiar to temperate environments. Consequently, there are many problems for which this technology is not entirely adequate and which only continuing study and invention within the tropical environment will solve. Among the general kinds of problems for which new technological inventions are needed are: the problem of harnessing waterpower from rapidly silting rivers and from rivers subject to sudden and raging regional floods; the problem of continuing control of the variety of insect and microscopic pests that beset man and his domesticated plants and animals; and the problem of highway upkeep in areas of heavy seasonal rains, high local humidity, and rapid weed growth. The application of some solutions has already had questionable effects. In insect control, the broad malaria-eradication programs, based on the assumption that what kills temperate bugs will similarly do away with tropical varieties, have now succeeded in naturally selecting DDT-immune insect populations. Farmers bothered by multiplying varieties of plant pests are increasingly resorting to insecticides so powerful that it is possible that they also may have been directly responsible for the deaths of some agricultural laborers and small farmers.

The problem of secondary development is not merely that it requires social inventions to utilize the technological innovations brought into the society. The problem becomes more complicated when the inventions borrowed are not designed to handle the specific adaptive problems of that society. Latin America must increasingly face the problem of handling its own technological development, as well as the more immediate and visible problems of social development.

A great deal has been written about the attitude of the Latin American *campesino* towards the land and the very special place it occupies in his philosophy and life plans. Discussions of Andean and Middle American Indians have sometimes idealized this relationship into one of almost mystical ties between the man and his land. The fact of the matter is, of course, that in subsistence agriculture the direct and immediate dependence of the man upon his land does give the land a very special meaning. Since the campesino is immediately concerned with physical survival, the possession of land at the best, and access to it at the least, is a matter of first importance.

The lower sector, however, has classically been the prey of those who had more knowledge of, and the ability to manipulate, the legal system. Ignorance and illiteracy have left subsistence agriculturalists at the mercy of predatory lawyers, both licensed and those practicing as empiricists. The legal profession has always been an important channel for ambitious men, and some lawyers have not hesitated to serve the interest of more powerful individuals of the upper sector in their quest for power.

In addition to the gradual encroachment of mestizos on Indian lands and of expanding latifundios into community and small private holdings, the problems faced by the subsistence agriculturalists have been vastly increased by the growing population. Many areas of peasant agriculture where land was sufficient thirty years ago are now areas of emigration. Subsistence agriculture, of course, has seen no increased efficiency or technical innovation to improve crop production. Thus while the saturation point of a particular technology in a particular environment may be somewhat different from that of another technology in another environment, it can be assumed that every environment-technology combination does have some saturation point.

However, just as surely as one area becomes saturated, so does the next, and the basic problem of increasing production and providing the subsistence farmer with adequate access to his basis for survival continues. Since much of the land in Latin America is still in large and often highly uneconomic holdings that are worked with still fairly primitive techniques, attempts to resolve the problem have usually revolved on either improving the technology of agriculture or forcing a social reorganization so that the land would be used more effectively. Improving technology has meant, obviously, mechanization and the introduction of scientific approaches to cultivation. Because of the fact that here, as elsewhere, the advanced agricultural technologies have been developed primarily in temperate countries, the scientific improvement of tropical agriculture has necessitated an entirely new series of studies and experiments. Much of this study has been done through agents of foreign universities and foundations, research institutes, and the establishment of ·local institutions. As with any continuing scientific exercise, many trials and errors have been necessary before any extraordinary advances could be expected. But there is no doubt that today the scientific development of coffee, rubber, sugar, and an increasing variety of tropical plants is beginning to reach the level that many temperate-climate crops achieved years ago.

The other solution that has been offered to the man-land problem has been social reorganization, more commonly known as land reform. Land reform in Latin America has tended to take one of two courses. It has either been essentially land redistribution with no particular innovation in the system of tenure; or it has been a revision of the tenure system, placing the individual in a new system relationship with the state. Land redistribution has usually involved the opening up of currently unused national lands for colonization, but has also at times involved the expropriation of unused private lands for the same purpose. Since in theory all Latin American states hold eminent domain, who happens to be in control at the moment determines whether the second step is taken or not.

Many Latin Americans will argue, however, that such redistribution of land really constitutes no reform at all since the same old process of latifundio expansion continues to operate. The efforts in Colombia, Venezuela, Guatemala, Peru, and various other places to move families to new and unused lands have not, claim the critics, served to provide any but temporary relief and are merely postponing the final solution. Instead, they argue, it is crucial that the tenure system as such be reformed, that land ownership be so reorganized that it becomes impossible for private capitalists to occupy and command the profits from extensive land holdings. The state should take over the responsibility and be ready to restructure the land system, turning to other forms of tenure besides that of private property. Thus far only Cuba has moved in this direction. The land reform of Mexico, now so well known, did in principle involve the establishment of specific limits on the amount of land that a given individual might own and did undertake extensive expropriations and the establishment of the ejido system. However, private capitalism has continued to flourish in Mexico, and the state has not undertaken any fundamentally new steps, although expropriations have continued.

Land reform has become a rallying cry of the champions of the lower sector in Latin America and has been converted into the symbol of a basic revolution. As is often the case in such instances, the term has taken on a thousand meanings, each created for the convenience of the user. For better or worse, the more extreme variety of reform has been so seldom practiced that it is difficult to evaluate its effect on the production process. There is little doubt, however, that the simple reallocation of land is not providing fundamental solutions to the problem of excess rural population. Improvements in agricultural technology have been almost entirely directed towards the large producer. From the point of view of national production, this focus is essentially necessary; from the point of view of the subsistence agriculturalist, it resolves little. The fundamental problem persists, however. What appear to be two different economic systems, the latifundio-supported upper sector, and the minifundio and laboring lower sector, are in fact intimately bound to each other. The former continues by virtue of the labor afforded by the latter; and the latter finds itself permanently and severely restricted by the power wielded by the former.

Basic
Agrarian Adaptation

In Latin America the term "campesino" is used to refer to almost all poor rural dwellers; it includes peasants who own their own land and rural laborers who may never have imagined owning land. The campesino is, however, among nature's most adaptive species. He may be found in the ever-growing group of peasants who spend part of their time in wage labor or among laborers who keep a small plot under cultivation; he lives in tropical forest clearings, in coastal fishing villages, in highland haciendas, in lowland sugar plantations, in independent towns. In some areas, such as the Andean highlands, the term has been used occasionally to distinguish a non-Indian from an Indian. Thus, the Bolivian highland Indians, when they wished to divest themselves of the degrading label of "indio," demanded to be called campesinos. This usage, as important as it is in understanding the events in Bolivia, need not deter us from adhering

$*$ 91

to a more general usage that does, in most places, also include Indian groups.

INDEPENDENT PEASANT AGRICULTURE

During much of the nineteenth century, and continuing in some areas into the present one, labor was relatively scarce in rural areas, and large-scale agrarian enterprises often found it necessary to resort to extreme devices to obtain the labor of individuals who preferred to remain as independent cultivators. Andean haciendas would gradually dispossess an entire village, leaving many families with no alternative except to go to work for the new owners. Elsewhere, as in the Guatemalan and Mexican highlands, some growing farms had to search neighboring areas for labor, and labor contractors developed a good business by getting Indians into the labor market. Expeditions to capture Indians for this purpose were not unknown. Over the past one hundred years, however, the population has gradually increased and communities of rural laborers have become more common. Whereas earlier it was necessary to force a peasant community into marginal lands so that its members would be available for seasonal labor, today the sheer increased size of the labor force has made it more readily available.

The result has been a change in the basic characteristic of peasant communities. While at one time they may have been mainly composed of independent cultivators, today it is uncommon to find a village that can support itself in its own habitat. Almost all peasant villages have taken up one or another of a wide variety of additional sources of income. Because the campesino's needs complement those of the large-scale agrarian enterprises, the most common source is labor on the haciendas and plantations. This system operates in two ways. In heavily populated peasant areas every generation produces a number of sons who cannot expect to survive on their increasingly diminishing lands. Of these sons, some seek further agrarian opportunities, while others go to the cities and the larger towns. In a sense, these individuals are lost to the communities, and many of them have little reason to return. Of equal importance, however, is the great number of individuals who seek out seasonal labor, thereby enabling themselves to continue residence for part of the year in their home town but obtaining the necessary supplementary income from outside. Sugar-cane cutting, cotton picking, coffee harvesting, or fruit picking, as well as seasonal work on other crops bring both ladinos and Indians out of the Guatemalan and Mexican highlands, Mexicans (until recently) across the border into the United States, Bolivians from the south of their country into northwestern Argentina, *caboclos* of northeast Brazil to the coastal sugar fields, and so on. Two important aspects of this kind of seasonal labor are that it enables the home villages to continue to flourish in spite of inadequate local resources and, at the same time, carries to those villages information and occasionally innovations from the outside.

The combination of wage labor and independent agriculture has become increasingly characteristic of peasant life in Latin America. Since it is no longer possible in many areas to carve out two distinctive populations—one of wage laborers and one of independent agriculturalists—the term "campesino" is especially meaningful. In any given area, a distinction may be recognized between the varieties, but as often as not a peasant father will have laboring sons. A review of the still rather scanty literature on rural labor in Latin America suggests that a hierarchy of preferences seems to characterize the views of the peoples thus far studied.

The most preferred circumstances are either those wherein independent peasant producers are so self-sufficient that they need not resort to wage labor at all or those laboring situations wherein the laborers have some successful independent organization such as a labor union. It is seldom the case that these two situations occur close enough together that the viewpoint of each concerning the other may be seen. Where peasants live close to laboring situations, they are usually heavily dependent upon that labor. The question of what makes a given campesino prefer wage labor to independent peasant existence, or the reverse, is not always easy to determine. Both of these situations are vastly preferred, however, to seasonal or periodic wage labor. The dependence on seasonal wage labor is, from the laborers' standpoint, a thoroughly dislocating and unsatisfactory situation. Nevertheless, most peasants would prefer this forced mobility to being wage laborers under the paternalistic power domain of a hacendado, a situation in which the laborer receives little or no effective protection by the law nor the services of a labor union. These colono situations that still mark Middle America and the Andean highlands continue especially in the more isolated areas. While they look unattractive because of the restrictions on the colonos, they are still generally regarded as being much superior to the situation of the laborer who has neither the protection of the law nor the protection of the hacendado, and who, unskilled and poverty-stricken, is completely at the mercy of a labor market controlled primarily by the employer.

The independent small-scale operator in Latin America seldom owns all of the land that he cultivates. The term "peasant" implies an independent operation but not necessarily ownership. Land distribution is uneven and a man will often rent from his neighbor. Forms of rental vary from place to place. Straightforward cash payment, payment in specific amount of crop, and a wide variety of sharecropping arrangements are all to be found. In Central America as a whole, sharecropping seems to be decreasing, but it is still widespread. In Santander, Colombia, and probably elsewhere, sharecropping is not a rigidly formal system but rather is used by the landholder as an alternative if the market looks bad. When the tobacco market is good, the owner hires labor and thereby gains most of the profits; if the market is bad, he will work his tobacco land by sharecropping, thus distributing the losses among all.

Peasant communities have long since developed methods of

organizing labor for specific efforts that require a concentration of human power beyond the capability of the single household. There are two general kinds of such effort: exchange labor and communal labor. Exchange labor is usually carried on between two individuals. One asks the other to provide him with help for a day, and at some future time the second requests the first to reciprocate. This kind of labor is most common between individuals who regard themselves as being on about the same socioeconomic level and who have no alternative way of getting the work done. This kind of arrangement is often called "giving a hand," and the unit of work is usually one day's labor.

Communal labor is somewhat similar except that it involves a large number of people and is used for such tasks as raising a house or for some kinds of field work. It is usually accompanied by eating and drinking and is often considered as much recreation as work. In the Andes and a few other places, it is used for communal projects such as erecting public buildings. Agricultural collective labor is usually on private property, although occasionally it will be used on communal lands.

Peasant agriculture is characterized by low production, limited storage facilities, involvement with the cash economy, and sometimes a dual-crop pattern, with one crop raised for cash and the other for subsistence. In the Andean highlands the distinction in specific crops stems back to the colonial period, when crops of European origin were introduced for purposes of tribute and native crops were raised for consumption by the campesino. Also very common is heavy dependence upon a single or minimal set crop. In Tobatí (Paraguay), 99 per cent of the *chacras* (plots) raised manioc and 95 per cent raised maize. In Saucío (Colombia), wheat was raised on the largest proportion of cultivated land but potatoes gave the largest quantity of yield, and the combined yield of these two crops was nearly four times as much as that of all the other crops. In Cruz das Almas (Brazil), 16 of the sample of 17 families grew corn, accounting for 61.7 per cent of the total cultivated area; also, 16 of the 17 grew beans. Of 466 households among the Tajin Totonac (Mexico), only one household did not grow maize.

The peasant's agricultural adaptation is rather specialized. A limited number of crops are cultivated, almost inevitably the amount grown is barely enough for survival, and as a result alternative sources of income are very commonly sought. The peasant's freedom of action, however, usually places him in a more flexible position than that of the resident hacienda laborer.

LARGE-SCALE AGRARIAN ENTERPRISES

A great number of campesinos are permanent laborers on large-scale agrarian enterprises. These enterprises vary from still surviving old-style haciendas, wherein the resident laborer— variously called *colono* or *huasipungo*—is involved in *corvée* labor, to the modern "factories in the field," where the laborers reside in a town or compound and achieve some protection through political and collective action. The old-style hacienda system permitted the laborer to live on the farm and provided him with a piece of ground for his own cultivation. In return, the owner expected certain services. In its more extreme forms, this system has become infamous throughout Latin America as one of the harshest forms of servitude to survive into the present day. From highland Ecuador, Peru, and Bolivia have come reports of up to 200 days of labor a year, plus the domestic services of the women of the family, and the rights to some of the offspring of the colono's domesticated animals. Much milder forms are still to be found in Guatemala, where a latifundio is held by an owner sheerly as a labor reserve, somewhat reminiscent of a colonial *encomienda*. The colonos are given complete rights to work subsistence crops on that land, in return for which they are expected to be available for two to three months of paid seasonal labor in another farm of the same owner, usually at the time of the harvest of coffee, sugar, or cotton. Laborers forgo the right to decide where and when they wish to work. In some instances, the colonos residing in these labor-supply farms live under better circumstances than the independent campesinos who suffer the pressure of increased population and may face a bad labor market.

Over the years there have been repeated incidents of agrarian violence in the Andes. Currently the best known is the *violencia* in Colombia that has in the past decades so combined local politics, banditry, and the international communist-capitalist controversy that it is often impossible to know which may most guide a particular incident. Violence in Peruvian highlands has been frequent, long before guerrillas undertook to enter the scene. It has usually involved campesinos who have been consistently restricted in their access to lands. The most famous such incident took place in the Cochabamba region of Bolivia and resulted in the agrarian reform that subsequently became national policy. Another case where independent action became a base for national action was that in the hacienda Vicos, Peru. There, a joint program by the National Indian Institute of Peru and Cornell University led to the expropriation of the hacienda in favor of its resident colonos. The fame of the effort spread to other parts of Peru and Bolivia and very likely contributed to further collective action by campesinos against landowners.

Contemporary writers have tended to refer to the colono system as a feudal one. Superficially, some features are common to both systems. It is important to recognize, however, that the system of hacienda labor being described here has not been formed, nor did it perpetuate itself, under feudal arrangements. Indeed, the contemporary survival of the old-style hacienda has depended upon the hinterland role played by Latin America in relation to the developing industrial economies of the rest of the Western countries. The owners of the haciendas did not form feudal societies, at war with one another; rather, they formed part of a national and international capitalist elite whose position in society depended upon the relative isolation of their enterprises.

The colono system, although possibly surviving in its harshest forms in the Andes, had its parallels among the great fundos of Chile, the estancias of Argentina and Uruguay, the *fazendas* of Brazil, and the haciendas of Middle America. Characteristic of these systems were: the residence of the owner and his family on the land; the extremely paternalistic attitudes and relationships that typified employer and employee; the almost complete control of the employer over the lives and welfare of his employees; and the nearly total inability of the employee ever to accumulate enough capital with which to embark upon his own enterprises. The particular legal form of the relationship varied. Most countries were moving away from debt servitude by the first half of the twentieth century but depended upon various local controls to obtain labor. Argentina's system was somewhat different, since the great estancias of the south were built upon the basis of European tenant laborers who, after arriving in the land of promise, found it all taken up. Their only recourse was to work as tenants on the properties owned by the resident Argentinians. The latter used the tenants to clear new lands for the gradual expansion of the cattle industry, and —through such practices as restricting their length of tenancy on any given piece of property—kept them to a living level little, if at all, better than that of the Andean Indians.

Just as the old-style hacienda was adapted to the needs of the earlier part of the industrial revolution, so the changing needs of the contemporary industrial world have gradually altered the character of the technology and social organization of the present-day hacienda. The modern plantations—such as the mid-twentieth-century sugar plantations of Brazil, the Caribbean, Venezuela, and other areas, and the now-declining banana plantations of Central America—reflect a distinctive internal organization. The paternalistic qualities of the older system are highly attenuated; labor now has, to an increasing extent, access to sources other than the employer from whom to seek means of adjusting labor problems. Although agrarian unions are still relatively weak throughout most of Latin America, governments such as Mexico's, and more especially Cuba's, and less regularly those of other countries, take a hand in the running of some of the enterprises or apply pressure to speed efforts to provide for the worker's needs. The tendency now, somewhat paralleling the elimination of slavery at an earlier period, is the attempt on the part of the enterprise to break the long-standing bonds of labor dependency and to avoid the increasingly complex labor laws that have been developed in almost every country.

In its organization, the modern plantation is a corporate concern; although sometimes held among members of a single family, it is usually run by an administrative staff and along lines thought to be rational. The goal is to make profit and to depend neither upon the government nor labor too much, but to effect control over both insofar as it is necessary to achieve the goal. This goal has led to a variety of specific forms of labor adaptation. In Chile and along the Peruvian coast, highly stable plantation communities are to be found in which both emigration and immigration are highly discouraged. In Puerto Rico, Central America, and Venezuela, labor stability on these farms is relatively high. Elsewhere, especially where speculative agriculture has made its appearance, the labor force is necessarily much more mobile, moving from one opportunity to another. Much of the mobile labor is composed of people who are actually seeking some place where they may undertake their own cultivation and so are not really enthusiastic about the laboring situation in any one location.

PEASANT MIGRATION

In contrast to the adaptation that the large enterprises are making to the changing demands and times, the peasants have been generally unable to find devices for improving their relative position without giving up cultivation in some part. Other alternatives besides rural labor have offered themselves, principal among which are migration to the cities and attempts to move into unused lands. The first of these alternatives will be discussed later. The movement into other rural areas for purposes of continuing peasant agriculture is of immediate concern here.

Throughout the length of the Andes, along the eastern edge of the western communities in Brazil and Paraguay, and in scattered regions in Middle America and elsewhere, there are agrarian frontiers receiving the growing agrarian population. Some planners have hoped to see in these regions the development of highly rational, large-scale production of crops for the growing populations of the countries. Unfortunately for the interested entrepreneur, transport and communication facilities to these areas are generally wretched, medical and extension services are either few or nonexistent, and the possibility of establishing a paying agrarian enterprise is discouraging. It is an old saying among Latin American planters that the man who first opens up a farm will go bankrupt, but the man who buys the semisuccessful concern from him is ready to make money from it. So, irrespective of the planners' dreams for the yungas, the montaña, El Petén, or the Gran Chaco, the people who find themselves propelled toward these areas are not so much the entrepreneurial, speculative, large-scale farmers, as the small-scale agriculturalists. In some areas, the latter are individuals who have long since operated in terms of a cash market and for whom subsistence production is but an unfortunate necessity. In other newly opened areas or regions formally colonized, the emigrating peasants carry with them the tools and knowledge that have served them in the past, and subsistence agriculture is their basic survival mechanism.

Although governments worry, plan, and sometimes intervene in extreme ways, the development of the frontiers of Latin America continues to extend the geographical area of primitive agriculture. In the Petén area of Guatemala there has been a gradual immigration of Kekchi Indians from the neighboring department of Alta Verapaz. This population, like that of so many other areas of Guatemala, has simply outgrown the capacity of its marginal peasant land and the laboring needs of the coffee firms of their district. The people must move. In this instance, the combination of being monolingual in an Indian language and having the open frontier within a few days' travel leads the Kekchi Indians in the direction of the frontier rather than the city. In Panama, the movement toward what Ofelia Hooper has called the "interior frontiers" is simply an extension of the pattern of squatting on national lands. The montaña of Peru and Ecuador has seen the gradual spread of highland populations over the past centuries. In earlier years, this migration consisted mainly of Indians, but today it also involves mestizos and foreigners. Mexican migration has involved both the movement of individuals north into the newly operating areas where irrigation has only recently been introduced and also the formal transportation of people from the center of the country to the southeast.

One pattern of movement occurring in many countries is that from highlands to lowlands. This pattern reflects a major change in the adaptability of the population in general. Classically, the highlands were the home of some of the major higher cultures at the time of the Spanish conquest, and the Spanish found the area reasonably attractive. Jungle and forested coasts, such as the Central American Gulf coast and the eastern side of the Andes, were not heavily occupied at that time. Early attempts to establish European colonies in these regions did not lead to flourishing rural centers, but in many cases led instead to the breakdown and flight of the colonists. Recently, however, migrations to lowlands have been much more numerous and successful. In part, they are probably due to the increased availability of drugs to handle the more obvious tropical maladies. Malaria can be controlled today with drugs in a way that does not make lowland living impractical. The efforts of many countries to eradicate malaria have succeeded—although probably only temporarily—through the elimination of much of the insect population that formerly made the warmer areas dangerous and threatening. The agricultural potential of the highlands has long been supplemented by lowland production from large-scale plantations, but now the population is so dense in most highland regions that it must overflow. Such interior lowlands as southern Costa Rica, northwestern Guatemala, the montañas and yungas of the Andes and the areas bordering on the coasts, as also northern Ecuador, southern Guatemala, northern Honduras and Nicaragua were, in many instances, little occupied until the past few decades.

Attention has been called to the deculturating effects of frontier living: the immigrant has to readjust his way of living to those patterns already invented for survival in the new environment. I would note that what makes migration of this type possible in many parts of Latin America is that the necessary readjustment is limited. While new kinds of manual skills may be necessary and new knowledge of the botany and climate of the region has to be learned, this adjustment does not involve a lowering of the standard of living. The Kekchis' forest huts in the Petén of Guatemala may be more isolated than their earlier homes in villages or on the large farms in the Alta Verapaz, but essentially the same bare items of living are to be found in both places, the same kinds of social relations hold with neighboring communities and with the dominant ladinos, and, withal, many Kekchis have considerably more independence in the Petén than they had at home.

The apparent breakdown that occurs in the way of life of northern Europeans and North Americans when they adjust to the Latin American tropics does involve changes that make the result look very different from life in the home country. Among these kinds of colonists, however, one finds an interesting range of possible adjustments. Some have given up whatever possibilities their northern technology might offer and have adapted entirely to the mode of agriculture and living of the local population. Others have forced the introduction of new crops and, by combining high motivation and work with tropical possibilities, have come up with incomes considerably better than they might have received at home.

Recent years have seen the establishment of more and more formally organized colonies. In some instances these colonies have been established in answer to demands for agrarian reform; and in others, simple recognition of population pressure has been the dominant cause. Many early efforts at such settlements met with varying degrees of failure, but now a number of features common to the new colonies are ensuring better success. Good road access is necessary; if the first crop cannot be removed, then it is likely that the people themselves will begin to drift elsewhere. Minimal medical facilities are now usually within call, though they may be nothing more than a drug store. Perhaps most important is the fact that the individuals now turning to these formal colonization efforts do so because they cannot turn back. They must colonize somewhere, and the land made available by the government may, in many instances, be the best there is. Thus, in most cases the government-sponsored colonization areas are surrounded by many private migrants who have moved in because the road made it possible, with the recognition that where the government is operating there must be a series of niches for others.

Although the campesino of Latin America is conditioned to survival at a low income level in a rural environment, he has enough experience with markets and the exploitation of his immediate environment to make a remarkably good adaptation to the city. Extensive rural-urban migration began early in the present century, and slum areas commenced to appear at least in the second decade. The new migrants brought with them rural values and patterns of adjustment. They continued a heavy dependence upon rural kinsmen and tended to create community organizations within the enclaved and marginal areas they gradually occupied. Their lack of specialization made them available for little more than domestic service and unskilled manual labor, and since the cities were not hives of industrial activity as yet, it was to such work that the migrants were put. As factories developed, so did the labor force. The tendency to utilize anything available in the immediate environment that characterized the campesino carried over into his city life so that he exploited the urban environment too. Shacks were made with poles and cardboard and sheets of scrap wood or metal in place of poles and palm fronds and adobe. A few animals were kept—chickens, occasionally pigs, and others. Gradually, of course, as income increased, the style of living improved; even more important, the longer the migrant stayed in the city, the more he gave up his country orientations and began to take part in urban activities. Moving to the city, however, makes the campesino population readapt in a way much more telling in the long run than does the change to full-scale plantation labor. From the plantation, a return is possible to subsistence agriculture. The new forms of living in the city, however, tend to so specialize the campesino population that the next generation has increasing difficulty in readjusting to rural living. There have been occasional reports of urban slum populations' moving to rural situations, but none of them has received direct study or treatment in the literature so far as I know.

CAMPESINO ORGANIZATIONS

Generalized adaptability is not necessarily a qualification for effective organization, and structured groups in which the basis of organization is the common interest of being a campesino are not common in Latin America. There have been three characteristic varieties of such organizations: rural unions, peasant leagues, and cooperatives.

The emergence of rural unions has usually depended upon stimulus from urban settings, and their structure has been rather similar to that of industrial unions.

The major campesino organization started in the Cochabamba area of Bolivia independently of the government and succeeded through local violence in getting rid of most of the local land-holders. The revolutionary government of Bolivia was too weak for the first decade to effectively control this campesino organization. What it did, therefore, was to attempt to balance the campesinos against the miners, or to balance both against their common enemy, the *rosca*. Since most of the common enemies were effectively eliminated in the revolution of 1952, the organizations have more often been used against one another. As was indicated earlier, the fact that these organizations were armed and constituted a militia meant that they could not be readily controlled by the army; this fact placed them in a somewhat different category from that of some of the other campesino leagues to be discussed.

The arming of such leagues was the object of a shipment of arms to Guatemala in 1954; but the army, presumably aware of the direction of events in Bolivia, commandeered the shipment. As a result, the government, being failed by the military, could not draw upon any armed group for defense when the country was invaded by a rebel group later in the year. Had the government been successful, it would have achieved the kind of control that could have bypassed the army and also served to counteract the landed interests.

The peasant leagues of Brazil have been of a somewhat different order in that they have generally not been armed groups. Rather, they have been separate organizations sponsored mainly by outsiders, usually representing the workers or peasants within a specific region. Many of them are recognized as legal entities by the government, and as such come under the restrictions and controls the government may wish to exercise. Some are sponsored by the church, some by local individuals who wish to use them as springboards for a political career. The same paternalistic character that existed in the older employer-worker relationship exists here, because the league, with its active political head, promises to obtain what the worker needs.

Among urban peoples there has at times been a deep fear of

some upsurge of the peasant masses, coupled with the notion that they will somehow sweep the countryside, descend upon the cities, and destroy civilization. Such fearsome daydreaming has little or no basis in reality, but it does color the reporting on peasant leagues and similar organizations. The nearest approach to such an upsurge has been the development of the Bolivian leagues; but, as could have been foreseen, the object of these leagues was to better the campesino's position, not to destroy the cities. The only possibility of using campesinos in any situation remotely resembling the daydream is if they were organized under careful leadership and were worked up to a feverish state over what they might obtain by sacking a city. Most campesinos are not much interested in such rebellion, although they might well be interested in eliminating the local landlords or the local merchants to whom they have long been in debt.

Peasant leagues offer a government the same opportunities that the unions offer. They are a device whereby a sector of the population may be controlled for action against some other sector. They are not, in any sense, an indication of disorder; rather, they are a firm step in the establishment of a kind of order and balance within the country that is unobtainable when the rural peoples have no means of organizing. While it is possible to establish rural unions—and they are, in fact, being established—they will probably never adequately provide for the interests of most of the rural population, partly because so many individuals are not laborers (or are only transitory or seasonal laborers and return to their own cultivations), and partly because the continued separateness of the farms makes rapid action and organization difficult. For the moment, the rural league provides a better organizational possibility.

Another kind of organization, usually thought of in more purely economic terms, is the cooperative. The cooperatives offer certain advantages to rural peoples. Depending upon the kind, they can be used by independent producers both to better their technical development and to improve their economic position with respect to the market, competitors, and middlemen. To date, there have been few instances in which cooperatives have been mobilized for political purposes, but it seems inevitable that they must be. They are organized essentially to achieve certain economic goals for their members, and, as is always the case, such entities must turn to political mechanisms to achieve these goals when the competition becomes too difficult to handle on a purely economic basis.

The problem in instituting cooperatives is that, unlike the peasant organizations and unions which require only some organizing competence, the cooperative requires not only organizing competence but also technical and economic competence in the activity in question and in the marketing of the product. As was earlier argued in general about economic development at the community level, cooperatives specifically require persons who are familiar with the pitfalls of organization in establishing them and who can also grapple with some hope of success with the technical and economic questions. However, an additional problem arises in the development of cooperatives in Latin America, and that is that productive agrarian activities have traditionally been individual affairs, not matters for cooperation. There is little tradition of cooperation in the planting and harvesting beyond that of communal or exchange labor in privately owned fields. The important issue is that the crop belongs to one person; it is not shared among the various participants. Cooperatives, at some point, require that the individuals involved collectivize some portion of the process—whether for shares of the profit, for marketing, or for something else. This, however, does not seem to be an insuperable problem, and cooperatives are, in fact, developing with some success.

The campesino in most areas is still organized mainly within the peasant system or the large-scale, extensive, agrarian enterprises. As will be discussed later, an aspect of this adjustment that is becoming more important is the mode of dealing with the larger society on other than simply liberal-economic terms. The appearance of peasant leagues and rural labor unions reflects a recognition by the campesino that his inferior position is due in large part to his political inferiority, and that he will be short on new technology, on education, and on other features of life that he knows are available in the cities so long as he is politically weak. To his generalized skills—long since effective in dealing with the habitat and the market—he is now adding the ability to deal with the larger society.

Workshops
and
Industrialization

~~~~~~

The fabrication of goods for the peasant and town dweller was, until the latter part of the nineteenth century, divided between home production and production by craftsmen in workshops. Latin America's essentially hinterland role in the development of industrial capitalism meant that the factory was rarely a significant part of the way of life of the region until the late nineteenth century, and in most of Latin America it became important only at the end of that century. In southern Brazil and Argentina, the growing industrial labor force was largely composed of recently arrived European immigrants, some of whom brought with them notions of urban living and industrial operation. In many areas of production today, the factory has displaced the craftsman, but in some, the individual artisan, whether independent or the member of a workshop, continues to supply the needs and desires of a large segment of the provincial population.

WORKSHOP PRODUCTION

The best study of a workshop community is that by Marvin Harris, treating of the pseudonymous Minas Velhas in Brazil. This particular community is an extreme case, as it is composed almost entirely of workshops, businessmen, government administrators, and civil servants of one sort or another. As such, it is a service town for the entire rural region. Elsewhere, it is more common to find a number of communities within a given region with small groups of artisans and storekeepers—shoemakers, hatters, tailors, seamstresses, carpenters, masons, weavers, barbers, blacksmiths, and so on. In some areas—such as the central highlands of Peru and the western and midwestern highlands of Guatemala—there is some community specialization, such that the furniture makers will dominate in one community, the basket weavers in another, pottery makers in still another, and so forth. Where this kind of specialization occurs, there is nearly always a widespread regional market system: different towns have markets on different days of the week so that the entire region is serviced by vendors from other communities as well as by itinerant and city-based salesmen.

Some workshops bring together a number of craftsmen who work under the auspices of an individual who pays them for their work and then takes the responsibility of distributing the product. These workshops are usually found in such centers as Minas Velhas, and in provincial and departmental capitals. These organizations are really collections of individual craftsmen and seldom involve any specialization in fabrication of specific parts of a final product. They, like the hacienda, involve an organization of individual laborers and usually show the same kind of paternalistic relationship that exists between the individual farm laborer or colono and the patrón.

INDUSTRIAL PRODUCTION

The growth of population in the provincial areas has placed as much strain on the artisan as it has on the peasant and rural laborer; in addition, many of their crafts are being, or have been, displaced by industrially produced goods. Among the first of the industrial products to compete with handcrafted goods were textiles. Textile industries, as distinct from the workshop collection of looms, were underway in some parts of Latin America late in the nineteenth century. Since cotton was grown locally, most of the production became essentially local, depending upon areas of primary development principally for dyes, machinery, and parts, and for technicians and administrators. Handwoven cloth—coarser, costlier, and available only in smaller quantities—was quickly displaced in many regions and continues to be pushed off the market. Picturesque Indian costumes, characteristic of regional populations, disappeared and were replaced by dreary clothing that only identified one's sex and socioeconomic position. In many areas, seamstresses continued to ply their trade, since the industrial production of finished clothing is only now filling the market. In the same way, metal, glass, and enamel cooking- and tableware have pushed handmade pottery into marginal markets.

The pattern of industrial development is still reflected in the nature of the largest concerns in Latin America. Among the earliest efforts were the establishment of railways and, somewhat later, the setting up of electric companies and petroleum explorations. These, combined with mining operations that were expanding after their decline in the late colonial period, are still among the largest investments in Latin America. Early consumer goods were principally textiles, beer, tobacco, and sugar products, especially alcohol. Of the 180 corporations—including the 30 largest corporations of each of the 6 major Latin American industrial countries—31 were companies whose major interest was in finance; next most numerous were 19 electric companies, then 15 companies involved in steel and iron, 8 in petroleum, 7 each in mining and textiles, 6 each in railways, automobiles, and beer, 5 each in sugar and alcohol, and in telephones. In other words, with the exception of automobiles, the upper 60 per cent of the major industrial and related businesses in Latin America still reflect the early stages of industrialization.

Factories have been set up in various locales, including major cities, provincial centers, and the countryside. Each kind of area naturally provides distinctive industrial advantages and disadvantages. Many major cities are national capitals and, being the centers of urban migrations, also have the largest available labor supply. Migrants into these centers undergo urbanization as they fit into the factory system, the factory being one of the acculturative devices which hastens their adjustment to city life. The greatest concentrations of factories are in the original major cities, although in recent years the petroleum and iron centers have been established in locales more appropriate to the materials, such as Concepción in Chile, Chimbote in Peru, Volta Redonda in Brazil, Maracaibo in Venezuela, and Poza Rica and the Coatzacoalcos in Mexico. There is no question that industries have expanded by virtue of the migration of labor to the sites of the factories. In many instances, the movement of people to the cities has not been inspired by a specific desire to join the industrial labor force; rather, the city has simply offered the best general alternative to the agrarian pressures being felt in the rural areas.

The establishment of plants in provincial areas has served to drain people from the larger cities only in the cases of larger installations. Small provincial factories have often obtained almost all their labor from the immediate vicinity; such was the case of plants in Cantel and Villa Nueva in Guatemala. As the industrial effort continues, however, it usually impels a long-term adjustment that is not precisely the same as the one at the beginning; the older provincial textile plants in Peru have tended to prefer immigrant highlanders over the locally born mestizos, as the former were more docile and took orders better. Provincial plants have tended to manifest somewhat greater stability of operation than urban plants, possibly in part because the strains inherent in the industrialization process are not compounded by those of urbanization.

The "factories in the fields" about which we know most at present are sugar refineries and the related field operations. Studies in Puerto Rico, Brazil, and Venezuela have revealed a variety of adaptations that seem to vary specifically with the manner of administrative control. The largest enterprises are corporately owned and administered by professionals. The smaller plants tend to be family-owned and are often administered by kinsmen of the owner. As we shall see later, these variations in administration make a crucial difference in the nature of the relationships established, more crucial than would be variations contingent upon the specific product or crop being processed.

Factories in the fields are, in a very real sense, forms that have adapted to both a rural and industrial situation simultaneously. Because they are not found in classic European industries, they have perhaps been thought of as "transitional" types. The factory in the field is an adaptation that will be present as long as the industrial processing of field crops can best be done near the area of crop production. But today these factories also provide a situation in which the rural labor force still belongs to the hinterland of the industrial revolution, while indoor factory work represents its more progressive sector. The apparent transitional quality stems from the fact that in the Western experience these two sectors have usually been separated by vast distances, even oceans. Most people in the West have lived their lives in one or the other context, but not both. Latin America is one of the locales in the world in which the two are joining into a single operating complex, and the nature of the phenomenon confronts Western-trained economists—be they capitalist- or Marxist-oriented—with a potful of problems.

The textile factory in the Indian town of Cantel, Guatemala, provides essentially a similar situation, but in this instance, it was not set up because of the locus of the raw materials but because of the locus of available power. In any event, the population in question has yet to take on the expected qualities of a proletariat.

In a few areas, the formation of a classic European proletariat has taken place. It is not easy to distinguish this proletariat from its very real European origins; in some areas, such as Argentina and southern Brazil, much of the early urban labor was in fact of direct European extraction. Elsewhere, as in Chile, Mexico, and Colombia, where industrialization emerged on a local labor supply, thorough proletarianization has not been so evident.

Two factors have contributed to alter the picture that we usually associate with European urban labor. One was that the labor force formed within each plant and factory in a pattern of organization that was already known in the New World. Celso Furtado has pointed out that the early Brazilian industry paid fairly high wages to the predominantly European labor force and that little or no conflict developed between labor and management. Charles Savage has shown the same pattern to have evolved with local labor in Colombia. Furtado likens this situation to the generally harmonious situation that already existed in the local agrarian picture. The early experience of the Argentinian di Tella organization certainly reveals a development of paternalism and labor-administrative relationships that comes much closer to the Latin American agrarian pattern than it does to the European industrial pattern.

The other factor that has tended to mold the labor force around the Latin American agrarian relations pattern rather than the industrial pattern of Europe is that much of the industrializing labor has been of recent rural origin. The first generation of incoming migrants tends to retain strong ties with the home communities, and this sets a series of constraints on the adoption of newer ways of seeing things and new varieties of social relationships. The continuation of the paternalistic relationship is particularly evident. Recent studies suggest that the introduction of government action on the labor front, combined with the intent on the part of some management to introduce more systematic management and production procedures, is serving to reduce this paternalistic quality. Cochran and Reina mention that in the di Tella Argentine enterprise in the period of Perón there was an annual labor turnover amounting to a total larger than the actual labor force. And Savage describes the shift away from paternalism that accompanied the appearance of engineers when the older owners absented themselves from a factory in Antioquia, Colombia. The shift is not yet overwhelming, however, as illustrated by Harry Hutchinson's description of a small Brazilian sugar factory in the field which is owned and run by a family and involves a classic degree of paternalism. He mentions that the larger corporate installations were attempting a return to the paternalistic system after having undergone extensive labor unrest with the organization of labor unions.

North American and European observers have tended to look upon the development of labor unions in Latin America as if they were carrying out the same role and attempting to achieve the same goals as they did elsewhere in Western history. It is true that many of the union developments were part of the general movement in the Western world since the latter part of the nineteenth century. However, a major situational difference produced the development of a series of organizations that even today look, in their general form, like labor unions elsewhere, but which are doing a fundamentally different thing. The difference lies in the fact that during the early years of this century Latin America was a hinterland; it was not an area that was being heavily industrialized. The size of the industrial labor force was still a minor part of the total population, even in those countries such as Argentina, where it was numerically important. The great mass of Latin American labor was agrarian, widely scattered on estancias, plantations, and haciendas, many quite isolated from each other and from the capital city and therefore quite impossible to organize or even to reach for purposes of indoctrination.

Many observers have noted the problems inherent in any attempt to organize both rural labor and very poor labor. During the years when Western industrial labor was organizing and the great efforts toward world labor organization were emerging, Latin America provided little substance for union development. One role that is often ascribed to the labor movement in the rest of the Western world is that of being a quasi-nonpolitical force that, through exerting its right to strike, gradually achieves legal recognition and is given certain other rights by the government. In the early days of labor in Latin America, it did somewhat the same things, although from its earliest days its anarchist tendencies made it of direct interest to the government. The major difference between what took place in Latin America and what occurred in areas of primary development was that the governments of the latter were growing strong with the expansion of industry, and they were not terribly inclined to pay any more attention to labor than was absolutely necessary. Long, and sometimes bloody, strikes and fights brought to the fore the needs of labor, and political champions began to appear and gradually to win for labor the legal rights that it was claiming.

Latin American governments, however, were not growing strong with expanding industry; in fact, they were weak from the control that already strong landowners exercised collectively over entire regions. It was quite evident that the campesinos—colonos, tenant farmers, plantation laborers, and peasants—were suffering varying degrees of poverty and were in no condition to be organized. Since most of the governments during the first part of the twentieth century were in the hands of individuals who represented the interests of the landowners, no organization of rural labor could have expected to receive help from them.

Some Latin American governments, as they began to grow in power and to exercise the responsibilities of sovereignty, found that labor was a force that they needed. Since the governments' major local competitors for power were the individual landowners, the governments had no way of exercising power independently of the landowners. Initially, the use of unions by the governments was concentrated upon the urban areas where unions were already active. In some situations, in which there were no unions, their formation was encouraged. The period of the 1930's and 1940's saw the development and utilization of unions by the governments of Argentina and Mexico in a way that permitted those governments to exercise their control over the wealth of the country. In the 1950's, Guatemala's government attempted the same thing, but was ultimately unsuccessful and lost power entirely. Thus in the second quarter of the century, when labor unions were visibly successful, they essentially served the governments in their attempts to become the recognized powers in the society.

This is not to say that labor unions have not succeeded in any of the efforts of the kind more often associated with them. They have struck, they have achieved higher wages, and have bettered the worker's situation in general. The degree to which they have been able to do this, however, has generally been strictly controlled by the government. Any specific successes the unions have had have usually been determined not only by what was deemed to be labor's best interest but by what was deemed by the government to be the country's best interest.

It is not strange, therefore, that we find many writers commenting on the continuation of paternalism in Latin American labor relations, but with the government now playing the role of the patrón. In fact, it is now the government that determines in great part what labor shall and shall not succeed in getting. In so doing, it places itself in a unique position over the laborer, not entirely dissimilar to that formerly enjoyed by the employer. From the point of view of governing a country, it is not only useful but almost necessary that the government allow occasional extreme (although not necessarily lethal) events to occur in order to achieve a balance between the various opposing interests that must exist within the nation as a whole. Permitting a strike, a walkout, or the stoppage of some service such as transportation can often accomplish this balance. Of course, some such demonstrations occur without government's approval and in direct challenge to the government. When they do occur, another force—the military—is called into play to balance the workers or syndicates, and it thus plays a crucial role in the attempt to maintain general balance.

There is little question that traditional Latin American labor stability and paternalism are related and are specifically responsive to the general power structure of the larger situation. The description by Sidney Mintz and Elena Padilla of two large sugar operations in Puerto Rico shows paternalism to be absent in a situation in which both labor unions and corporate management are given some attention by the government and to be present where the government has taken over as the owner of the plantation. In the first instance, the laborer stands in a multiple domain, with the labor union and the government holding competitive positions over him; thus, either management or the union can turn to the government for action and support of their arguments. In the second instance, however, the laborer stands in a unique domain. Management and the company are incorporated into a single entity, and the union cannot ask one to take sides against the other. Labor, in this situation, has no alternative source to which to turn and therefore paternalism tends to be perpetuated.

It is impossible to examine the process of industrialization in Latin America without arriving, sooner or later, at the question of the role played by the government. The early period of industrialization in the West, marked as it was by rather flamboyant free enterprise, cannot be expected to have a parallel in the industrialization currently under way in Latin America. In some sectors of the Anglo-American society, free enterprise is now a political symbol, monumentalized with a nativistic reverence. One gets the impression from some literature that sweatshops and substandard working conditions are absolutely necessary to continued development. On the positive side, Western industrial expansion brought in its train the growth of universal education and literacy. Whether fortunately or unfortunately, it is the goal of many Latin Americans to avoid the social injustices so manifest in the industrialization of North America and northern Europe and to hasten the gains in education, housing, diet, and luxuries that are assumed to be the more positive fruits.

The urban industrial population of the temperate zone became a political force by virtue of the fact that threat of a strike posed a serious problem to the welfare of the total society. Crucial was the fact that the society had become increasingly dependent upon the products of industrialization. In Latin America, whole sectors of the society can continue to operate for extensive periods even if the industrial elements do pose a strike. Reliance on supplies from the rural hinterland and the ability to retreat to the village countryside if things become really difficult tend to neutralize the power of the proletariat as it was known elsewhere. Consequently, too often the only sector that can exercise sufficient pressure on the industrialist to respond to industrial labor's needs is the government.

Concerning Mexico, Raymond Vernon has commented that it is not always possible to distinguish the public from the private sector, as the government is involved in so many ways with industrial and commercial operations. The same may be said, in some degree, of many Latin American countries. The Cuban revolution obviously did nothing to alter this generalization. The current efforts of the Chilean government under a political moderate, Eduardo Frei, are not to replace the private sector—

to eliminate foreign private ownership of the great mining operations—but to enter as a partner in them so as to begin to gain control over a sector of national activity that has remained more responsive to the needs of the United States than to those of Chile.

The attitude of the active industrialist in these circumstances is that the actions of the government in controlling prices and imports of crucial materials, in taxing exports, in setting labor legislation, or in exercising preferences in labor courts are all part of the real economic environment, and that the successful enterprise must operate in terms of these risks as well as of those more commonly recognized in the past. It is possible, however, to find many segments of what would have been called liberalism in the nineteenth century. The great industrial complex of Monterrey, Mexico, developed in a situation some- what separated from the general social development of Mexico. Although Monterrey was connected by rail with Mexico City late in the nineteenth century, the general attitude of the development strongly reflected the private-enterprise prac- tices of its northern neighbor. A few years ago Monterreyans even started a technical university to train "apolitical" industrial managers and engineers. A somewhat similar development oc- curred in Antioquia, Colombia, where the semi-isolated locale permitted remarkable industrial development, relatively free of the governmental controls so evident in Lima, Mexico City, or Rio de Janeiro. The development of industrial complexes as such quite obviously cannot be ascribed to isolation, but the establishment and maintenance of an essentially nineteenth- century philosophy of industrialization, coupled with an ad- vancing twentieth-century technology, can be.

The varieties of industrial development in Latin America are a response, in part, to the problems generated by the relative degree of dominance of industrial hinterland and city. In ad- dition, there is the question of which sector of the society shall take the lead in integrating the various parts into an operating nation. In almost all instances, the answer has already been decided in favor of the government. How this integration comes about is a problem of social invention—whether through explicit government control, as in the case of Cuba; or through actively balancing labor against management, as in Perón's Argentina, in Peru, or in modern Mexico; or through a regional contrast, such as that between Monterrey and the Veracruz coast, wherein the latter is dominated by government-owned oil operations; or through government partnership or sponsorship, as in Chile and Venezuela; or through some other means. Common to all solutions is the attempt to encourage and control enterprise to achieve a better distribution of the fruits of industrialization than was evident in nineteenth-century Europe.

FUTURE PROBLEMS AND POSSIBILITIES

It cannot be assumed for a moment that the above implies that all Latin American governments have things well in hand. The important aspect of the entire picture is that the government is the only entity available that can even attempt to have anything in hand, and that the diversities witnessed in the current scene derive from the varieties of attempted solutions. In genetics, the comparable process is called random variation and refers to the various adaptations to a new environmental situation that are tried when there are many different entities making the attempt. It is inevitable that some attempts will not work, but it is also improbable that all will fail. No matter what else characterizes Latin America today, diversity does. It is unlikely, if not impossible, that any one specific solution will supply answers to the problems of all the countries.

Industrialization in Latin America involves not merely the increase in production of goods on a greater scale, but also concomitant increase in numbers of industrial consumers. The problem of distribution of wealth is thus as central to industrialization as it is to production. This problem has so far been attacked only by extremely revolutionary governments, but there is a growing sector of commercial interests that regard the home market as fundamental.

Secondary development is little understood in the northern nations. Their manner of industrialization has led to theories of development that place special emphasis on the forward thrust of technology and on the adaptations that society can make to new technological demands. Some Latin Americans, also educated in the northern schools of thought, similarly assume that development may follow roughly the same path in their own lands. However, industrialization of a formerly hinterland area is a process that may involve two phases, and each of them is thorny. One is the introduction of existent technological complexes. It is this process, and the necessary massive readaptations of the social order necessary to make it possible, that I am calling secondary development. A further process, however, and one that no Latin American country has really attempted intensively, is the transformation of secondary development into primary development. This second process, as was suggested in Chapter 1, seems to involve extremely high costs in social readjustment, so high that they have thus far been paid only by countries involved in extensive world conflicts.

At this point in time, the major issue in Latin America is not converting to a primary-development phase, but undergoing the strains of secondary development. It is a phase of evolution that is uniquely cultural and does not share its basic structure with biological or organic evolution. The diffusion of new technology—the learning by adult members of a society to adapt to the skills, social relationships, and general patterns of thought and emotion that are engendered by the new behaviors—is hard to achieve on a purely trial-and-error basis. Planning is of extraordinary importance, and planning can only be fruitful if it occurs in a context in which the plans have some realistic possibility of being carried out. To be realistic, the governments of Latin America are in most instances the only entities that can even hope to plan for long-term results, and the fact that they fail in so many cases does not mean that there are other entities that can hope for greater success.

Entrepreneurs, Economists, and Capital

Among the changes that have taken place in the structure of Latin America over the past hundred years two are to be noted: a different kind of individual has become active in development, and he draws upon different sources for his capital. In what has been called the "mixed economy," the change in these two factors has been notable during the twentieth century.

DEVELOPMENT OF ENTREPRENEURIALISM

Under nineteenth-century liberalism the entrepreneurs were principally agrarian-domain holders who combined cheap or essentially free labor with very inefficient farming methods to produce a crop that entered an export-market system. Coffee from Colombia, Middle America, and Brazil, wheat and beef from Argentina and Uruguay, and sugar from the Caribbean were produced for export. Mineral operations in Chile, the Andes, and Mexico followed essentially the same formula. The capital was drawn from exporters or merchants who, in turn, received it from private banks. The appearance of family fortunes did not discourage speculation, nor did it develop flexibility in agricultural planning and rational production.

There were also large agrarian establishments producing for an essentially fixed internal market; inefficient production marked these efforts too, but an internal market made the returns somewhat more sure, though smaller. The production of sugar, tobacco, grapes, coca (in the Andes), and the local staples supplied the cities—as well as rural peoples—during off seasons and when their crops were poor. Whether for export or the internal market, the system worked under the general patronage of the government, in that government personnel were either one with the landowners or each supported the other in its exercise of power. Labor was either employed at very low wages, in keeping with very low production per capita, or it was kept in a mobile-tenancy, debt-peonage, or colonal status. Under such conditions, laborers had little choice as to whether they could leave the land.

The twentieth century brought changes into almost every aspect of this system. Industries were initiated and, needing labor, had to provide a better basis of employment than merely giving the colono a little land or relying upon debt peonage. European immigration to the east coast, especially Brazil and Argentina, provided a new laboring force with a background quite different from that of the local mestizo population. The notion of land as the principal basis of wealth prevented the European immigrant from becoming wealthy, because the accessible lands were already owned, and since many of the newcomers were city-bred, city life was somewhat more palatable; from this group came some of the most important early entrepreneurs in the industrial area. From the very outset of Latin American industrialization, foreigners participated almost everywhere at the entrepreneurial level and in restricted areas in the labor force. In a few regions, such as in the Antioquian region of Colombia, local individuals took the lead in economic development.

Credit and manner of production in the new enterprises were generally not too dissimilar to those governing the older agrarian production. Output was low and rational production was not a major feature of the process. Ownership tended to be a matter of family control; administrative personnel came from among the circle of friends and relatives. Nevertheless, industrial production in the expanding population was basically different from the agrarian production that preceded it because, among other things, there was competition from the outside. It was also necessary to find a new class of individuals, the professional and technical specialists. Much of the labor force was trained on the job; but operating spinning and weaving machinery, dealing with the technical problems of laying a railway roadbed, or preparing drinkable beer depended upon technicians who often had to come from outside the country. Although credit was available from local banks in some instances, foreign interests also made their appearance. Local banking and commercial houses were unaccustomed to the risks of industrial production, but investors from outside the country found them less strange. As industrial activity increased, so did foreign investment.

Industrial entrepreneurialism was, to a considerable extent, imported into Latin America along with sources of credit and with technical personnel who undertook the finer details of operation. But, encountering the Latin American agrarian environment, it rapidly followed the same pattern of low production, family ownership, and paternalism. The next really significant change was the onset of the contemporary challenge of development, when the increasingly visible social injustice inherent in the agrarian mercantile system erupted in the Mexican Revolution. The revolution, however, followed no plan

—not even so much as was the case in the Russian Revolution that followed shortly thereafter. The growth of urban populations in some areas, especially in South America, together with the action of rural peoples in Mexico, set the entire continent to thinking in other ways.

The years between the two world wars saw much ideological experimentation, but also a considerable growth in the industrial entrepreneurial sectors of the larger countries. At the same time, Latin American governments were finding themselves in the role of handling industrial and labor disputes. It also became evident that powers in the outside world were inadvertently providing them with a means of dealing with their own internal problems in ways not possible a decade earlier. In protecting its own interests—such as the Panama Canal and the investments of its citizens—the United States found it advisable not to contest the Mexican expropriation violently. Weak Central American and Caribbean governments served no purpose for the United States; in fact, it was advantageous to have stronger governments in those countries, governments that could at least be responsible for the payment of debts and the protection of foreign investments and nationals. Hence, the sending of Marines to Nicaragua and Haiti was done in the hope that the United States could establish there what it liked to think of as more stable governments.

Government Participation in Economic Growth

The growth of strong central governments was most clearly felt in the entrepreneurial field after the Second World War, although earlier events in Mexico provided the prototype. The question of who was to undertake development was automatically answered in the manner of the West: private enterprise. But it was increasingly evident to those in responsible government positions that private enterprise had serious failings. The entrepreneurs were chronically short of capital; their choice of investment possibilities was determined by what they felt would be most profitable in the short run and not by what might be best for the country at that point in its history; and their relations with labor throughout the first half of the century had been marked by working conditions that were increasingly condemned in some industrialized Western countries. Indeed, it was quite clear that some foreign investors found the Latin investment market attractive because of the low labor costs, a feature that permitted them to enjoy luxuries denied them at home. Thus it was that the governments themselves began to become involved in the investment issue and to undertake enterprises, to share in the costs of establishing industries, and to exercise more and more legal controls over the activities of private investors. The post-World War II period saw the real emergence of the so-called mixed economy, the varying combination of public and private investments.

The development of railroads was one of the first major steps in the development of the infrastructure necessary for economic development. During the first half of the twentieth century, the highway systems also began to grow through government efforts. In some instances, road development was spurred by the concern of the United States for a connecting route between the various countries. The major efforts have been and still continue to be undertaken on major commercial arteries rather than on the multitude of feeder roads necessary to join isolated farms and subsistence-agriculture areas with central markets. The governments developed roads in response to the demands of the larger producers and export interests. Here, as elsewhere, the campesino's voice was unheard.

In more recent years, one of the most important institutions established by governments has been the development agency. These agencies have played widely diverse roles, depending upon how they were conceived and how they evolved within the particular country. In most instances they are primarily credit institutions, combining some variety of technical services with supervisory functions. Some become involved directly in investment, whereas others supplement or initiate investment in the hope that private interests will buy in after the initial costs have been thus taken care of. Many specialized development offices have also sprung up. Some are directed towards the building of municipal establishments, including plants, sewer systems, and water systems. Others are aimed at specific industries or agrarian sectors, and a few have even been established to try to provide credit and technical and extension services to the campesinos. These latter have usually been specialized: their efforts have been aimed at the *ejidatarios* (in Mexico), or the Indians (in Guatemala), or the colonists, or others. Really imaginative and effective broad-scale aid to the lower sector has not approached the magnitude of that which has contributed to develop the upper sector.

It has often been pointed out that the participation of government in the affairs of private investment is hardly new, strange, or peculiar to "socialist" nations. The United States government has long been so involved, as have governments of every other Western power. The reason it has occasioned so much attention is that the growth of government control in Latin America has in many instances been rather recent. Although the situation varies, both from place to place and from time to time, the Latin American government generally has more potential legal controls than is the case in North America. These, however, are used sparingly and sometimes in a rather unpredictable way. When the government exercises its power broadly, as in Mexico, the private investor must pick his way through a varied network of official decisions.

A number of activities form these governmental processes. There is the matter of making political decisions as to what the government shall do, and there are the hosts of technical problems that require an understanding of the background and consequences of actions made on such decisions. In the past two or three decades, the economist's advice has become more and more crucial to the decision of the politician. The economist, handling matters that have to do with the relative allocation of funds and resources, finds himself in a position of unexpected power. Although his vantage point does not guarantee that his recommendations will be followed, his technical analysis commands attention. Thus, for the private investor, the government economist plays a very important role because it is he who sets the limits to private-investment activities.

Most economists are trained in the local national universities, and most faculties of economics are concerned not with classical economics but with socially oriented theories. The role of the foreign investor in general, and of the United States in particular, in the history of the country is ordinarily a matter of considerable suspicion. Although nationally trained economists tend to be strong nationalists, most influential Latin American economists have been trained outside the area; they are not, therefore, provincial, or ignorant of many of the alternative and competing theories. Since few come from wealthy backgrounds, the position of power in government that their training opens to them is attractive. The government economist tends, by ideological training and position, to be in favor of a strong government role in the development of the country. This does not mean that he is categorically against private investment or private gain. It does mean that the private investor must subordinate his investment interests to those of the nation; and the economist sees his job, among other things, as that of a watchdog.

Many new kinds of technical professionals have taken their places in the government, but few can match the economist's position of power in general development practice and policy making. The professionals in medicine, geology, agriculture, and engineering occupy positions of control within their respective areas of knowledge; but the economist's decision-making position allows him more influence in the over-all political process. The growth of the economist's role in the political process is not unlike the gradual encroachment of science upon the dogma of religion. As each area of decision making becomes more dependent upon technical knowledge, the area of the politician's independent judgment is narrowed. Of course, the politician can ignore the technician's advice completely, but he does so at the increasing risk of his own political welfare. The rise of the economist has marked the relative decline of the lawyer. Matters that used to require decisions based on legal matters are now so technical that the lawyer has lost what was once a rather central position in the social structure.

THE ENTREPRENEUR'S SOURCES OF CAPITAL

The private investor or entrepreneur continues to be an important force throughout Latin America, but his role must be seen in terms of the kind of operation in which he is engaged. In the first place, there cannot be said to be a class of private investors, or entrepreneurs, as over and against the government bureaucracy, the shopkeeper, the peasant, or the professional. The interest and desire to become involved in private gain are as widespread in Latin America as anywhere in the world. Culturally there are restrictions, particularly evident in peasant towns and villages that limit the kind and degree of entrepreneurial action in which a person may hope to achieve success. Certain activities are recognized to be appropriate within a community, and the individual who ventures too far from the understood patterns is apt to be censured and ridiculed. This attitude prevails especially in smaller communities, whether isolated by habitat or culture.

A peasant may expand his land holdings, but if he becomes excessively wealthy or unusually successful, the only possible explanations are (1) that he has been dishonest; (2) that he has been lucky in finding some unexpected lump sum, such as by winning the lottery or finding buried treasure; or (3) that he has been involved in some kind of magic that has enabled him to do so much better than his peers. It is notable that none of these things are entirely inhibited by traditional overt sanctions.

The problem the peasant faces is whether he wishes to live among people who suspect his actions. If he does, and his sons are successful in keeping or expanding his holdings, then his family rises to a local position of prestige. Equally often, however, he finds it unpleasant and decides that the more rewarding way to enjoy his gains is to move, renting his properties or leaving them in the care of a relative.

The person concerned with gaining wealth today faces different problems than was the case when wealth could be readily equated with control of large extensions of land. Today there are other important, though limited, sources of wealth. One may: (1) have his own or his family's fortune; (2) marry into money; (3) have friends who are wealthy and who can be counted on to provide some capital; (4) have access to some standard credit agency, such as a private bank, a government loan agency, or development agency; or (5) hold some position that can serve to make it worth someone else's while to contribute, whether willingly or not. Those with access to the first of these wealth sources are obviously few; it is a source that can be used only by the very wealthy. Not all scions of such families become forceful entrepreneurs, but they are important contributors to development in terms of how they decide to invest their funds. A standard complaint is that much of Latin America's wealth is not reinvested in Latin America. This is unquestionably true; but it is a rational economic decision that leads to investment abroad, a thing that most private investors should be able to understand.

In many cases, the wealth of the very rich is held either corporately by a family or in parts by various members of a family. The assumption that one can trust kin more readily than strangers (or even friends, since they have their own kin to answer to) means that the tendency is to keep wealth within the family. It is difficult to know whether this concentration of wealth is as true of the newer fortunes as it has been of the older ones; but there is evidence that some government restrictions—such as Mexico's—on the amount of land that a single individual may own have served to stimulate family members to cooperate closely in financial matters.

The use of friends as sources of capital is usually merely the basis for beginning business negotiations. While few friendships are strong enough to obligate an individual to invest in a friend's enterprise, it is more often the case that the friend evaluates the possibility of the venture and decides to invest on the basis of this judgment. The importance of friendship lies in providing a basis for initiating the negotiations. It is also assumed that the entrepreneur will not run off with the money of a friend. Friendship does not preclude this possibility, but it reduces it.

The use of credit agencies, both public and private, has become an increasingly important answer to the credit problem. Since older private banks tend to be fairly conservative in their lending policies, many governments have instituted new banks to make credit available to the commercial and industrial investor as well as to the farmer. In both private and government agencies, however, the importance of knowing people in the right places continues to be great. This is not unique to the Latin American scene: one must have credit on Wall Street too. But Latin America does face a greater scarcity of funds. With requests for more capital than is available, it is obvious that the better known will receive preference. Among the new credit agencies are the development institutions mentioned earlier. Also of some importance has been the expansion of foreign banks—from both Europe and North America—that have brought with them a philosophy of investment somewhat varied from that of the older local banks.

Most of the courses mentioned thus far have to do with investors and enterprises of the upper sector. For people of limited means, resources are still severely restricted. Aside from one's friends, the most important wealth sources are local individuals who make a practice of advancing cash, tools, or food as credit on a new crop. The local financial entrepreneurs usually select their clients on the basis of direct profit or of whether the collateral offered—usually land—will provide good income or sale value. Storekeepers are the most common source of funds involved in this business; their interest is special since their debtors will use their stores if they expect continuing credit.

Another means of gaining capital is through graft—using one's particular position as a lever by means of which one can pry funds out of someone. There is every reason to think that graft follows the principles of free enterprise. It occurs between private individuals, as when a newspaper prints articles critical of local concerns when these fail to advertise in the paper, or when heavy tolls are demanded for crossing one's lands. Much more important, however, is the shifting of funds to and from government personnel. Most governmental jobs place an individual in a position in which he can exercise pressure if he wants funds. Some jobs are classically lucrative, such as customs posts, the granting of licenses, the building of roads, the letting of contracts for any one of a thousand jobs, and so on. Similarly, the government itself is a source of funds. Money that goes out to private individuals may be tagged with a percentage to return to the officials who sent it. Books in the national library can be sold to European and North American book dealers. Government funds for per-diem payments for people working in provincial areas may be paid regularly to office holders who never leave the capital city. As Charles Erasmus has pointed out, the assumption of immorality in these dealings is generally present; that is, even though both or all parties are agreed that they will resort to graft, they do not advertise it but try to keep it quiet. There is also an assumption that such payments have occurred whenever a person who occupies a position in which he could be expected to extract money by graft manifests sudden wealth. Since the goal of most individuals is to obtain a surer income than graft can provide, a great deal of grafted money is invested. This money is used to buy land, to start businesses, and to initiate other investments.

The existence of graft emphasizes the importance of government intervention in the process of free enterprise. Although the more industrialized countries have long since controlled certain sectors of potential graft, they are not without it. An important aspect of growing government strength is that only a strong government can reduce graft. Graft within a government simply indicates that there has been a proliferation of control centers; more people can act as they wish in their own interests and not bend their efforts in the interests of the country. Widespread graft is a symptom of governmental weakness, and to ascribe immorality to it clarifies little.

The whole process of secondary development provides the basis for—and indeed requires the extensive participation of— many different kinds of entrepreneurs and investors, politicians, and technicians. The roles of these individuals, however, do not divorce them from their other positions, that is, from their roles as members of a society in which prestige symbols are costly and capital and cash are not easy to come by. One Latin American remarked that "In the United States there is enough graft to go around." Whatever may be the case in the United States, there is a clear insufficiency in Latin America. The individual— whether he does or does not hold a fervent ideology for the development of his nation—must face up to the question of survival at the level of living to which he is accustomed and, if possible, of an improvement of that level in terms of his view of the prestige system. There is nothing in Western history to lead us to think that more advanced countries have any greater proportion of entrepreneurs than do industrially backward countries, though they do have greater entrepreneurial opportunities and more sources of wealth. Opportunities and capital for enterprise increase with markets; like most other factors in development, they cannot be created out of whole cloth.

Scientific Revolution and Education

~~~~~~

Only for analytical purposes is it possible to separate knowledge—and specifically, scientific knowledge—from the various topics that have been already discussed. Technology is, at its core, knowledge; and the inventions and theorizing that may have contributed to the improvement of technology were as profound a part of the industrial revolution as were its material and social aspects. The changes in the scope and structure of knowledge that have been referred to as the scientific revolution diffused to Latin America as did other aspects of the industrial revolution. Scientific knowledge, however, exists only within the process that produces it. It is an intellectual and observational endeavor, often involving a laboratory for controlling the conditions of experiment, as well as a particular frame of mind toward the things being studied. There must be doubt, but of a constructive kind, and there must be willingness to make countless mistakes before a fruitful answer is found. All this means that the professional scientist benefits from a somewhat protected environment for operation.

THE GROWTH OF SCIENTIFIC KNOWLEDGE

In the industrialized world there are two educational phases of science. The first phase is the existence of a relatively educated sector in the population, sufficiently literate to take advantage of the products of science and to supply enough youngsters to work in the area as creative individuals rather than technicians. The second phase is the presence of centers of learning that provide the core and continuity of the pioneering work in research and the training of new scientists. This responsibility has, in great part, been carried by the universities, although both industrial firms and governmental bureaus have become increasingly involved in basic scientific work.

Latin America has been slow in joining the scientific revolution—just as it was slow in participating in other aspects of the industrial revolution. Illiteracy has been, and continues to be, widespread over much of the area, and universities have predominantly been professional schools, heavily concerned with the education of lawyers and doctors. Continued pride has been taken in what is felt to be the rich, humanist tradition of the continent, and this is contrasted with the crass, materialistic tradition that is ascribed to the North American scientific and technological world. The term "science" has been used to refer to minor experiments by talented individuals who so involved themselves because of idiosyncratic preferences. So long as much of science was a matter of observation, so long as it consisted primarily of natural history, some Latins were numbered among the great observers and travelers of the western world. When science began to demand greater professional competence, a more rigorous methodology, greater professional preparation, and a more consistent expenditure of time, Latin American society was short on the space, resources, and interest necessary to encourage scientific activities. Private industry scarcely existed, and government's most excessive interest was barely consistent enough to do any more than maintain libraries and museums (and these often in a deplorable condition). Many of the great Latin American natural scientists have been Europeans and North Americans who came to the area for longer or shorter periods, having been educated elsewhere.

UNIVERSITY REFORM

The process of secondary development has become evident in education and science as well as in the material aspects of technology and society. The great Latin American universities that were established in the colonial period found themselves, early in the twentieth century, the target of a profound "University Reform," in which students demanded a greater part in the control of university affairs. In itself, this was a revolt against what was seen to be the almost total incompetence of the universities to cope with the changing world. But the goals of the reform were insufficient and too misdirected to bring the universities rapidly into the twentieth century, although it did in some instances so disrupt the university structure that governing faculties were forced to accept a somewhat more flexible coalition with respect to matters of curricula and administration.

Of probably greater importance, however, was the conclusion that adequate higher education in many fields, especially in engineering and applied sciences, could not be entrusted to the older faculties and universities. This led to the establishment of technical and engineering universities that patterned their curricula after those of modern foreign universities. These universities were started sometimes by private interests and sometimes by the government and include the technological school in Monterrey, Mexico, and the Instituto Torcuato di Tella in

Buenos Aires, the Engineering University in Lima, Peru (earlier a polytechnic institute), and a number of Brazilian universities. A characteristic of the more technical of these institutions was the tendency of the students to be less interested in the national political life and its problems than were students at the older universities.

Following the University Reform, the older institutions continued as before to be centers for student sorties into national political life. The universities had traditionally been sanctuaries, and in the colonial period they were under the control and dominance of ecclesiastical orders. In the republican period, any semblance of order that may have been derived from their former church relations was lost, and the universities subsisted as the poorest of governmental stepchildren. Since the number of individuals in the early twentieth century who received university educations was small, it was not surprising that they played a role in the national political scene out of proportion to their numbers. This role became especially important following the Second World War, when the issue of nationalism became increasingly explicit in Latin American intellectual circles. The universities provided a ready-made mob for both student-sponsored and nonstudent-sponsored demonstrations against the government or some particular event. Demonstrating against visiting dignitaries of countries whose politics the students did not like was one such form of protest. The treatment accorded Richard Nixon in Peru and in Venezuela was perhaps somewhat exaggerated, but a similar reception had been granted Alfredo Stroessner, the President of Paraguay, during his visit to La Paz, Bolivia, in 1958, and minor steps were frequently taken against other disfavored individuals. Under these circumstances, some universities have been periodically closed, and the process of education has come to sometimes extended halts.

Another source of university endeavor for reform appeared in

Catholic universities, and in a few instances in Protestant missionary-sponsored colleges. The sponsors of these schools were interested not only in furthering the faith, but were also concerned with keeping continuity in the educational process. As might be expected, costs of the Catholic schools had to be borne by the local wealthy, and the majority of the students who went to these schools were of conservative Catholic backgrounds. In recent years, these colleges and universities have attempted to strengthen themselves specifically to counteract the political freedom usual at the major national universities.

GOVERNMENT, TECHNOLOGY, AND THE UNIVERSITY

The private university in Latin America, unlike its predecessor in North America, is the latecomer, and the contemporary national university has the long history. Consequently, the private universities are for the most part small and suffer from uncertain annual financing because endowments are small or nonexistent. Many of them depend upon government subsidy. Until recently, however, the national universities were not in much better shape. Presumably, the emerging variety of universities reflects increasing perception of the needs of a society involved in industrial development. But the national need for more highly educated specialists is beginning to be met at home. Only in extreme instances, as in Cuba's case, has the university system been entirely converted to the single interest of the nation as defined by the incumbent government. An attempt to make this conversion following the Bolivian revolution in 1952 was greeted by a year-long university strike, during which the various universities in Bolivia were closed and were occupied by the peasant and mining militia. In the end, the militia retired, and the universities continued as they had been before.

In the Bolivian instance just cited, the universities directly challenged the right and ability of the government to nationalize them, and they were successful in that challenge. The situation throughout Latin America varies greatly in this respect, from complete state control over administration and policy (as in Cuba) to a combination of state control over administration and considerable university control over policy (as in Brazil) to cogoverning of universities by students (as in Bolivia and Honduras). (I am speaking here only of the public institutions, not the private universities mentioned earlier.) But in one respect most of the universities seem similar. Few, until recently, have taken the national lead in advancing education or in developing a level of operation beyond their immediate operating funds. In general, when the universities have taken major steps to improve themselves, it has often been under the pressure of the government.

As could almost be assumed from the above, the universities have similarly failed to take much of a lead in technological development, and their role in the scientific revolution, perforce, has been slight. North American educators have tended to lay the blame for this lack of development upon the heavy emphasis on theoretical training and on the lack of emphasis on laboratory and experimental procedures. To place the blame on the form of education in use, however, hardly explains a thing. The fact of the matter is that for the nineteenth century the traditional Latin American university was still quite adequate; scientific training had begun in those places where technical phases of the industrial revolution were taking place, and Latin America was not among them. Education in the national universities was sufficient to answer the business needs of agrarian mercantilism and to teach the cultivated conversation necessary for living in the upper sector. The attempt in recent years to introduce scientific technical training directly into Latin American curricula has met with heavy going for exactly the same reason that other phases of the technical-change process have encountered difficulty. The problem confronted by those who have tried to introduce such changes has not been so much a lack of ability to comprehend the scientific needs as it has been a severe lack of motivation to come into conflict with the social relationships that are current.

The general conclusion has been that the only way to alter the curricula and the operating procedures of Latin American universities is to effect a fundamental reorganization of the university and to improve the financing of the institution. Both solutions are precisely those that many Latin Americans have long recognized to be the only ways in which major changes in any sector of life will be achieved. Both, it is clear, stem directly from the nature of the problems inherent in secondary development. Since the universities have not grown consonantly with the growth of advanced and complex technologies, the sudden introduction of a whole complex of new concepts, procedures, and methods is as difficult for college professors and administrators to handle as are changes in agricultural technology for the peasants. The attempt to introduce new curricula is difficult when there is no way of rewarding those who initiate improvements. The reasons for introducing new technical subjects may seem unnecessarily obscure when they are not readily identified with things going on in the university. Prestige considerations still draw many of the best students into medicine and law, since the potential income and social position in those fields are more readily perceived.

Academic freedom in Latin America embraces the broader, European version of that concept. It involves not merely the right of the professor to teach what he pleases, but also the freedom of the student to study what he pleases. Quite obviously, when a curriculum very distinct from the traditional one is introduced, the most likely response of the student is to ignore or oppose it. Since such innovation reflects unilateral action by the administration, the student sees it as an infringement of his rights. When the novelty is identified as North American in origin, it is even more unacceptable. Consequently, such innovations are perhaps among the most difficult adaptive changes in Latin America.

A further problem, especially in the technological area, is that many technological skills and concepts are regarded as somewhat private by the organizations that use them. Companies with research laboratories are not likely to give away the secrets to processes and products that they have invented. The efforts to initiate a textile program in a South American university were partially neutralized by the reluctance of the local textile companies to release their own secrets for laboratory work. Secrets owned by a foreign company are even more likely to be denied release, since a growing nation is seen to be an expanding market.

University education in Latin America is still a very restricted matter. Many classes are held at night, and students often carry full-time jobs. Libraries are generally small, and the time spent on courses and work leaves the student little time for reading. For this reason there is still emphasis upon the lecture, which, in turn, is often substituted for by the "copy book," a mimeographed set of lecture notes or a discourse that the student can usually buy from the professor. In this way, the materials taught are unique in some respects to each professor. An intelligent student can pass a course without attending many lectures.

The professional schools are generally operated at the undergraduate level, with little or no postgraduate work. It is only in the major universities, such as those of Argentina, Chile, Mexico, and Brazil, that one finds significant postgraduate programs.

The internal structure of the universities is such that each university is usually composed of a series of independent schools that control the entire curriculum for the student who embarks on a degree program. There is little or no effective intercourse between these "faculties," and whenever the same course is needed in two or more of the faculties, it is taught independently in each, usually by different professors. The autonomy of the faculty within the university is matched only by the claims to autonomy of the university itself within the national structure.

It is perhaps paradoxical that the effort called the "University Reform" is preventing universities from playing the role they might play in the nationalizing process. Also, the basic compartmentalized structure of the faculties of contemporary Latin American universities is as durable a power structure as is the hacienda; the agrarian base has, in some cases, been more seriously challenged than have the universities. But the effective national development of a country requires institutions that are much more responsive to national needs than are most universities in Latin America.

Just as the universities have been slow to adapt themselves to the late arrival of the industrial revolution, so also have they been slow in providing any leadership or stimulus for the wider development of education within the countries. The normal schools have generally been at the secondary level and have been operated directly from the ministries of education. This system has produced a fairly rigid, nonexperimental approach to education, determined as much by political expediency as by pedagogical concerns. Few ministries of education can afford extensive research into problems of education; in many countries they have been unable to provide regular salaries for the teachers. The normal schools are, in many instances, the only access many individuals have to secondary education of any kind. As a result, the normal schools handle a task that should be shared with various secondary schools that are preparing people for other careers.

Responsibility for public education in Latin America is highly centralized in the national education ministries. Not only do they run the normal schools, but they are usually responsible for the overwhelming number of primary schools, both rural and urban, including upkeep and personnel. In most Latin American countries, government administration below the level of the central government is too poor to attempt to run its own school system. The general poverty of the community and the municipio affects the real possibilities of the development of even primary education at the local level.

EDUCATION AND POLITICIZATION

A major disadvantage of the Spanish colonial heritage was its lack of any genuine tradition of public education. Except for the early work of the missionaries, who deemed reading important for purposes of conversion, the new republics of the nineteenth century found themselves with essentially little by way of a tradition of education for the public. Today, literacy, the minimal educational tool, is still unavailable to large numbers of Latin Americans. It is significant that studies of rural migrants in the urban areas reveal that a small percentage of people regularly cited urban educational advantages as the major reason for migration.

Basically, public education is the device that has been invented by civilizations to indoctrinate a people into their own culture and to provide each succeeding generation with the means to survive within the environment as it is known. Urban civilizations, which Latin America has had for centuries, have required literacy as a basis of the operation of the city and the structure of political control and economic exchange. This base, however, was not necessary for the rural hinterland, and the advent of the industrial revolution did little to change this situation. The Latin American peoples, although long part of the literate Western tradition, entered the twentieth century essentially as illiterates.

The need for literacy comes suddenly upon an emerging nation, as do other needs of secondary development. Where the educational organization is weak and the tradition of literacy is absent in a major part of the population, the introduction of literacy becomes a matter of large-scale readjustment. Where literacy programs have been tried and have failed, their failure has been due more to poor organization and lack of support provided the program than to any reluctance on the part of the population to learn. Latin American governments have generally attempted to increase literacy through one of a variety of social inventions that have proved less than satisfactory. The standard method has been to establish within the regular school structure an additional system for educating adults to read. This has meant, almost inevitably, that the rural school organization, composed as it often is of a few underpaid teachers, had to assume additional responsibilities. Introducing literacy to adults is fundamentally a problem of adapting a population to a new form of behavior. Most rural teachers have minimal training themselves and are therefore not readily equipped to take on new technical tasks. The addition of an adult literacy program often places them in the position of being the only agents pressing for important change within a given locale.

There has been sufficient experience in rural areas to indicate that campesinos—except possibly those in monolingual Indian communities—generally recognize the importance of learning to read and write. Also, it is commonly felt that once a child has learned to read, to calculate, and to write, he is sufficiently educated and should turn to the work on the land. This recognition is a realistic one from the standpoint of the campesino. The other abilities that are taught in primary schools—detailed memory work on the geography of the country and elementary scientific ways of looking at the world—are not of immediate use. For the individual who sees his general goal to be survival within a rural context, the ability to calculate, read, and write is an essential tool for dealing with storekeepers, government agents, and other representatives of the larger world. But matters of content, that is, what to read, what is written, and what the calculation can accomplish, are felt to be implicit in one's way of life and need not be learned from a schoolteacher.

The point of view of the nationalizing governments on literacy is frequently ambivalent. If increasing control and centralization of power were one of the major goals of the government, it would seem to follow that pushing for extensive literacy would be a most important device. Political communication can be accomplished in a limited way through radio, but more detailed knowledge and arguments that need inspection have to come through the printed word. But few Latin American governments have recognized this necessity. Instead, the concentration of power is still seen to be a matter of urban concern, and the potential power of the large rural population is still not effectively mobilized. At present, the proponents of the revolutionary vigor of Cuba seem to have much on their side when it comes to teaching literacy. The context, however, is instructive. Cuba provides a situation in which the government has succeeded in concentrating its power and eliminating competitors within the national context. It therefore has a good basis for controlling what people will read. Given this base, the extension of literacy becomes of immediate use to the government, since there is a specific ideology that has to be taught. Without literacy, the introduction of an ideology is more difficult. When the government has no ideological direction, the urgency of literacy is simply not recognized.

Secondary schools play a particularly important role in Latin American life. Since university education is available only to an exceptional few, secondary schooling is the major educational device available to the individual for improving his social standing. Urban areas have both public and private secondary schools, but the secondary education available to rural and provincial people is as often as not part of the normal school system. While teacher training is a major goal of many of these schools, many graduates do not enter, or long continue, the teaching profession. The fact of the matter is that the normal school is still a major means of social mobility, and, as such, it is used by many individuals for that purpose.

From the standpoint of nationalism and development, the

secondary school plays an additional important role. It is the major locale of politicization. Action by secondary-school students is as important as that by university students. Since most secondary-school students live in cities, and in many cases these are capital cities, they are immediately available for political participation. The identification of national devils and heroes and the political view of the world are first encountered here. Here, also, literacy finally becomes effective. The amount of reading done by adult primary-school graduates is minimal and is usually restricted to legal deeds and public announcements. The secondary-school student, however, enters the world where the newspaper is a standard item of daily life and where living requires communication through reading.

In Latin America, education in general is regarded as one of the most important problems in the development of the society, but it is also one of the slowest to be solved. Historically, education has not been primarily a tool for changing the societies involved, but, rather, a device for perpetuating their current structure. The problems of introducing literacy, of establishing a more directed and dynamic university system, and of diversifying the intermediate educational institutions suffer from this common characteristic. Education in Latin America cannot be held responsible for the failures in development. Unfortunately, educational institutions tend to reflect the operating order of the society as it stands. Universities are changing and literacy is being inculcated, but the change is occurring no faster than are changes in other sectors of the culture.

The difficulties of introducing social invention are nowhere so patently obvious as in the educational structure. Reluctance to allow for change in the agrarian picture has been ascribed to ignorance or lack of education. But clearly these cannot be the reasons for failure in the educational system. Rather, the situation of the educational structure of a country makes perfectly clear the fact that individual motivation and education may be quite irrelevant when the structure is supported by the nature of the country as a whole. Change thus far has taken place in two ways: by supplementation, as by the appearance of new universities; and by substitution, as by the complete renovation of the Cuban universities. Supplementation is difficult in the educational system as a whole, and substitution presupposes a radical shift in national power.

Family, Household, and Kinship

~~~~~~

It is widely recognized that the family, in its various forms, plays an important role in the operation of Latin American society. It has been difficult at times, however, to sort out just how the family is structured, because most of our systematic information comes from relatively few actual studies. The purpose of the present discussion is to call attention to some of the features of the family organization that seem to be especially adaptive.

The Family

In general, the basic operating unit for most Latin Americans is a household kin group, a group composed usually of a married couple and their children, if they have any, possibly a dependent parent and his or her spouse, and/or children of one of the children. In areas of poverty, of short-termed residence, or where males are few, the woman-headed household is very common. In some areas, specifically Brazil, it is not uncommon to find a large number of closely related families living in the immediate vicinity, thus forming a large, extended kin residence area. Even with important extended family ties, however, the specific set of kinsmen who form the household often continue to form the crucial unit.

Within the household kin group, the basic dyadic relationships are to be found: mother-child, father-child, husband-wife, and siblings. The mother-child relationship is one of the most important within the whole system, and it is one that is congruent with a number of patterns that relate to the larger system. One should not err in assuming that because the mother is so important in the Latin American family structure, all the Freudian assumptions familiar elsewhere in Western European cultures are applicable. The mother, to the Latin male, is a person of respect to whom one has certain obligations. The overt show of this respect does not affect his business abilities, his general personality characteristics, or other features that might be assumed in United States society to be so affected. The mother pays special attention to the male child, and it is still common that the hierarchical order of authority in the family places the sons, even though still young, above the mother. The basis for the strong mother-child relationship is to be found in a number of aspects of the family situation. One reason is that the father is often quite distant to his children, sometimes because of real absence from the home and sometimes because of the custom of regarding the home as a place for women and children. The men often find their recreation outside the home, and the women are both excluded from it and expected to find their pleasures in the home.

The variations in familial relationships are enormous. Among the poorer households, there may be no resident husband at all, and in such a case, the mother-child relationship is further enhanced. The reverse of this situation is increasingly reported for many upper-sector families: the wife participates more with the husband in recreation, and the husband spends relatively more time with his household kin. A somewhat similar relationship is also found in some peasant and farming communities, but it is of a different origin and cannot be said to be widespread.

The consequence for the male child is that he may have to learn the culture of manhood from sources other than those within the household. This problem increases in the lower economic strata, where there may be no man in the household at all. One result is that inability to relate to a father in his own childhood makes it no easier later for the grown man to relate to his son.

The mother-child relationship is directly related to the other two immediately relevant dyads, the father-child and the husband-wife relationship. When the mother-child relationship is especially strong, it is usually the case that the husband-wife relationship is somewhat cool and perhaps even unstable if the family is poor. The strength of the father-child relationship, however, appears to vary directly with the strength of the husband-wife relationship: when the husband—instead of retiring to the club or cantina—enjoys recreation together with his wife, then the father-child relationship is also strengthened. By spending more time at home, the father strengthens his relationship with both his children and his wife.

Situations in which the household members coparticipate in more than eating and sleeping are particularly evident in two phases in contemporary Latin American life. One is the campesino household, in which available forms of recreation are either slim or nonexistent, and the man is usually active in keeping up with the necessary chores; the amount of time spent with the family is determined basically by the needs for survival. The other situation is found among middle-income families in which the woman has been educated and lives in a community of similar families. Under these circumstances, the woman can often support herself if necessary, and the man, to keep his home in order, must spend more time in it. Also, the educated woman simply demands more participation, in the style of the enfranchised woman of other Western countries.

Marriage, as an institution, takes a number of distinctively different forms. Formally, the vast majority of Latin Americans are Catholic and, being under the influence of the church as well as other sectors of the society, regard marriage as the necessary and proper condition for adult living. In at least two kinds of cases, however, this view does not hold, and in some others marriage cannot be realized. The first example is to be found in woman-headed households and is quite common: many women will prefer to establish an alliance with a man rather than actually marry him. Their argument here is that, when married, the woman reduces herself to the inferior position of a wife, and the man may treat or mistreat her as he wishes. If she remains independent and simply lives with him, then to keep her he must behave himself, thus allowing her to exercise her own preferences more widely. In the second case, found in many Indian and also isolated mestizo regions, marriage is recognized as an ideal state for a couple to live in, but the cost of marriage and the tradition of living in a free union often delay marriage. A formal marriage may not take place at all, or may take place only late in life or when a priest comes around with the strong intent of getting everyone married that he can. As one rises in the social scale, formal marriage increasingly becomes a requirement, but the husband-wife relationship is not necessarily a dominant one. Rather, the marriage role is an obligation for couples living together if they wish to hold a respected place in society. While sexual rights are definitely enjoyed by virtue of marriage, extramarital privileges are differentially accorded to men and women. In the upper portion of the society, men are often assumed to have both brief and extended sexual alliances outside of marriage without necessarily threatening the solidarity of the marital union. Sanctions against women who are discovered exercising such freedom, however, have been severe. As one moves into the lower sector, women increasingly exercise such freedom, even though the ideal may remain as exercised among the more wealthy. The variation noted earlier—that among the poor, both stable and unstable unions exist—holds here too. The difference is that in poorer families sexual activity outside the marriage more often leads to dissolution of the union. The presence of inherited wealth tends to strengthen the formal marriage union, even though the husband's and wife's personal relationship may completely lack affection.

It is sometimes assumed that the lack of formal marriage among poorer people indicates familial or household instability. Such is by no means the case. Among many Indian and transitional populations, local custom regards the household as a very strong unit, even though formal marriage is not central to it. Formal marriage in Latin America has a somewhat irregular role, since government efforts to exercise secular dominance have led to the existence of a variety of differences between civil and religious ceremonies. In some places, as in Brazil, it is possible to have either a civil or a religious wedding. Elsewhere, it is often the law that the civil ceremony must precede the religious rite and that the latter has no legal status. For centuries, marriage by the church was the only binding formal ceremony, and it is still felt to be so in many areas. The result has been that among really orthodox Catholics and in some provincial areas it is necessary to undergo two ceremonies. To the poor, for whom the expense of even one ceremony is a problem, the prospect of two contributes to avoiding the formal ceremonies entirely. Household stability sometimes produces a negative association with formal marriage, as among the Guatemalan Indian populations, where there are very few woman-headed households and equally few marriages. In urban Guatemalan mestizo populations, both formal marriage and woman-headed households are more numerous.

The sibling relationship in Latin America is usually one of

responsibility. At all levels of society, an elder brother is expected to show responsibility for his younger sisters. If there is any question that a young lady is being pursued by improper or irresponsible suitors, the elder brother is often expected to take the matter in hand, make the rascal perform correctly, or, if real offense has been incurred, to punish the offender. However, since collateral relationships are often tempered by the quality of the lineal connections (to be discussed shortly), the warmth of the sibling relationships varies. When inheritance is a question, siblings have both the common interest and the competition implicit therein; and when it is not, the expected form of responsibility may hide real feelings of distaste. The strength of the sibling bond was well illustrated by the relations that have held between Fidel Castro and his nonsocialist brother. Since it was assumed that one would show preference and protection for a brother, when Fidel Castro's brother insisted on retaining his private land, Fidel had to denounce him publicly in order that the society at large would know that he was canceling his obligations to him as a brother. Otherwise, it would be assumed that the brother's continuation of an anti-communistic attitude was acceptable to Fidel.

HOUSEHOLD ECONOMICS

Economic support of the household is a central feature of the household kin structure. Ordinarily, the basis of support is the husband's work. In the wealthier sectors, however, this may be supplemented by income from holdings of the wife, but the wife does not usually earn money. In the poorer sectors, the wife or woman may have to supplement the man's earnings or even provide the major support for the household when there is no man present. In the middle-income groups, there is some differentiation. Here the men are still assumed to be financially responsible, but whether or not the woman has earnings depends to some degree upon the position taken by the man in the family and the degree to which the woman desires to emancipate herself from the older role. When women earn money, the older role of the man as the protector and the "boss" in the household is weakened. This consequence has long been observed in the lower-income sectors, but is now evident in the middle-income population too. The woman who earns money outside the home—who deals with men, perhaps working near or next to them on the job, and so on—is not uncommon today. The traditional Latin male would regard such a situation as an insult, a breach of the sanctity of the home, and would never let it occur in the first place. When, however, a woman does not wish to remain in the passive role, she will start working after finishing school or college (in white-collar positions or in other nonmenial work) and will give up her job only when she decides to prefer marriage. Some continue working after marriage. It is difficult to know the degree to which such work contributes to the actual upkeep of the home and the degree to which it is carried on simply because of its symbolic meaning.

In poorer homes, particularly in urban areas, it sometimes falls on the women to support the entire establishment. They will often depend upon additional sources of income. The most important is the use of the children. In the cities, children, like women, can find odd jobs such as shoeshining and washing cars, and miscellaneous jobs in large homes, factories, or business establishments.

The household, then, is a basic kin unit in Latin American society. Its particular form and the quality of the relationships within it are set by the source and amount of wealth that it has available, the amount of education the women have been able to obtain, and the degree to which the husband gravitates to or away from the company of men for his recreation and to other women for his fun.

KINSHIP

In all levels of Latin American society, the wider groups or networks of kinsmen and friends to which a person turns for aid or companionship form the basis for important economic and political relations. These kin groups may be discussed in terms of two major categories: kinsmen and fictive kinsmen.

The most common device in Latin American society for recognizing kinsmen is the tracing of the linking relatives of household kin groups; the extent to which such relatives are recognized, that is, how distant are the kin who are recognized, is determined by specific factors that lead to common interest. The direction of the recognition, that is, whether it is disproportionately accorded collateral relatives of the same generation or relatives standing in a specific lineal relationship, also depends upon the nature of the interests which the relatives may have in common. Only under rare circumstances may corporate familial kin groups be said to exist.

When one examines a microscopic portion of the kinship universe, it appears that the major operative relationships are dyadic. Certain of the possible relationships have been singled out because of some specific common interests between the individuals involved. A question that needs answering, and one for which we have only some initial suggestions, is: What are the dominant kinds of common interests that determine this choice of recognized relatives, and what are the patterns that seem to characterize the choices made?

It is quite clear that the interests that hold among members of the old elite and wealthy families are quite different from those held in the middle-income sectors and violently different from those of the poor. The wealthy have properties, the inheritance of which is of considerable common interest. Literally, relationships are important, and the degree to which relatives are recognized collaterally will vary with the degree of active lineal recognition. When wealth is great and is retained within a single set of kin, one will usually recognize those relatives who are linked to the households of the various coholders of the property. It therefore appears that a lineal principle operates in the recognition of kin, but the importance of the lineal relationship stands specifically in terms of the availability of wealth or property. Even in Brazilian society, where kinship is reported to be particularly important, students agree that the classic patriarchal household and attendant recognition of kin, based upon the ownership of and succession to plantation properties, is greatly weakened today.

The importance of land as a basis for recognition of kin has been and is being supplemented by that of industrial and commercial wealth. Many of the major industries and business houses in Latin America started and continue as family enterprises. Kinsmen are preferred for administrative positions because it is assumed that the common interest of kin in the maintenance of good operations will guarantee loyalty to the concern. If an individual from another family is employed, then a real competitor may be brought within the fold. If someone with no wealth is employed, he may be more dependable because his welfare stems from his position in the organization. Thus, the marriages of girls from well-to-do families to proper, able, but relatively poor men who work in the business are not uncommon.

In the lower socioeconomic stratum of manual workers and poor white-collar workers, the recognition of kin is also made on the basis of common interest. Here, however, there is usually little to inherit, and common interest is based on mutual aid. This kinship system is best illustrated by the net of kin relationships that extends over areas of migration where the economic circumstances within a large region require some individuals to move in order to survive. Two widely separated movements provide examples: that to Buenos Aires from the neighboring rural areas, and that of Mexican migrant labor to the United States. Both of these areas have widely recognized kin networks. Since the basis of these relationships is not common inheritance, lineal depth is not the device used to identify which collaterals may be important. Rather, the household kin groups are known in the Texan-Mexican population through a series of linking relatives, and the households thus linked may extend over an area as great as that from northern Mexico to Michigan and California. These relatives are known, as are their addresses, because they provide a network of help for the individuals who must go elsewhere to look for work. Just as the Peruvian highland Indian or mestizo upon arrival in Lima first looks up relatives and stays with them, so the migrant is taken care of by his geographically distant kin. Some Mexican-American women in Austin, Texas, could name up to 500 specific relatives.

In Argentina, a similarly extended set of kinsmen is recognized for exactly the same reason, but the possible gaps in a network are tied together by intervening individuals who stand in a fictive kin relationship or who are believed to stand in some sort of uncertain genealogical relationship. The former are usually *compadres,* and the latter are just *parientes* (relatives) or fall within the category of *concuñados* (people who are related by virtue of being married to siblings). With this variety of possibilities, one can create an ever-widening adaptive network of kin to meet the immediate problems. One feature of this adaptive extension of kinship is that it seems to operate most effectively within one's own generation. If aid is needed, one goes to an individual of his own generation; the obligation is not felt to be so strong between individuals of different generations even if their genealogical relationship may be closer. This same tendency to concentrate on a single generation is reported from Puerto Rico.

The wide network of known relatives identifies individuals in terms of the location of their homes and those of the connecting relatives. Among Texas Mexicans, when a connecting relative dies the entire membership of that household, as well as more distant kin linked through it, may drop from the network of recognized kin.

The *compadrazgo,* or the system of relationships established by asking an individual to serve as godfather to one's child on the occasion of his baptism, confirmation, or marriage (and in some areas extended to other events as well) has received a good deal of attention from students of Latin American social organization. As may be surmised from the discussion thus far, the compadrazgo has been used in an increasing variety of situations so that it is hard to identify any particular kind of relational niche to which it has been restricted. In some places it has provided a method for formalizing the paternalistic relationship that exists between members of the wealthier employing sector and their employees. Elsewhere, it has been used to strengthen specific kin bonds. In still other places, it is used to relate individuals who need a specific bond for economic or political purposes. Thus, a rural supplier may have a compadre relationship with a town or city middleman; or a politician on the make will attempt to take on as many godchildren as possible in order to bring within his circle as many compadres as possible, thereby laying claim to their support and votes. Compadres, no matter what other features they may manifest, are usually characterized as persons of *respeto*, that is, persons to whom one shows special deference because they are proper people and know how to behave. The older expectation under compadrazgo, that the *padrino* (godfather) be available to help the *ahijado* (godchild) should he become orphaned, seems to be little observed anywhere. Few padrinos today expect, or are expected, to provide for the orphaned child unless there are no available genealogical kin or friends who can take on the responsibility.

It is sometimes asserted that the importance of kin relations declines as industrialization advances, and that the demands for flexibility and mobility make it impossible for the individual to take advantage of aid from a kinsman. This view is somewhat misleading. Kinship is proving to be as viable as any human social structure, and it is adapting to the new demands of an urbanized and industrialized age. If it is declining in importance, it appears to be doing so in parts of the middle-income group in which individuals seeking prestige and power find many kinsmen of no help and, in some cases, see them as obstacles. Given this kind of situation, the individual tends to limit himself to those kin who can be of greatest help. But the alternative, that of finding dependable individuals beyond the kin network on a friendship basis, is still far from adequate in Latin America. Associative relations tend to answer directly some of the newer demands; but in as many cases as not, the kin-based relations are being called in to adapt to those new demands. Our knowledge about the operation of contemporary kinship in Latin America still is much too defective. It is clear that it continues to be important, but that the quality and variation of this importance are ambiguous.

Community, Region, and Nation

THE NATURE OF THE COMMUNITY

The community occupies a peculiar place in the social history of Latin America. It has given rise to a remarkable intellectual enthusiasm that has lifted it far above its rather humble reality. It has been seen as the microcosm of the nation, acting out in miniature all the major problems that face nation-states. It has been seen as the principal contemporary unit of Indian life. More recently, in the hands of community developers, it has been seen as the energetic base for the development of entire nations. The discipline of anthropology, in particular, has focused on Latin American communities, and the best systematic descriptions of Latin American life are to be found in the community studies that have been carried on over the past forty years. No other writings so clearly display the recognition of the interdependency and integration of the life of the individual within the complex set of relationships that affect him.

Yet, to focus on the community is, in a sense, to focus on a thing that hardly exists in and of itself. A community may be compared with a stage on which a play is being acted. Unlike the audiences of other plays, the audience here needs to be aware of what is going on offstage in order to make sense of what is occurring in the play. The community is, in its simplest form, merely a piece of territory within which sets of social relationships are played out from year to year. Intense and complex, these relationships have regularity and rationality because life requires that one at least be able to predict the simplest things. A man in search of a doctor seeks one nearby, and the relationship is thereby a community fact. A man seeks a wife, and it is easier to find one nearby; thus, the action becomes a community fact. The storekeeper obviously has most of his clients from the neighborhood; the farmer makes most of his purchases within the community. The community exists by virtue of spacial proximity.

The community is also something more. The concentration of things that occur because of proximity produces a network of social relations, and an identity is formed among those who share in these experiences. A community, in the general sense in which the term has been used in Latin American studies, can be defined as a minimal piece of territory with a name, whose population calls itself by a name usually derived from the territorial name. Thus, the native of Muquiyauyo is a Muquiyauyino; and of Monterrey, a Regiomontano. If the population becomes too big, the relationships become too extensive and spread over too great an area to be identified as a community. The fact of the matter is that when relationships cease to be made because of proximity, the communities do not merely change; in a very real sense, they disappear.

In Latin America today, however, the majority of people

still live in communities. They live within a system of relationships established in great part because of proximity, and they are restricted from many others for the same reason. The territory that sets them apart from other similar groups of people has a name, and it is the custom to know a person by the community whence he comes. There is nothing sacred or eternal about the community within which a people lives; it is a delicate thing and can readily be destroyed. Nor are any two communities alike; they are profoundly different insofar as they have benefited from discrete histories and face distinct environments.

Students of communities in Latin America have placed great emphasis upon the community's quality of closeness, of inward focus, and of intense local identification. Eric Wolf, in a classic paper on the subject, drew an important distinction by pointing out that only some communities seemed to show these characteristics and that, in fact, it was specifically the Indian communities—residues from the great states and empires of Nuclear America—that most commonly appeared this way. Wolf called these communities "corporate" communities because, he stated, they held corporate control of the major resource, the land. Land was not individually held but was communally held, and no individual could alienate the community land. These corporate Indian communities had a distinctive internal governing organization that served to focus the attention of every member inward, toward the interests and needs of the community.

One important feature of Wolf's distinction was that most communities are *not* corporate and, in fact, do not show this communality of interest. Rather, individuals living in communities have many relationships that extend far beyond the community's limits and are little coordinated or adapted to the fact of community or proximity. In addition, communities could develop the inward-focusing quality (and evidently had done so) only when they found it necessary to mobilize their members for defense. For example, the little town of Tusik, a Mexican community chosen by Robert Redfield as an example of a "primitive" community, was, in fact, one that had been armed and organized defensively against the Mexican government during the War of the Castes. However, the quality of corporateness is not necessarily peculiar to "primitive" groups; in fact, there is good reason to think that it is more related to defensiveness, for it appears in some advanced communities. Even more important, the quality is apparent in the behavior of nations as they emerge as specifically defensive organizations.

COMMUNITY STRUCTURE

Whether corporate or not, communities often manifest similarities of internal organization. Among the features found through much of Latin America is the subdivision of communities into *barrios,* comparable in a way to the wards of the North American city. Barrios are subsections of the "urban" territory of the community. They are not subcommunities, because the inhabitants are usually not known by the barrio name. Barrios are important because they form the basis for factionalism. Occasionally, barrios are endogamous, but it is rare today that they significantly affect the marriage system. Rather, they tend to serve as a basis for political, religious, ethnic, or other social differentiation. Historically, it is not always possible to know whether the barrios were established on the basis of factions or whether the factions formed in terms of barrio membership. We know, for example, that some communities have been formed by distinctive ethnic groups. Archaic terms for the Barrio of the Mestizos and the Barrio of the Indians are still to be found in communities in Middle America and the Andes. On the other hand, the so-called Indian barrios to be found in some Middle American communities today are simply poor sections of town where the least acculturation has taken place.

Barrios provide a community with natural lines of cleavage

for any issue on which the members of the community must take sides. When Protestant evangelicals came to convert, it was not uncommon for them to find their universe of converts limited by the fact that the first converts were in one barrio and not another. When politicians come seeking votes, it is often the case that adherents in one barrio guarantee them the enmity of a large sector of another barrio. Modern urban development has found the barrio system convenient for expansion, since entire new sections of a town can be established as a barrio, a unitary subdivision. Since in larger towns and cities each barrio usually has some official responsible to the municipal government, barrios proliferate with urban growth.

The relationship that holds between municipal government and community organization is one that has often been confused in the literature and that should be clarified. The difference between the municipio and the community lies in the fact that the municipio in Latin America is a territorial subdivision of the state. Municipal boundaries did not come into being by the gradual growth of communities but by statute, often based on parish boundary lines or land claims dating back to colonial crown grants. In some cases, these boundaries were based on pre-Columbian community boundaries. In recent years, the boundaries of municipios have been decided by the national governments. When a municipio's population grows too large or diminishes to a point at which it can no longer function, it is either split into two or amalgamated with another. The wishes of the dwellers have often not been respected in this matter; whether or not action is taken depends upon politicking in the national capital.

The *municipio* (or *distrito,* or *cantón,* depending upon the country) consists, then, of a territorial extension in which is located a town that acts as the capital of that municipio. Each municipio population includes, therefore, both a town (urban) and a country and hamlet (rural) component. Unlike the town-and-country system of English-speaking countries, here there is but one single government for both town and country. The barrios of the town and the hamlets lying elsewhere in the municipio frequently have appointed auxiliary officers who are responsible to the municipal government. They are often unpaid, however, having to serve their time as a public contribution.

The municipal governments are so structured that it is not easy to represent satisfactorily the interests of both the town and the countryside. The town dwellers, being closer to the municipal officers, receive the major attention of the government. Country dwellers are usually unable to make their needs felt. "Civic government," as the term indicates, refers to the town and not the entire population. By the same token, the townspeople face problems that are indigenous to town life and have little effect on the country people. The upkeep of the town as a physical entity is a problem that has little interest for those who do not actually dwell in it, and the municipal government is limited in what it can do for the town itself.

Of even greater consequence is the fact that the municipal government is a subsegment of the national administrative hierarchy. As such, it is at the command of the state government, or of any of the intermediate administrative bodies, such as the department or province. Taxes are often drained off and sent to the national government, leaving the municipio dependent upon a national grant for its expenses. Municipal budgets, meant for the government of a territorial area and not for town upkeep, are usually completely inadequate for the town. This lack of funds has led townspeople to seek other ways of guaranteeing themselves resource support for their needs as townspeople. One solution has been the formalization of a community organization around some set of special interests of the residents which are distinct from interests common to all inhabitants of the municipio.

Community organizations have reached an extraordinary development in parts of Peru, where they usually control the resources that are regarded as belonging to the town rather than to the inhabitants of the entire municipio. These resources are classically community land, irrigation water, and, in recent years, community enterprises such as electric service. Another way in which such organizations have emerged is through the purchase of land by a group of interested people and the formation of a community organization around it. Thus, haciendas have been purchased by the tenants who then organize themselves as coowners. In some instances, an organization forms around the exploitation of a specifically local resource. The people of a hamlet who are dependent upon the sale of forest products may organize themselves into a community of woodcutters.

The administration of a municipio may nearly parallel the administrative organization of a community. However, the first is at the service of the nation, and the second may be said to have been created to protect itself against the demands and threats of the national scene. In the Andes and Meso-America, some of the community organizations of the Indians date back to the colonial period; during the nineteenth century they evolved into strong protective structures. The classic Indian community structure consists of an age-graded hierarchy through which an individual must pass, serving in each of a series of religious and civic offices before he may achieve a position of recognition as a person of responsibility in the community. These organizations, combining posts specifically related to Catholic Church organization on the one hand, and local civic activities on the other, have been shunted aside as municipal governments became stronger. They were especially characteristic of corporate communities and comprised the community government that served to protect the community's land or other resources from predatory large landholders and church interests.

The kinds of organizations just described are established when inhabitants find they have some strong common interest that requires organization for the purpose of solving problems connected with that interest. Specific events may also create such local interest where it was either nonexistent or all but dead. The establishment of the Mexican revolutionary ejido is a case in point. Here the national government provided land under the stipulation that there be an organization to control its allocation and, in some instances, its very utilization. So it has been that within Mexican municipios, communities of ejidatarios have emerged, just as they did in the colonial period. But the ejido communities have to be recognized as being very different in structure from other community organizations, since they rely entirely upon the nation-state to protect their rights. Instead of being created to defend against the encroachments of the state, they have been created by the nation to compete politically and economically with larger landholders.

In addition to the municipal government, some other important administrative forms exist in Latin America, which usually are not found in municipal capitals or in hacienda or plantation situations.

Scattered throughout Latin America are communities—sometimes of mestizos, sometimes of Indians—in which, irrespective of the particular municipal government that may be official and recognized, the people allocate their right to decision making to some individual or clique of individuals who stand for and represent them before agents of the national government or any other outside group. The term "cacique" has come to be used for these local boss-middlemen. The cacique stands in the position of being mediator between the group and the larger political and economic structure and also as a mediator of disputes within the group. He acts for them when they need to confront the outside. The community grants him, or is coerced into giving him, the right to tell the community what to do with respect to the outside. Thus, the position of the cacique depends on a delicate balance between satisfying the wants of the people of a community and satisfying the demands and wants of outside powers. So long as he can satisfy both, he continues in power. But if the people lose faith in him and he loses the power to coerce them, or if the outside agents decide that, for some reason, they want to bypass him or to deal with some other agent, his position is threatened and may be lost. If he can hold the monopoly on either the people or the outside agent, he can usually bring one or the other to bargaining terms. Sometimes, the role of the cacique is so highly regarded in the local community that factions form around individuals or groups of individuals who compete for the position.

The hacienda or plantation community organization is quite different from any of those already described in that it is part of a production organization. Under most circumstances, the laborers and employees have little or nothing to say about the way things are run, and their only mode of expressing a complaint is to leave or to cause enough disturbance that they get fired. Whether this is easy or difficult depends upon the labor market. Under the older hacienda system (still operating in some places), there was usually a labor shortage and the hacienda would exert special effort to discourage laborers from leaving. This was done, classically, through the institution of company stores or through government-supported debt peonage. Vagrancy laws were another means of assuring that labor would remain. Also, the recognition among hacendados that a laborer who misbehaved on one hacienda would do so on another hampered mobility. Hacienda communities—because the control of power lay in the hands of an essentially separate social sector and because they were directed toward one end— seldom maintained the picturesque cultural characteristics that were to be seen from time to time in more independent communities.

Three of these community organizations—the civic-religious hierarchy, the cacique, and the hacienda—have been disappearing in recent years, and the roles they performed have been taken over by other elements of the society, both within and outside the community. The establishment of political interests outside the community has provided the basis for the destruction of the civic-religious hierarchy. Young men enter the picture by being given access to power from the outside that permits them to introduce innovations within the community. Similarly, the cacique is bypassed when outside agents deal directly with community members or set up a series of individuals in the community with whom they can deal. Almost inevitably, these processes of change generate factions within the community. Those who generally favor the change because of what they may gain from it oppose those who are destined to lose.

Two general processes underlie these changes: nationalization and population growth. Nationalization is responsible for the replacement of local government forms when they obstruct the action of the national government. Population growth increasingly forces the community to face up to new problems of land allocation, of individual support, and of handling new practices brought in by returning migrants. How a community reorganizes to accommodate changes, however, depends on a number of factors. Many of these factors are peculiar to the community, such as the resources on which it can count, the varieties of experience of its members, the enthusiasm that can be engendered for innovations, and the passivity that may be anticipated in the face of adverse events.

Today communities are being asked to play a role in the development of their respective nations, and in some instances this role has been interpreted as a major one. The community, however, can seldom go beyond the limits set for it by the region and nation of which it is a part. Unless it can reach beyond the radius of its resources, it is limited in what it can accomplish. Because so much attention has been paid to community development elsewhere, it is worth some space here to indicate why the Latin American community is not entirely appropriate for the role assigned it.

NATIONALIZATION AND COMMUNITY DEVELOPMENT

Most Latin American countries are involved in a nationalizing process; they are states becoming nations. In nationalization, the most successful process to date has not been the incorporation of communities as such within the national system, but the incorporation (often coupled with their creation) of other organizations. Labor unions, agrarian reforms, and collectivization (in the case of Cuba)—when used as devices to gain the loyalty of, and control over, a population—have not been used with communities as such, but with relational systems that intersect and form parts of communities, such as a rural proletariat or an urban laboring population. The relation of the community to the state is not such that the community necessarily forms a convenient unit of nationalization; rather, nationalization is achieved more easily by dealing with categories of individuals that cut across community lines. Indeed, the community organization itself may be a specific target of nationalizing.

Nationalizing involves breaking down whatever bonds may exist within a community that inhibit communication from, and control by, the larger political structure. The community loses autonomy and control as the state gains them, the organization of the community changes so that its leaders become not merely local people with local or regional interests, but local people with national interests. The nationalizing process also involves controlling the various population segments and resources in such a way that the nation acts as a redistribution center for its various segments. The state decides which of the communities, among other entities, will get the scarce resources that it controls. Through favoritism by certain people or through interest groups, some communities have greater access to the nation's wealth in the form of road building, development money, health services, agricultural extension, and the like. Since there is not enough wealth for all, the state has to select from among possible recipients. This selection in some instances may even mean deciding that certain communities shall be abolished or be left to die natural deaths, as when a hydroelectric installation requires the flooding of an area, or when a new port is built, causing an old port to cease receiving trade.

Besides assuring that community concentrations of power are broken up, a nation must also constantly reassure itself that no community is concentrating power in a way that may become a threat to the integrity of the nation. In the light of this necessity, it requires a relatively well-developed nation to pursue intensive development of a community, unless the nation is sufficiently strong that it can regard a local buildup of power as being no threat. National support of any community will always be balanced against the relative power of that community among the aggregate of communities within the nation, and against the specific threat that the community may pose against the nation itself.

Since no two communities boast the same human and natural resources, the fact that the nation will inevitably behave differently toward each one of them guarantees that no two communities can develop in the same direction and at the same rate. Uneven development is not a question of policy, but an inherent characteristic of communities and community-nation relationships.

There is some lack of agreement as to what is the meaning of community development, but I believe it must include at least three central processes: (1) the economic development of the community, that is, increased income per capita; (2) politicization of the community: the political integration of the community into the developing nation; and (3) economic integration of the community: the increasing interdependence of the community with other countries of the state. Specifically not included here is the mere reorganization of community activities or the creation of goodwill. Community reorganization is required to achieve some of these processes, and goodwill may be crucial lubrication; but these factors in themselves do not constitute an end goal of, but rather a means to, community development.

In examining each of these processes, we find that they all presuppose a nation that has achieved some degree of development or, in the case of economic development, access to the resources of such a nation. To raise the level of production of a community, the community members must have access to new techniques and new knowledge. The basic techniques that still dominate peasant communities, primarily the use of hand tools, yield a low maximum production even if there is enough land available. Adding more land and more people does not substantially change the upper limit of production that is still very low. The knowledge and techniques necessary for development must not only come from somewhere but must also travel a cultural path that permits them to reach the community in an acceptable form. Communities are not likely to reinvent the major technological processes that are increasing production elsewhere in the world. Specifically, there must be a developed area concerned with providing the community with the techniques, the implements, the credit, and the education necessary for the actual utilization of the new technology. One peasant community has very little to teach another. In addition, it is necessary to the whole operation that there be meaningful communication between the sources of the technology and the potential users. To make this communication possible, there must be common cultural forms and common words with common meanings—in short, some common culture. If this common culture is to exist between an urban center and an isolated rural community, there must already be a considerable degree of nationalization. Quite clearly, the economic development of a community simply cannot occur unless the state itself is in a somewhat advanced condition of development so that it already has elsewhere the facilities and experience to bring to the community. For, to repeat, the community itself can rarely be expected to invent these things.

Political integration of a community also presupposes certain conditions that will be present only in a developing nation. As in economic development, a common culture is also necessary for political communication; these common cultural forms must include a national language or a set of national languages. Moreover, the notion of what participation in the national political process involves must be present to some degree elsewhere in the nation before it can be introduced into a given community. Similarly, the concept of the legitimacy of government must be fairly widespread before a community may be said to be involved in the political process. And finally, the recognition that there is such a thing as an alternative political ideology must come from the national-international level. Local community politics usually circulates around issues of local concern, not around matters that need be raised to the level of ideological principles. But the concerns of the nation operating at the national level will be expressed in terms of ideologies. These national-level ideologies must already be available if they are to penetrate to the community; and if they are to exist at that level, the nation must already have taken considerable steps toward nationhood.

The third component process of community development is economic integration of the community with a larger society. This integration means that the community exports more and imports more and consumes less of local produce. Quite obviously, to have this situation it is necessary to have a widespread communication system and an adequate transport system, both items of a fairly well-developed nation. Further, there must be a good market for the goods produced in the community, and a wide assortment of goods must be available to import into the community. Specialization of production—a thing inherent in the economic development process—entails greater dependence of the individual consumer. A community clearly cannot be expected to integrate with an economic exchange system that is unable to provide consumer goods for the products it receives. Thus economic integration of a community, perhaps quite as much as political integration, demands that there be a larger area, already *more* developed than is the community, with which it can integrate. In a sovereign state, this larger area must clearly fall within the nation-state.

In view of the above discussion, it is strange that there has persisted for so long the notion that community development could provide a grass-roots answer to the problems of national development. Quite the contrary is true. A considerable degree of national development is a prerequisite for community development, since the community must have a source to which to turn for new knowledge, new technology, and the necessary credit and financing. It must also have an effective set of complementary productive organizations that can provide it with its needs as its exports to the national market increase. There must be factories and large farms producing reasonably cheap goods that can be used by the villagers. And there must be a nation to which the community pertains, and within which it can find its new organizational place.

Experienced community-development people have increasingly recognized that they cannot rely on the elements of a community to develop themselves; rather, they particularly need help in doing so. What has perhaps been lacking in community-development thinking is the explicit recognition of the nature of the larger political entity that must be present for community development to be effective in more than a merely pilot project way. There has sometimes been a tendency to blame the community for not jumping at the chance, as it were, to raise its production. But the real problem obviously lies in the nature of the relationship between the community and the nation. If the nation does not have the things necessary for development, it is hardly possible to expect the community to develop itself in a vacuum.

In human social systems, the community as such has probably not been a significant unit of survival since early neolithic conditions held. Ever since communities have recognized regions —which surely goes back before the invention of agriculture— there has been a maximal system within which communities operated; and ever since the beginning of the state, this maximal system has been systematically restricted to the state. The nationalization process uses the state as the basic territorial organization and consolidates power and control both within state boundaries and against competitors from without. Under these circumstances, communities are not units of survival; any indication that the members of a community think they are may lead to sanctions, if not reprisals, by the government of the larger and more inclusive system.

The development of communities needs not only resources of the nation-state, but in many instances it needs what amounts to permission. Through systematic differential treatment, the nation-state can provide for the development of one community and for the dissolution of another. Of greater importance, however, is the fact that since the resources for development are scarce, they must be allocated unevenly if they are to be effectively concentrated; and since the internal organization of relationships within any particular community will be different from that of any other, some will be ready to take advantage of whatever resources are available, whereas others will be unable to do so, even if faced with abundance.

On this view, the nation has quite obviously become the principal unit of Latin American social organization. This is not to say that it always has been, nor that it always will be. The emergence of supranational blocs suggests the specific form of the newer unit. The community increasingly appears to be a microscopic segment within these larger developments, and much of the welfare and development a community may expect to enjoy depends on the organization of these larger segments. This conclusion does not alter the fact that the community, for a large part of humanity, will continue to be the locale of central importance. It does mean, however, that the social environment of the community will increasingly play a larger part in the affairs of the community and its members, and that the local organization will more obviously be a segment of the careers of the national and supranational bodies.

Government

A thesis of this volume is that the government has a particularly important role to play in areas of secondary development. The argument behind this thesis is simple. In order that economic development take place, extraordinary changes in the social order may have to be made; and since economic development is important for national well-being, either the government must take the leadership, or the task is not likely to be accomplished. The question naturally presents itself as to whether the governments of Latin America are equal to this task. Reading the North American press and savants would convince one that the round of revolutions, totalitarian governments, weak governments, or governments too far to the left and too far to the right have marked the region for some kind of political limbo. The question, however, is not whether the governments of Latin America can work such changes, but how in fact they are bringing them about.

It has become popular in some circles to see the governments of Latin America and other less developed parts of the world as undergoing "political development." Insofar as this term refers simply to the increased political participation of the population, there can be little objection to it. Unfortunately, however, much that is said in the name of political development seems to be a mask for a normative fad among those who would control the political destinies of other nations. Somehow, the immature nations are those that fail to conform to practices beneficial to the United States. Development in politics, however, can hardly be compared to the process known by the same name in economics. Political change is more of an adaptive process, one involving social inventions and the introduction of new values. There is, thus far, no conceptual way to handle political development that permits it to be as measurable as economic development. Our approach to these problems is still crude.

Latin American governments are participating in secondary development, but, at the same time are themselves among the things that are changing as a result of that development. The changes in which they are participating involve such profound issues as nationalization, increases in power, and a concentration of that power. They are trying to resolve problems generated by such uncontrollable forces as vast population increase, the extension of cold-war ideologies and hot-warfare military techniques, severe underdevelopment, and economic competition not merely with underdeveloped countries, but also with the world powers. It is little wonder that some of the governments appear inadequate to the task.

However, there are some features of the Latin American approach to governing that are generally recognized, although it may not be clear how they came to be. While these features may change under some conditions of development, they are surprisingly well adapted to secondary development, and so may well continue indefinitely. The two features of interest here are (1) the concern for power (2) and the related tendency toward formal centralism.

THE CONCERN FOR POWER AND LEGITIMACY

The concern for power that characterizes the upper sector of Latin American societies is also extremely evident in government. It marks both the internal operation of the bureaucracies and the role that government itself is seen to play in the life of the society. This "concern for power" should be distinguished from the hard power realities of government. The latter are found in all governments and in no sense can be said to be uniquely Latin. The bases of power upon which a government rests, the manipulations necessary, the balancing of interests and controls, and so on, are all to be found in politics and administration anywhere. The "concern for power," however, is specifically important in Latin American governments; the manipulation of power by politicians is given a value quite beyond its utilitarian foundations and indeed may be said to be a matter that is raised to something of an art among its practitioners.

The concern for power is illustrated by bureaucratic behavior. The position an individual holds in a bureaucracy can often be guessed by the pattern of obsequious and domineering behavior that is shown toward superiors and subordinates respectively. These behaviors may reveal little about the bureaucrat's personal character, but merely indicate formal conduct that he is expected to follow in his position. Government offices that serve the public directly are usually ready to give special attention to those with special positions of power. The outer office of bureaucrats may be filled with petitioners, but few will complain about the fact that an endless number of others are brought in before them to see the official in question. It is almost recognized as good form that a public official keep subordinates and clients waiting far beyond their appointment time. Indeed, power is treated almost as if it were a kind of quality which needed to be displayed in order to validate it. Part of the style of politics is behavior that displays this quality; it can be used at any bureaucratic level. No matter where you stand there will be someone some time over whom you have power—whether you are the minister of state who casually keeps a waiting room perpetually full of petitioners, or the janitor who slams the gate just before closing time and opens it tardily in the morning.

It is argued that much of this behavior occurs in contexts where the available techniques of public administration are not up to the complexity of the tasks they must handle. But interestingly enough, improved public-administration techniques seldom simplify these tasks. Rather, while they provide a sometimes more orderly and efficient way of doing them, the style of performing them remains the same.

This manner of power exercise relates to the question of legitimacy of authority, another quality of government that is particularly marked in Latin America. Like the concern for power, it too may be related to the situation of secondary development, and if so, it seems also to rest on equally firm foundations. Politically aware Latin Americans may draw a sharp line between the office of a public official and the individual who holds that office. The government of the Latin American nation-state is firmly separated in thought and action from the nation-state itself. Loyalty to the nation is expressed through loyalty to one's party or to one's particular political leader, not necessarily to the government. If the government in power is favored, then one will obviously show it respect and loyalty. If it is not, however, there is no obligation to show it respect, and it may actually be anticipated that one will go out of the way to indicate extreme displeasure with it.

This situation may be contrasted with some recent events in the world of primary development. In the United States there have been severe attacks on the government, the state, *and* the nation by groups of Negroes who take an extreme "black nationalist" position. They reject not only the government's activities, but they reject the entire notion of responsibility to the United States as a nation. They claim they should have their own separate nation. Such a situation would be uncommon in Latin America. People who are on the "outs" will reject the government but not the nation. The *guerrillero* groups in the Andes and Middle America in the 1960's have been outspoken in their rejection of the incumbent governments and in their overt intent to replace them with socialist regimes. But in rejecting the governments, they do not reject being Venezuelans, Guatemalans, or Colombians. Quite the contrary. They feel strongly that the very reason that they have chosen the guerrillero role is that they are *better* patriots than are those who run the governments.

Basically, this position holds that a government is legitimate only if it follows the rules set by the particular group, faction, or party making the decision of legitimacy. If a government comes into power elected under a constitution, the question will be asked, "Whose constitution?" Those who have not been involved in the preparation of the constitution simply claim that the document is fraudulent, and that no legitimacy can stem from it. The concept of legitimacy has served well in analyzing the governments of Europe and North America, and it has apparently been assumed that it also has analytical value elsewhere.

The question of legitimacy is closely related to the manner of handling constitutions. There are men of public service in Latin America who have written more than one constitution for their country. While this strikes some North Americans as odd, there are reasons that constitutions are so replaceable. The North American constitution was developed at a single point in the history of the United States. It was a major social invention and is certainly one of a few of its kind in the history of the world. As is the case with *technological* inventions in the primary-development process, alterations on this *social* invention were also made very gradually, long after pressures resulting from changing technology had made themselves felt. The United States constitution has survived extraordinary changes in the society through gradual reinterpretation and occasional amendment.

Latin American countries, when they entered the period of independence, found it easier to copy the North American document than to attempt a violently divergent and new invention of their own. The independence of Latin American countries was in no way the beginning of a new social order. Yet the documents that were drawn up as constitutions often reflected as ideals the elements that such a social order should include. As such, they necessarily represented the goals and interests (not always selfish by any means) of those who penned them. As governments changed, so did the sentiments of the rulers, and so therefore, did the constitutions. It often proved easier to rewrite the entire document than to simply amend the old one. In a minor way, each new constitution has been an attempt at social invention, an attempt to design a form of government that would both produce those forms of social life and governmental activity that were desired, and would take into account the social facts that existed at that time in the country. Constitutions became identified with their writers and, therefore, became dispensable when governments of radically different positions came into power. The legitimacy of a constitution was tied to the legitimacy ascribed to the government that produced it.

FORMAL CENTRALISM

The other general quality of governmental style that I want to deal with here is formal centralism. The governments of Latin America have, in a sense, always had this quality. Historically it clearly is derived from the colonial period when the imperial government kept to itself many rights, both economic and political. Those familiar with the history of the evolution of government during this period have suggested that the emphasis on form, the notion of *obedezco, pero no cumplo* (obedience without performance) that was supposed to be the hallmark of the creole official's response to imperial orders, has in some degree carried over into the pattern of government of modern Latin American countries. Be this as it may, this derivation is at best a tracing of the formal origins of the trait, and it tells us nothing of why such a trait might continue today. It is necessary, I believe, to recognize that formal centralism has operated effectively over the years since the colonial period. While it is not possible to trace such a history or series of histories here, a few points will illustrate the argument in terms of the concepts of development here being used.

In the nineteenth century, most of Latin America was strongly controlled by regional foci of power. Central governments expended much time in trying to assure that specific regions of the country were in fact loyal. Since there tended to be strong divisions in local loyalties, central government ruled in distant provinces through powerful local political chiefs as often as through any direct interest or control over the population. Most typically there was general oligarchic agreement that those who controlled the land were responsible for local government. Hacienda owners were really political bosses as well as economic controllers of the local scene. The church served as the bureaucratic scribe for many local tasks such as registration of births and deaths, and provincial centers evolved their own strong leaders and families of importance. A "central government" did exist under these circumstances, but it was a government that was generally weak and that ruled through the local power of the regional rulers.

Under such circumstances the chief of state, whatever his formal title may have been, varied between being a chief among chiefs—whose tenure depended in some degree upon his not upsetting the system too much—and being a promoter of the nation-state who was gradually trying to bring the regional and locally semi-independent bosses within national control. The success of this early nationalizing depended upon the strength that the chief of state could mobilize. Consequently, it was essential for him to keep to himself all the power that he could obtain. The decentralization of the little power he had, spelled certain revolt and probable disaster for the regime.

Over the past one hundred years each Latin American country has been following its own path toward nationhood. Argentina has done it through the emergence of many urban centers and a sharp dichotomy between the provincial, colonially oriented hinterland, and the urbanizing, foreign-oriented coast. Mexico initiated nationhood during the years of Benito Juárez and Porfirio Díaz, with the destruction of the conservative hand of the church and of the Indian communities, and with the encouragement of economic growth. Each country, in short, has gained nationhood according to its own circumstances and means, and at its own speed. But in almost every case, nationhood has been accompanied by the continued emphasis on the strength of a chief of state. In some instances, this strength has been supported by the church, as by the Catholic Church in Colombia. In others, nationalizing has seen long periods during which the only visible change was the emergence of a dictator who spent his years in strengthening his position rather than allowing the growth of new bases of power within the country. Whatever the mode, the general pattern has been one of a continued concentration of strength in the hands of the chief of state.

One consequence of this concentration of power was that revolutionary coups were relatively easy to accomplish. Since the control of the government rested so much in the hands of a single individual, the removal of that individual permitted another party to take control. Competing parties, usually liberals and conservatives, continued to exist side by side, each sometimes refusing legitimacy to the other, each biding its time until it could muster the forces to eliminate the rule of the other. Similarly, the individual who could muster the adequate tactical force for a coup could take over a government with surprising ease and establish himself for a time as chief of state. For the same reason that his predecessor wished to keep power in his hands, so did a new chief of state.

During these years the agrarian oligarchies began to change their shape; provincial power began to move to the capital city. It became evident that as governments were becoming stronger, the wealthy interests could not be effective from the country-side. Jockey clubs and union clubs became the scenes of eco-nomic—and thereby to an important degree, political—manipu-lation and control. In the same way, the provinces became less important politically.

The pattern of centralized government had, of course, defi-nite effects on the nature of government in the country at large. Local communities were not supposed to be ruled by representa-tives of local interest but by representatives of the interests of the central government. The municipio system, which exists in one way or another in almost every Latin American country, emerged as the basic form of regional government. Under this system, the country was cut into successively smaller hierarchi-cal chunks, with the municipio being the lowest territorial unit governed by a representative of the national government. A municipio had at last one principal town, usually with the same name as the territorial unit. A single government served both and was regarded not merely as a government to handle local problems, but also as a local representative for the na-tional government.

One response to this situation has been to create new local governments to handle problems that seem of little interest to the national government but that are important to the local people. In Peru, particularly, a number of towns have long since created "communities," new governmental forms that op-erate semi-independently of the national government and pro-vide a device for the local people to produce and carry out solutions to their own needs.

Another consequence of the concentration of power in the central government is that the paternalism of local patrons and bosses shifts to the central government. This situation, though stated simply here, is actually rather complex. The fact of paternalism in Latin America has been often noted. It has, however, often been confused with, or better said, not distinguished from, a quality of personalism. Because of this lack of distinction, the ascription of paternalism to social organizations implied a psychological characteristic of personalism that attached itself to the master-servant relationship and to similar political relationships. I believe the structure of the situation to be rather different.

Paternalism is surprisingly close to what the name suggests. It is a relational quality that appears wherever two facts hold. The first is the presence of a unique power domain, wherein there is but one superior to which an inferior can turn for derivative power and for the satisfaction of needs beyond his immediate grasp. The second is the use of a kin or familistic model for the behaviors that attach to such a relationship. Obviously the archetype for paternalism is the familial relationship between parents and children. Young children, in most Western societies are responsible to, and only to, their parents. The pattern is one of condescension, care, nonreciprocal behaviors, coaching, correction, punishment and rewarding, and so forth.

Paternalism in Latin American society, stemming from the imperial past, evolved in the situation of regionally independent political and economic domains where hacendados, or plantation owners, were the virtual rulers of a locale or region. In order to get their crops out, it was necessary to behave as a father to the laborers, be they slaves, Indian colonos, indentured servants, or tenants. As regionally unique domains gradually gave way to the centralism of government, and as the laboring and rural population gradually moved out of the power domain of the regional bosses and came under the control and direction of the government, the government increasingly became the major power within the country. Where this shift of power has occurred, the quality of paternalism that formerly was manifest on farms and in workshops has been transferred to the government.

The structural relevancy of the unique domain to paternalism was very clear in Guatemala during the revolutionary period of the governments of Arévalo and Arbenz. At that time, labor unions were introduced into the countryside. These unions had derivative power from the government and provided an alternative access to power that bypassed the formerly unique domains of the farm owner. Given the new multiple domain, the paternalistic attitude that held between the farm administrations and the laborers rapidly disappeared. Over a period of a few years the formerly paternalistic relations became hostile and unforgiving.

Centralism and the concern for power are, then, two qualities that pervaded Latin American governmental operations. They have remained remarkably consistent over the years, although it is clear that they have not hung on because of any mystical psychological propensity on the part of Latin America. Rather, they have been adaptable and utilitarian; and it may be predicted that until some better form of organizational behavior comes along, they will continue.

GOVERNMENT IN THE STRUCTURE OF POWER

The governments in Latin America have changed not only in the quantity of power that they control, but in the entire structure of power that characterizes a nation among nations. Nationalizing not only reorients the internal structure of a country, but does so also as a part of a larger structural reorientation. Nations evolve and develop as members of communities of nations. Inherent in the very definition of a nation is the fact that it is but one of a number of competitive, sometimes predatory, entities. The settling of national boundaries, a severe problem until recently between Nicaragua and Honduras and a problem that still troubles some countries along the interior mountain boundaries of the Andean region, is quite obviously an issue of nationalism and sovereignty as existing between nations. Similarly, the determination to expropriate foreign-held oil installations in Mexico, and like action in a yet more extreme form in Cuba, each reflect the process of nationalizing as seen in external relations.

Nationalizing establishes a network relating the various power foci of a country with comparable parts of other countries. In this extremely complex network, the lines of power and influence run across national boundaries. However, the central concentrations of power within each country are usually in the national government, although there are, from time to time, serious competitors. Nationalizing is also the process of establishing and maintaining the concentration of power within a country in such a way that it is not successfully challenged by other power concentrations either inside or outside the national boundaries. It really makes little difference where the competing power foci may be located, but it is important from the point of view of the utilization of power to keep some balance between the outside and the inside. The government that fails to achieve this balance may find that it is unable to mobilize power as it needs it. Derivative power from the outside, such as American or Russian military assistance or diplomatic pressure, or independent power from the inside, such as the control over labor unions and the exercise of import and credit restrictions, need to be available to permit a government viability and flexibility.

In nationalizing, then, a government is asserting its rights and responsibility to occupy the central position of power. For a Latin American government to achieve such a position, it is indispensable that it change from the nineteenth-century purveyor of private interests, both domestic and foreign, to an entity that can keep itself somewhat separate from the specific oligarchic and foreign interests. Independent domestic power cannot be based primarily on oligarchic interest groups and still be nationalistic. The network that marks the operation of nationalization also marks the direct articulation of the government with various entities of the society. To be a nation a country must effectively incorporate diverse interests and entities into a reasonably operative whole; a government that fails to effect this incorporation has, to that degree, failed to nationalize.

This position takes some issue with that which argues that a government is nothing more than the cat's paw of some limited set of interests. From an analytical standpoint, it is true that all governments must at any point in time be more favorable to some interests than to others; also, all governments must to some degree stand apart as separate and distinct social organisms within the complex of relations that form the society as a whole. The fact that a government has two distinct aspects, each of which must be examined if one is to understand precisely how it is operating, should not obscure the fact that nationalizing increasingly demands that the government be a focal point in the network and that it decrease its role as the agent of a special set of interests.

The contemporary governments of Latin America manifest a variety of postures with respect to nationalization, and they change these postures with some regularity. The process of secondary development, however, is common to all of them, and it involves a set of consistencies. Among these are the fact of increasing centralization of power and the increasing dependence upon both externally derived power sources and on new internal power bases. Each of these processes sets a series of questions that must be answered by every government.

The increased centralization of power sets the question of who, in fact, will control the increasing power of the government. Over the past two decades in Latin America, there have been four major kinds of answers: (1) continued control by the oligarchy (no longer purely agrarian, obviously); (2) control by the military; (3) control by a nationalist group, in the sense of the type of government described in the immediately preceding paragraph; and (4) control by a socialist government (Cuba being the only successful one to date). Within each of the first three types, of course, there are great varieties; and while one of these answers may be dominant at one point in time, it may rapidly be replaced by another.

All governments that have either a sizable amount of externally derived power or have achieved a position of sufficient internal strength can successfully juggle external powers. The questions faced by governments with respect to externally derived power is whence it should or must come and how are they willing to pay for it. The Latin American countries that rely heavily on the external support of the United States or on European communist powers pay a particularly high price for the benefits of such assistance. Their foreign policies must necessarily reflect this dependence, and their relations with other Latin American nations are frequently rocky. Basically, however, this is the price they must pay for such support.

The countries that are most in need of externally derived power are, naturally enough, those that are weakest at home. Development at home involves the elaboration of both new local bases of power and an absolute increase in the amount of available local power. The major question facing governments in this aspect of their affairs is: Which of the local sources ought to be encouraged, supported, and backed; and which are those that need to be curtailed, restricted, tightly controlled, or entirely nationalized? Since part of the nationalization process is the extension of governmentally derived power to previously weak segments of the population, the process is naturally threatening to the older power holders. The extension of support to formerly weak segments of the population thereby becomes one of the most serious threats to the government itself, since other powers, both internal (such as the agrarian and commercial establishment or the military) and external (such as the United

States Department of State or Department of Defense), may regard such moves as of sufficient threat to their interests to warrant intervention and overthrow of the government.

Nationalization, therefore, is a process to which each country subjects itself because it is seen as the road to survival and development; it also creates for the government the most difficult of problems. To nationalize is to take power from those who have it and to distribute it selectively among those who do not. Obviously it is impossible to achieve this redistribution of power in the same way in each of the twenty-one republics.

Violence
and
the Military

The role of the military in developing nations has received considerable attention in the professional literature and in the press, and recent events have made it abundantly clear that the armed forces occupy a profoundly more important part in the internal politics of Latin American nations than is the case in contemporary western Europe and North America. The reason for this difference is that differing political processes are found in primary and secondary development. In Latin America secondary development is characterized by recognition of violence as an instrument of action, by acceptance of the military as the arm of violence for the government as well as the judge and court of last appeals of governmental action, and by familiarity with activities ranging from periodic civil disobedience to insurgency.

✳   **193**

Violence as an Instrument of Action

Violence usually appears in one of three contexts: (1) as a threat used in the process of exercising power; (2) as opposition to or defense against violence; and (3) as a method of accomplishing a task directly. While the first two are generally found in all societies, the last is much more a matter of cultural conditioning and definition. Every society defines the recognized contexts in which violence may be used. This does not mean that the members of the society approve of such action, but merely that when it does occur, they have already culturally agreed upon its meaning and can therefore understand it.

In Latin America it is widely recognized that violence is used directly as an instrument of action and as a means of doing a job. Both governments and other groups or agents in the society may initiate violence without any prior use of threat. This pattern is manifest in widely divergent cases: for instance, in 1966 the Argentine military sent troops unannounced into two university faculties where they beat up both students and faculty; and in Colombia during the 1950's and 1960's widespread depredations, known collectively as *la violencia,* took place.

In both instances violence was generally not used as a threat to accomplish any particular goal but instead was used directly. Part of the same pattern are the periodic military coups in which troops are sent into the streets and governments are toppled. For the most part, such coups are planned in secret, no prior warning is given, and the troops are used to accomplish the act directly. Revolutions are one of the standard ways of changing a government.

There is no reason, I believe, to hold that the Latins are merely psychologically more disposed toward violence than people of other nations. Rather, violence is used for reasons that are inherent in the structure of secondary development. One reason is that there is relatively little power available, and the direct use of violence or force is often easier and more effective than attempting quieter exercises of power through threats, be they subtle or obvious. Peasant groups really have little power to use aside from organizing as a group to threaten violence; and once organized, it is often easier to proceed with achieving the goals than to give warning and allow countermeasures to be taken. A second reason is that the attempt to concentrate power in the hands of the government inevitably menaces the position of some previously strong power holders. Since the government is knowingly removing power from these power holders, it does no good to threaten the government with reprisals. Rather, the rational thing to do is to counter the governmental threat with direct action, which usually means violence.

This second reason is the same one that stimulates the United States to resort to violence in some Latin American dealings. To counter what it regards as an obvious threat of communism, the United States was ready to provide cash to Castillo Armas, to disembark over 20,000 troops into the Dominican Republic, and to support the Bay of Pigs operation. If one looks further back in history, there is also the earlier use of troops in Mexico, Nicaragua, and Haiti. It should be obvious that virtuous and schoolmasterly criticisms by the United States against the Latin American revolutionary methods for changing governments fall on rather unreceptive ears in Latin America. The United States' propensity for resorting to violence in its own foreign affairs makes the argument rather fatuous.

Violence cannot be expected to decline seriously until the power commanded by a government is so great that it is widely recognized that violence will not accomplish its goal. Currently, however, violence is a very promising way of getting political action. For violence to stop, a population must recognize that their government is in fact taking some cognizance of their needs. Even in a country as relatively well developed as Mexico there have been agrarian disturbances in the past few years over the lack of available agricultural lands. One response of the Mexican government was to speed up agrarian-reform activities in at least one of the areas, thus showing that a little bit of violence can be very useful. More real gains have been made for peasant and campesino populations through resorting to some violence than without any violence at all. The Bolivian revolution, the Mexican revolution, the short-lived Guatemalan agrarian reform, and the Cuban revolution all required violence. Irrespective of what foreign political planners may think, it seems reasonably certain that Latin Americans will continue to resort to violence for political ends for many years to come. As will be noted shortly, there are groups such as the guerrilleros who are explicitly devoted to violence as their means to power.

THE MILITARY IN THE STRUCTURE OF POWER

Military (including naval, marine, and air) forces are a government's formal devices for the exercise of threat of violence. Into the twentieth century, problems of international boundary delimitation led to wars between various Latin American nations, but the last major conflict was the Chaco War of the 1930's. Given this record, and ignoring the fact that many of the countries formally entered the Second World War as a matter of foreign policy with respect to the United States and Europe, it can be argued that the Latin American nations are among the most peaceful on earth. In Latin America there is nothing like the Israel-Arab problem, or the threat of invasion that Sukarno held over Malaysia, or the deep semimilitary troubles that punctuated the establishment of independence in the Congo. Nor are missiles poised and air crews alert as is the case between the United States and Russia.

These generally amicable international relations, however, have in only a few cases seriously reduced the size of military establishments, and the members of the military hardly regard themselves as being superfluous. The military forces in Latin

America see themselves as being important for a number of reasons, and only one concerns serving the government as its means of force or violence. Most of the reasons revolve around the relations that link the military and its interests to other components of the nation and to other nations. These relations are apart from the standard organizational responsibilities that attach to the military both in Latin America and elsewhere, such as contributing to the maintenance of civil order. Among the features that we may single out for discussion are the place of the military in the general middle-income strata of the society; its articulation with other military establishments in the hemisphere; and its role as both a nationalizing and an anti-national device.

A number of authors have placed great stress on the importance of the middle-income sector (usually referred to as the "middle class") in the economic development of Latin America. While I believe (see Chapter 3) that this focus has been excessive, there is no question but that this growing segment of the society is important in many respects. The middle-income sector is the major source of the educated and highly skilled people necessary for continuing economic development. The signal thing about the military in this respect is that it is composed almost entirely of individuals from this sector of the society, and it is organized specifically as an instrument of violence. The importance of this feature of the military is made clearer if we realize that in most Latin American countries relatively few individuals reach secondary school and that the paths of social and economic mobility are severely restricted. A free education and a promising career through the local national military school can be very attractive. The military, that is, the officer's corps, is composed to some extent of individuals who have been self-selected because of aspirations both to mobility and to the security of the organized life of the military.

This status of the military entails certain other characteristics. One is that the general culture and aspirations for social position imitate, as in the rest of the middle-income strata, the upper class. The "good things in life," involving in great part material items such as household appliances, canned and bottled foods, furniture of a particular style, and so on, are sought by the military as they are sought by most upward-looking middle-income people. A second characteristic, derived from the organizational character of the military, is that there is relatively little association between the members of the officer corps and the larger society. Barracks life in provincial garrisons, participation in the officers clubs, and so on, have naturally developed a self-supportive subculture that marks the military man in most Latin American countries. In some instances the military establishment gives positive rewards for staying separate from the civilian community and inhibits its members from taking university degrees or pursuing further education beyond that encouraged by the military establishment itself. The military man's origin and the organizational characteristics of his establishment have formed the military into a segment of the total society that sees itself in a special light, having access to special privileges and control of special powers. It is not surprising, therefore, that from time to time some military men come to believe that they also have special access to knowledge and special rights and responsibilities that may well override those of other sectors of the society.

As with the nation as a whole, the military is also a node in the network that stretches far beyond the national boundaries. The most important of these extensions is that which relates the particular national military establishment to other similar organizations. This relationship exists formally through the United States military missions resident in most countries and through the Inter-American Defense Board and Inter-American Defense College, as well as through the special training given to Latin American officers at various foreign military-training establishments. There are, in addition to such formal links, strands of informal relations that hold between certain officers from different countries.

The most important relation, however, is based on the interest of the United States Department of Defense in the general question of inter-American security. "Security" refers to the prevention of the establishment of a communist or socialist government in the hemisphere, and the prevention of excessive international communist influence. Toward this goal the United States annually allocates funds for the building up of select portions of the Latin American military. Besides the training of officers in special skills, this United States participation involves approving the sale of excess military equipment, grants of other kinds of equipment, and direct participation of specially trained officers and men, usually in counterinsurgency operations.

The Latin American military establishments are both grateful and reluctant to participate in this program. They welcome the additional strength that the supplies and training provide, but they are not entirely happy that the integrity of their own military organizations be destroyed by their North American colleagues. This reservation makes for some uncertain relations on a personal basis and makes the North American military advisors careful to maintain effective relations wherever possible.

Perhaps the most important, yet the hardest to estimate, of the effects of this inter-American articulation is the degree to which the political preferences of the United States military are reflected in the activities of their Latin American colleagues. It is far from clear whether there would be greater variation in politics among the Latin American military were the North American source of supplies and contacts reduced. There is evidence that the background of the Latin American officers allows them as much leeway politically as it does the rest of the members of the middle strata. Politically this sector engenders both rightists and leftists, both capitalists and socialists, and above all, nationalists. As with the rest of the middle strata, there is often a strong anti-United States feeling, relating both to specific military and more general cultural factors. Given this variety of backgrounds, the political interests of the individual members of the military in Latin America do in fact vary; and there are instances, such as the case of Arbenz in Guatemala and of Perón in Argentina, where the political ambitions of one officer led a significant segment of the military establishment away from the path preferred by the United States.

One reason that the importance of this internal variation is hard to estimate is that, for the most part, the integrity of the Latin American military establishment generally rests on the right. The major revolutions of the hemisphere—in Mexico, Bolivia, and Cuba—have led to serious reorganizations of the entire military so that at least for a time the military played a relatively slight political role.

THE MILITARY IN NATIONALIZATION AND DEVELOPMENT

A third structural feature that characterizes the military in Latin America is its ambivalent role in the nationalizing process. The military, as the arm of violence of the government, is a crucial element in centralizing power in the government. With few exceptions, it gives the government the force that is periodically necessary in trying to incorporate regionally distinct elements into the national system. At the same time, however, like most Latin Americans, the members of the military make a severe distinction between the government and the nation and do not necessarily feel any loyalty to a given government. Coupled with this characteristic is the organizational integrity mentioned earlier; we find that the military sets itself slightly to one side of the general government, seeing itself as a special repository of rights within the government. In this capacity, it stands as an element that may at any point in time decide to compete with the existing government and usurp the central position of power.

Since nationalizing requires centralization, this separatist quality of the military acts as an antinationalist force always lurking at the margins of any government's attempts to proceed with the extension of power to other elements of the population. Since it is highly institutionalized itself, the military cannot effectively act *as* the government, although it tries on occasion to play such a role. It stands instead as a potential source of competition to the government, all too ready to decide what is the best way to get things accomplished.

The military of some countries started a few years ago to play a direct role in the more peaceful aspects of the nationalizing process; in recent years they have been encouraged by the United States Department of Defense to extend this role. These efforts, generally going under the name of "civic action programs," involve the army in literacy programs, road building, public-health work, and other development efforts. In some instances the activities of the military require a larger budget than that allocated to the civilian ministry. In some countries of the Andes and Middle America, where much of the noncommissioned personnel of the army is made up of Indians, military service trains the recruit in literacy and forces him to learn about the country beyond the region immediately surrounding his own village. This role of the military has been recognized as being an important adjunct to development and obviously contributes directly to the process of nationalization. The role, however, has never been taken so seriously by the military as to divert it in any way from what it sees to be its major responsibilities.

This perception that the military have of themselves has been characterized by some as the "supermission." Under this rubric goes the complex of ideas whereby the military take upon themselves not only the power but the right and the responsibility of seeing that the national government and its challengers do not upset the system too ₊much. Since the Second World War, fully one half of the national governments of Latin

America have been taken over by the military, with the expressed intent of saving the country from economic ruin or communist domination, or both, and with the promise of setting things aright in order that the nation could be returned to civilian rule. During the earlier of these cases the military regimes did in fact reestablish civilian regimes, and in some cases, such as in Venezuela, effective governments have resulted from the change. In some more recent cases, however, such as in Argentina and Brazil, the incumbent military governments have given no indication that they intend to relinquish power. This stand is significant not only for the particular countries in question, but also for an understanding of the role that the military may choose to play elsewhere in Latin American secondary development.

Certainly it could be argued that if secondary development were to be carried on in the most efficient and possibly inhumane manner, a totalitarian government under strong but developmentally oriented military control might institute changes responsive to the demands of advanced technology. In part this course has been followed in Cuba under the Castro regime. To the degree that one can argue in favor of the Cuban experiment, it is equally possible to argue in favor of attempts of other military regimes to institute the same kind of process. Students of politics would, of course, make a sharp distinction between the socialist goals espoused by the Cuban regime and the fact that the military operations would usually reflect interests of the commercial, agrarian, and industrial upper sector, along with those of foreigners in the country. But sheerly on the basis of the question of whether military elements should be in control, it is difficult to differentiate the cases.

This coincidence of the strength of the military and the fact that an incumbent government needs such strength places the military in a position of special importance in secondary development. It can be argued that only under circumstances where governmental support has successfully been gathered from other sources, can a Latin American government expect to pick its way through the complex and divided interests of society to direct economic development without the backing of a military force.

Counterbalancing the Military

If one approaches this problem from the standpoint of asking who or what might be used as a substitute for the military, there have already been some answers. The Mexican case is probably of such relative antiquity that it is of less relevance than are the more recent cases. The Mexican military situation following the revolution was, in some respects, more similar to the warlord situation in China of the same period than it is to contemporary Latin America. The military was made up of semi-independent local and regional armed forces, and each local chief generally had a military force upon which he depended for his needs. Today, the military of all Latin American countries is reasonably centralized; and to the degree that there is regional separatism, it is based on command differences, not on local military chiefs.

One case of a successful effort to counterbalance the military was that of Bolivia. The revolution of 1952 saw the emergence of a series of local militia (both among campesinos and miners) and the virtual disintegration of the army. The effective balance of military power was held by the miners and campesinos for a decade, and it was only because the two militia groups could find no basis for coordination that it was possible for the army to reform itself and eventually to take a position similar to that which the army has held in other countries. In Guatemala, the government of Arbenz found itself increasingly uncertain of military support and planned to establish a campesino-based militia through the agrarian-reform committees. The army knew of the effort, however, and commandeered the arms that had been ordered to equip the new force. In Cuba, the Castro regime made a very public and efficient display of killing off many of the Batista army officers, and many others fled the country. The army was then rebuilt, along with the establishment of a broad base of militia in the general population. The popular militia, however, was gradually weakened as the new socialist army came into being.

The Bolivian experience, the Guatemalan failure, and the Cuban success, together with the increased strength of the military, have contributed to the significant change in the strategy of political competition in Latin America. Insurgency has a respectable history in Latin America, but its marked success in Cuba was rather new. The success, however, was not due to a more effective insurgency, but to the luck of some of the circumstances. The most popular model for such action, that of Sandino in Nicaragua in the 1930's, ultimately failed, not because of the failure of the guerrilla action itself, but through treachery on the part of Somoza, who had Sandino shot under a flag of truce. The success of insurgency is very dependent upon external circumstances. Castro's success was due in part to the favorable climate afforded by the entire hemisphere to his efforts. His subsequent overt switch was possible only because Russia was willing to provide the necessary counterbalance of power at the international level in order to neutralize the displeasure of the United States. Insurgency makes sense only if there is significant derivative power to support the tactical activities of insurgents.

The international interlocking of hemispheric militaries is paralleled by a similar interlocking of insurgents. The establishment in Cuba of a communist government, with the avowed goal of establishing socialist governments throughout Latin America, has provided antigovernment forces in each country with a permanent base and constant source of derivative power that has never before been available on a comparable basis. Although world events and the fortunes of the socialist nations elsewhere may bring temporary strength or weakness to insurgency efforts, there is every reason to believe that they will continue to be active in the Latin American social and military environment for years to come.

The strategy of the insurgents openly admits ideological support from the Cuban base and in some instances publically states that the goal of the insurgency is to establish a socialist government. Of interest is that this recourse to violence with no compromise fits into the pattern of Latin American violence as discussed earlier in this chapter. The ideological agreement does not mean that the insurgents of the various areas are necessarily closely coordinated. It has even been the case that rival bands have existed from time to time, as in Guatemala. For the most part the guerrilleros are nationalists who have decided that a full-scale social upheaval and a socialist government are their primary goals, although it may take years to achieve them.

The extreme position taken by the socialist insurgents is helped by the fact that they follow in a long tradition of discontent in the Latin American countryside. Civil unrest has marked the Peruvian highlands, was widespread in Colombia, and has occurred from time to time elsewhere. These outbreaks of civic violence—based on the simple circumstances that the rural population is increasing and the relative amount of land available to them is not increasing—have generally been put down with little or no change in the conditions. Today, however, the combination of nationalism and the threat of insurgency is leading a number of governments to pay more heed to the situation that has engendered the problem.

Violence in Latin America has become a recognized mode of political action. It is used by governments through the military or by the military on its own; and it is used by campesino populations as well as by students and by others through demonstrations; and finally, there is emerging an institutionalized insurgency, a new continuing revolutionary effort that at the present time fluctuates from one country to another. The growth in strength of the military on the one hand, with the increase in insurgency on the other, means that violence will continue to be an important device. Presumably, it will decline in importance only when power is distributed more widely and the various elements of the population share more widely in the fruits of production and development. To reach this goal is no simple task; to achieve it there must be more power, and that power must be less concentrated than it is now.

Religious Institutions

~~~~~~

RELIGION IN LATIN AMERICA

One of the most obvious features of the general culture of Latin America is the debt it owes to the inheritance of the Catholic Church. Elements of its Catholic background run through its art, advertising, common daily expressions, the annual calendar of celebrations and vacations, rituals surrounding otherwise nonreligious events, and so on. As is the case with culture in general, however, these formal qualities of Catholic origin give no direct clue to the relative importance of either the religion or the church in contemporary life and social structure.

The establishing of the independence of most Latin American countries from the Spanish empire in the early nineteenth century technically also separated them from the imperially supported church and its officers. But in fact, the church continued to play an important role, just as some of its agents had played roles on both sides of the wars of independence. Under the

Spanish crown, priests not only had important functions in the society at large, but often also occupied offices of state, making the distinction between the religious and the secular somewhat meaningless.

Given this history, the church has long been accustomed to playing a political role, both collectively as an institution and individually through the activities of particular clergymen. In the years following independence, the relations of the church with the rest of the society differed from one country to another. In very few of the countries did close relations continue unabated during the entire period. In some, such as Mexico, Guatemala, and later Cuba and Panama, there were strong constitutional separations. In most countries, the church gradually lost much of its power. But nowhere did the church lose interest or potential to act politically. It is a central characteristic of the church in Latin America that it feels the right, just as does the military, to express strong favorable or unfavorable reaction to governmental action in matters not directly related to its central concerns.

A classic illustration of this stand may be seen in the case of Perón. The church gave him strong support at first, helped him to gain power, and then later issued strong criticism, probably contributing somewhat to his downfall. Similarly, in Guatemala the archbishop issued a pastoral letter against the spread of communism in the country during the Arbenz regime. Political activity on the part of priests may be illegal under national law, but the strong expressions of preference at the parish level are common.

Varying claims are made for the degree to which the church is directly or indirectly implicated in the political parties and movements that go under the general name of Christian Democracy. For the most part the parties are nationally identified and claim complete independence from the church, holding that participants may be of any religion. In fact, however, there is direct financial support for some of these parties from parareligious institutions abroad, and the strongest local supporters of these parties are often deeply involved in church affairs.

The severe separation of religious institutions from the state that was inscribed in the Constitution of the United States clearly derived from a cultural situation of divergent Christian religions in which such a separation was the only way to insure that the state would not meddle in church affairs on the one hand, and that no one religious group would dominate state affairs on the other. In contrast, in Latin America at the time of independence, the governments could hardly operate without elements of the church, and there was no divergency among churches to necessitate the second caution. Clearly the history of Latin American society involves the church as a political force; and the gradual separation during the nineteenth and the first part of the twentieth century was not some superficial attempt to imitate the pattern of the United States, but a necessary concomitant to the emergence of the state as the national leader.

The fact that varying degrees of separation were achieved does not mean that total separation is either necessary or desired by the nations involved. For some, such as Peru, where the formal links between church and state have been particularly strong and continuous, Protestants have been able to work with a minimum of governmental interference; and the identification of Peru as a Catholic country has something of the quality of the statement that the United States is a Christian country. The fact that many Latin American countries have special church-state ties is less remarkable than are the penetrating cultural features that reflect both the past and present roles of the church in the nation at large.

It has often been recorded that the church and the Catholic religion have been to some degree abandoned in Latin America, that the nations that are overwhelmingly Catholic are in fact apathetic and effectively nonpracticing. There is no question that there are significant differentials in overt participation, such as attendance of Mass and taking of the sacraments. While almost everyone is baptized, Mass attendance averages only 15 to 20 per cent of the nominally Catholic populations and varies from as low as 3 per cent to as high as claims for total participation. In any case, both Catholics and Protestants have felt that the religious situation in Latin America leaves much to be desired. The Catholics have seen in it insufficient support and effort; the Protestants deem it so short of true religious conviction that it is wide open for evangelizing.

Protestantism, which elsewhere has been related to industrial development, entered Latin America in a role that reflects more its adaptation to the Latin American environment than its earlier history. The most successful sects have been those which —because they emphasize egalitarian relationships and possibly because they have provided some welfare work in their missionary activities—have contrasted with the often distant, authoritarian, and alms-seeking hierarchy of the older Catholic establishment. Baptists, Presbyterians, and Pentecostals have been especially successful. The greatest conversion has been achieved in the poorer sector of the population. I remember a large tent meeting during my first field work in an Andean mountain community. In discussing the phenomenon of conversion to Protestantism with some of the Catholics of that community, I was told that "only North Americans and Indians are Protestant!"

While the appeal of Protestantism to the poor is obviously neither consistent nor universal, it generally reflects the frustrations felt by so much of the population about being effectively blocked from access to the symbols and values controlled by very few people. The egalitarian quality of Protestant churches is evident. Each meeting or church is essentially in charge of its own affairs; and each individual within the congregation has an equal voice and is not only allowed but also expected to voice his interests. This expectation has some appeal both to the individualism so strongly characteristic of much of the Latin

American population and to the hope that many entertain for a better way of life.

To Indian peasant communities Protestantism sometimes makes an additional appeal. Unlike many of the mestizos, Indians in Andean and Meso-American communities are cut off by language and culture from participation in the prestige system that characterizes the rest of the population. In many of these peasant communities there exists a strong motivation toward gaining wealth because, as among non-Indians, wealth is the major known channel to the prestige symbols within the Indian society. In that context, hard work is the only way to wealth, and the value placed on being a good man with a hoe, plow, or machete is high. The traditions of the Catholic Church have long involved the Indians in *cofradía* organizations, which have institutionalized the expenditure of wealth on annual rituals. The advent of Protestant missionaries with their emphasis upon frugality, hard work, temperance (liquor was high on the list of expenses of the Catholic fiestas), and reinvestment in land and business for further income had a distinct appeal to some of the Indians. Protestantism promised a way out of what appeared to be an otherwise completely restricted situation. It also appealed to some of the wealthier Indians who were gradually taking on the prestige values of the larger society, although the ability to make more money moved them further away from the Indian society and way of life.

Protestantism was not the only alternative ideology and social organization that made its appearance during the early years of the twentieth century; an understanding of its appeal must be seen in a broader context. The efforts in the 1920's to develop an ideology that would reflect social justice and, in some instances, echo the specific organizational characteristics of the Communist Party, gained a significant number of adherents among younger intellectuals. Latin Americans were traveling in small numbers and often in difficult circumstances to Russia. The United States was beginning to project itself as an economic and materialistic giant which, with the arrival of Marines in Haiti, Nicaragua, and Mexico, was a new devil behind the incredibly poverty-stricken way of life of peasants and laborers over much of the continent. The general social protest movement known as *indigenismo* was active, and specific organizational efforts, such as the Aprismo in Peru, were making political gains. In Mexico, the revolution was still developing its own solutions.

Many of the individuals who in the 1950's were active in political movements against the surviving nineteenth-century agrarian controls began as dissidents in religion or as political exiles during the years preceding the Second World War. Protestantism, then, played a role not entirely dissimilar to that of political-reform movements. It is obviously senseless to equate (as some conservatives have done) the motives of Protestant conversion with socialist political efforts. But it is clear that the two efforts entered the social context of Latin America at much the same time and for many of the same reasons. The fact that both serve as areas where dissidents and marginal people find rewards suggests that, irrespective of their ideological differences, they are playing parallel roles in the adaptation of Latin American societies to development.

CHANGING BASES OF CHURCH POWER

The processes of secondary development and its current idiom of nationalizing have changed many of the rights and privileges enjoyed by the church at the time of independence, and indicate that the church is operating from a fundamentally different position of power. It has lost some sources of derivative power but gained others; and while being shorn of certain of its independent bases, it has sought out new ones. Needless to say, the specifics about to be described hold only generally, and the actual situation varies from country to country.

With the establishing of independence, the church continued to have many of the responsibilities that it had had under the empire. It was responsible for keeping almost all vital statistics, primarily through its parish priests. It handled almost all the education and ran the hospitals and charitable institutions. It oversaw and controlled marriage and advised on family life. It owned properties, sometimes extensive haciendas and productive farms, as well as vast extensions of idle lands. It had the right to eliminate competing sects and in many areas had complete political administrative control over entire Indian communities. As under the empire it was difficult to distinguish derivative from independent power because, under European arrangements, the church was given various secular powers and the state exercised certain ecclesiastical rights.

The century and a half following the declarations of independence saw various of these prerogatives gradually taken from the church. The state began to institute educational enterprises and in some places finally removed all state support from church-supported schools. The keeping of vital statistics was gradually taken over by the state, and church record keeping was reduced to those statistics concerning purely sacramental affairs. Formal separation of state and church was reached in various degrees and under a variety of formal arrangements. Marriage and dissolution of marriage came under state control or was set up in such a way that the citizen could'choose either the religious or civil ceremony. Some countries, specifically Mexico and Guatemala, expropriated church properties, thereby removing the income derived from the estates and making the clergy dependent upon the alms of the parishioners and upon support from the state. Dissenting sects were not only allowed but in some instances were actively encouraged to come in. Until a few years ago, Protestantism was relatively weak; but as many Protestant missionaries were eliminated from China, Latin America was declared a prime area for North European and North American missionary efforts. The numbers of sects and converts have multiplied significantly since that time.

Analyzed in terms of sources of power, the losses of the

church not only removed its economic base of operations, but made continued activity dependent upon power derived from the state. Recently the church has made a few gains in the very areas lost earlier. In Guatemala, for example, after some 80 years of liberal and revolutionary governments, the church was given back its *personería jurídica*, whereby it owned land, and religious personnel were allowed and encouraged to come into the country. Mexico, while keeping many anticlerical laws in its books, in fact ceased to observe them, and the clergy in that very important country have grown significantly in strength.

For the most part, however, the losses inherent in the gradual differentiation of the church from the state are not recoverable. The state has generally taken over all the major activities relating to education, hospitals, vital statistics, and civil status, and has also in many cases specifically banned priests from holding public office. Sketched in broad terms, these losses may not appear to be so great; but if looked at carefully, it will be seen that the church has generally lost control over all the major life crises except the sacraments, as well as over the indoctrination of children and the determination of whether divorce may occur. Where it occurred, the loss of landed properties was staggering.

The church did for a period become progressively weaker. The losses sketched above were, until well into the twentieth century, generally uncompensated. The years following World War II, however, saw the arrival of missionary priests as well as Protestant missionaries—partly the result of the loss of China as a missionary field. This was the beginning of an increase in the number of foreign priests that brought with it both renewed pastoral and welfare activities, and a change in attitude on the part of many church officials as to the proper role of the church in Latin America. Many of the new priests were more liberal in attitude than their predecessors and also brought financial support from their home countries. A great proportion of the foreign clergy seem to come from countries which may be overproducing clergy. In 1960, Germany, Holland, and the United States accounted for over 12,000 priests, with Spain alone being the source for over 7,000. Some Latin American countries, specifically Mexico and Colombia, are also exporting religious personnel, mainly women.

The church has found an important new derivative source of power in the informal cooperation with the United States Department of State and the Agency for International Development. The latter agency, in particular, has found resident priests in the countryside to be potentially important elements in community-development programs, and in a number of instances financial help to some minor projects has been promised on the fact that a priest would be responsible. Both the Department of State and AID are strongly in favor of encouraging the work of the clergy in those areas where it can be seen to have some developmental or educational results. While there may possibly be also interest in supporting the church as such, the specific goal is to use priests as politically dependable agents for development. It is assumed in general (although there are exceptions) that the priests will not work in support of things that are likely to turn out to be socialistic.

Certainly these new sources of outside support for the church cannot replace the unique position that the church enjoyed in the colonial period; but then the issue is not to compare it with the colonial period, but to understand the real possibilities and alternatives for the church today. In the long run, I believe that the new sources of independent power toward which the church is building will prove to be much more important than the current derivative sources. Particularly interesting new power sources are found in four areas: rural work, university education, the Opus Dei, and new lay associations.

Perhaps the most widespread and diverse endeavor of the church has been in the rural areas, among both campesinos and rural laborers. These efforts range from the specific work of enterprising parish priests to experiments by priests with single-channel receiving sets for reaching parishioners in various countries. The major thrust has been to try to reach the lower sector and to institute effective parish work. Some countries have Catholic action organizations among campesinos. While these organizations have been used particularly for doctrinal purposes, they are also seen as potentially useful politically.

Another important effort of the church is in the area of education. Parochial schools have long been common in many countries; and church-supported universities have been particularly important, since the training and education of students therein are less likely to be interrupted by student demonstrations and strikes than is the case in the national universities. The United States Agency for International Development has been particularly interested in providing aid to some of these universities, both in the development of basic subject matter and in those fields that would influence the ultimate political and economic opinions of the students. Here again it is impossible to attempt to separate the church's effort at education from its political component.

One of the most interesting developments in Latin American Catholicism has been the appearance of the relatively new order, the Opus Dei. This order first emerged as an organization that mobilized people in the upper sector. It has encouraged its lay members to seek positions of wealth and influence, specifically positions of power, in order to contribute more fully to the glory of God and, not incidentally, to the order. I do not know currently how widespread the Opus Dei is in Latin America. Its strong and rapid development in Franco's Spain suggests that it will find ready acceptance among the conservative members of upper-sector Latin America. One of its peculiar attractions is that it makes the heaping of profits an ecclesiastically sanctioned activity, especially so when it involves spreading the influence of the church. The Opus Dei is particularly interesting organizationally because, by attempting to obtain adherents in many professions and occupations and by keeping rather quiet about its successes, it grows as a semisecret network that could, under some circumstances, exercise extraordinary influence. Among the clergy it is not viewed entirely benignly; the success of the Opus Dei with the upper sector has posed a serious threat to the influence of the Jesuits who have, until now, exercised considerable influence in that area.

On the local level, the formal organizations through which the church has operated have been changing. From colonial times into the twentieth century, organizations of laymen called *cofradías* or *mayordomías* were established by the church as a means of collecting money to support fiestas and other church needs. Now, these organizations have been generally replaced by associations run by laymen.

The cofradía was a system whereby an individual or group was named annually to be responsible for the celebration of the day of a particular saint during the ensuing year. In earlier times, the individual or group was named by the priest; but as the clergy became scarce in many areas during the nineteenth century, cofradías invented various devices for selecting future patrons. To be a patron of the cofradía was a matter of high prestige, and candidates were usually available. It was, however, a costly matter, and there are accounts of long years of debt for many who accepted the responsibility. Each community customarily had a number of confradías, ranked in terms of relative importance. Cofradías did not have exclusive membership, although the number of individuals who could afford to sponsor a fiesta was limited. The membership issue was not crucial, since the fiesta (consisting of home and church services, a religious procession, and dancing) was usually open to everyone. In those areas that observed social distinctions, certain saints were traditionally allocated to people of the upper strata and others to lower-strata individuals. The cost of a given fiesta indicated the relative prestige of the cofradía. Over the years, the use of control of the saints took on social significance, and in some instances the wealthy used this control as an additional means of exploiting the poor. In one particularly flamboyant Guatemalan case, the controlling ladino family in a predominantly Indian community kept the statue of the saint in their home and charged Indians a fee for permission to pray to it.

Recently there has been a general breakdown in the traditional cofradía system. This breakdown has arisen from various causes, but it would appear that its survival is related to the maintenance of some sort of corporate control within the population. Thus, cofradías still operate in Indian communities that have maintained cultural isolation from the mestizo society. More important, the survival of cofradías is correlated with the community's ability to continue large celebrations at the expense of one or a few individuals. The increasing tendency in some places has been for the annual *mayordomo* to solicit financial help from his friends and neighbors. Formerly, a number of officers were usually named for the annual celebration, each of whom was responsible for some of the items required. This gradual defraying of expenses has tended to mark out a specific circle of individuals to whom a given mayordomo would turn, thus establishing an informal membership.

The cofradía has been replaced by lay associations which have regular membership and which are collectively responsible for supporting the saints' festivals. These associations also tend to be marked socially; different groups tend to represent specific sectors of the local society. The declining participation of poorer men has left most such societies in the lower economic sectors in the hands of the women. Even in the upper sectors (although a few men will be active) women carry much of the responsibility for the maintenance of the societies. Membership in religious societies is sometimes supposed to reflect political conservatism, but this tendency does not always hold. In the larger cities, active work in these societies is indicative of such conservatism, but in the provincial areas and especially in small towns, some of the societies may actually be politically progressive.

In some areas, especially Brazil and the Andean countries, religious societies have evolved into dance societies that are particularly active on the occasion of some event in the religious calendar. Most famous of these societies are the groups organized for the carnival, the celebration marking the beginning of Lent. In Brazil, Bolivia, and Peru this has been a traditional celebration of great pageantry, and to some degree, license. Dance groups are engaged for months ahead in preparing for their performances in the major parade, and a great deal of money is spent on the celebration.

The perpetuation of these groups, emphasizing the purely secular aspect, illustrates again the separation that the church is experiencing within the society at large. The church has not penetrated secular activities, but secularity has instead penetrated religious activities. Moreover, the religious associations, as opposed to the older cofradías, draw support from a much larger portion of the population, since all members theoretically contribute to it. However, the associations also serve to differentiate people socially. As the population and a middle-income group increases in size, the formation of closed groups has helped to draw lines of distinction.

The power structure of the church today is unquestionably under change, and in the main it is adaptive to the broader changes that are taking place elsewhere in the social structure. There are still cases, some outrageous, of priests or higher authorities of the church acting in concert with the government and with members of the upper sector to crush campesino or other lower-sector group efforts to organize for bettering their situation. But these cases, while they may be expected to continue, are increasingly being balanced by the activities of priests who are devoting time to the wider problems of their parishes. Within the clergy itself, there are important conflicts over the degree of freedom a local priest should be allowed to have, and the cold hand of the authoritarian structure too often transfers priests when they are proving themselves to be especially capable of working successfully for the betterment of the campesino.

The encyclicals of Pope John XXIII, together with the concerns of the Twenty-second Ecumenical Council, have unquestionably laid the foundation for a much broader approach to pastoral and political action on the part of the clergy. Whether the church in the various Latin American countries will rapidly seek these wider horizons is hard to predict. The temptation to continue to depend upon the support from the upper sector will inevitably inhibit the development of power bases in the lower sector. The emergence of new networks such as the Opus Dei suggests that there are adaptive devices at work for the continued preservation of the church and of those aspects of the society on which it heavily depends. The increasingly international character of the clergy in Latin America unquestionably will pose problems as the national clergies grow in size. The presence of so many foreigners already brings nationalistic reactions on the part of Catholic laymen who sometimes feel that the church is acting as an arm of penetration of foreigners (most particularly from the United States), and above all, that it is an antinationalistic institution more interested in the service of the Vatican than in the nation.

THE CHURCH AND DEVELOPMENT

It is tempting to see the peculiar history of the church's decline as a part of the general underdevelopment of Latin America. In fact, however, the change in the church's role has been part of the process of development. Since the authority and power of the church lie in an international establishment far beyond the national limits of any specific Latin American nation, the process of development has required that the clergy be gradually excluded from control of national life. The church has generally contributed little of a positive kind to the developmental process. While it is analytically wrong (and futile) to blame the church for Latin America's developmental problems, it is also misleading to allow it much credit for having tried as an institution to help resolve these problems.

The church is much more a reactive institution than an innovative one; it has proved itself to be a generally poor social inventor. In rural development, the origin of the idea that a single-channel radio can be used for educational, doctrinal, and political purposes has been ascribed to a priest in Colombia; but whether the idea originated with him or not, the church as an institution can hardly be regarded as the innovator. Individual churchmen, both at the level of parish priest and higher in the hierarchy, do act as innovators from time to time. To make their innovations work, however, they have the double task of convincing their ecclesiastical superiors as well as the population at large. Over the past twenty years "progressive" elements in the church have been trying to change the traditional role and image of the clergy. Even this attempt, however, must be seen in the somewhat pessimistic light of an adaptive reaction, stimulated as much by the desire to save the church in Latin America as to save Latin America.

The preceding paragraphs are written neither to condemn nor to condone the church. It is not in the design of this analysis to seek institutional scapegoats for Latin America's problems. It is important, however, to understand where institutions stand in the complex and slowly evolving process of development. The place of the Church is unique. It has outside connections, commitments, and obligations, in which it resembles the international communist movement or the interests of foreign investors; it has local responsibilities, in which it resembles agencies of a national government; it is centralized in its hierarchy, but priests at all points in the system have a high degree of individuality and autonomous action. Finally, it is the historical progenitor of many aspects and parts of a cultural heritage over which it has little further control. The church is rather like the Latin American campesino; it has a great ability to survive, but its condition has improved only slightly, if at all, over the years.

PART III

Patterns

Power and Economic Development

The pattern of development in Latin America has been, and continues to be, significantly different from that of the rest of the western world. New techniques and knowledge are not being born within the society and finding their social adjustments as they originally developed, but rather, are being introduced as large complex wholes that require major social readjustments. Instead of experiencing a gradual growth of power within the society, Latin America has had a whole new series of complex power sources and bases thrust upon it. The response has been the elaboration of the power system and changes in the allocation of decisions about economic development within the organization of power.

The remaining chapters are concerned with exploring the structure of sociocultural alterations that are taking place as a part of secondary development. Various phases of these alterations have already been described in Part II; here I would like to examine them in terms of more inclusive structural changes. The present chapter is specifically concerned with the nature of the changing power bases and with the effects of power on economic development.

EXPANDING POWER BASES

The amount of power in a society may be increased from either of two sources. First, there may be an expansion of the power base—those areas of the environment under human control and therefore available for controlling other men. Second, derivative power may be made available from another power domain; while this derivative power is not directly controlled, it may be drawn upon in times of tactical need. Such power can never be as easily manipulated as the direct control enjoyed by an independent domain, since it is subject to the decisions of another control center. Nevertheless, whether the power comes from one source or another may be quite irrelevant in a specific event since it is the tactical use of power at a specific time that will determine the outcome.

There is, however, an important difference in the way power from the two sources is utilized. The control of a specific environment may be fairly complex. Government control over the operations of private investors and entrepreneurs, over the guerrillas that may be operating in marginal areas, and over the votes of peasants is much more complicated than is the organization of force and the decision making that may be available from some external domain. Military and technical aid from the United States or Russia are easier to arrange than is the elimination of guerrillas through military action.

The control of derivative power is basically an administrative and organizational matter and therefore involves a large amount of individual activity of a bureaucratic nature. Organizational development and study in recent years have shown that there are features common to many organizations even when their substantive parts and purposes differ. It is easier to learn the organizational phases of power control than it is to solve the more diverse control problems within one's immediate environment. The relative ease of organizational manipulation, together with the increase in power exercise necessary for a population to adapt to new technological or economic devices, has generated within the Latin American countries a deep concern with power and its control.

The increase in power bases in Latin America has come about in a number of ways. The emergence of new technological processes provides bases of power that may be handled independently of the organizations that the processes may spawn. Institutions of higher education have to teach this knowledge if it is to become part of the ongoing culture. Universities in Latin America are not uniform in matters of control, but they have often maintained a degree of autonomy in their operations— from the business-industrial community, on the one hand, and from the politics of the government, on the other. Thus, the growing importance of the institutions of higher education makes them important power bases. One way of controlling this power has been to start new universities with the express intent of focusing education in specific areas relevant to development and of retaining control of that education so that certain things will not be taught.

The engineer and the architect are occupying new positions of importance. Since industries need trained engineers, the competition for good men is severe, and the speed of training such men is still inadequate. Trained agriculturalists are also in increasing demand as large-scale farmers realize the importance of scientific agriculture and mechanized farming. Industrialization places increasing reliance upon the specialist, and both the specialist's utilization of his own skills as a marketable entity and the control of specialists by manufacturing firms and by governmental bureaus provide all of them with new bases of power. The economist also has a power role. His technical abilities are relevant to commercial and governmental actions as well as to industry; and the position he holds is quite similar to that of the engineer, although more viable.

Another kind of new power base is found in the increase in the amount of material goods being produced and consumed within the growing whole of Latin America. The economic growth in parts of Latin America—though by no means so rapid as is considered either necessary or ideal—is exceeding the population growth. Also, the growing diversity of production sets up differentiated power bases as individuals become involved in administering the processes. Manufacturers and middlemen engaged in producing and marketing steel, iron, plastics, and petrochemicals have grown in importance compared to those who have traditionally handled such products as textiles, furniture, and beverages.

The increase in power derived from the control of credit and capital may be the most significant of all. The largest single Latin American operation, in terms of big business, is financing. One study suggests that of 180 of the major firms in the entire area, over 30—the largest single group—are involved in financing. Bankers, both public and private, are occupying more and more positions of extraordinary power, since they can slow or hasten the entire development process.

Of major interest in this context is the increase in the numbers and kinds of human organizations that are directly and indirectly involved in economic development and in the rapid growth and urbanization of the population. It is characteristic of human culture that people will organize when they have some common interest that becomes of particular importance to them. In Latin America, the twentieth century has seen a rise in the importance of labor unions and syndicates, of peasant leagues, of agrarian organizations such as the ejido committees in Mexico, of rural laborers who combine to purchase land for their collective ownership, of wealthy farmers and industrialists, of politically inclined groups of businessmen, and the like. Perhaps the most visible but politically least understood source of power in Latin America today is this proliferation of human organizations. Indeed, these organizations have been more effective than many of the other power sources dealt with here. The actions of the Bolivian peasant and mining organizations, the controlling of unions by Perón, the political use made of the Brazilian peasant leagues by some rising politicians, the manipulation of a large variety of these organizations by the Mexican government and its major political party—these, as well as the controls exercised over private enterprises, are all examples of the developing power that organizations of people make available.

Finally, the constant increase in armaments and new skills in many Latin American military establishments has meant the increase of sheer force. Arms and force in Latin America have traditionally been sources of social control, and the increase in the power they afford is not being disregarded by any of the competing interests.

DECLINE OF OLD POWER BASES

This review of the bases of expanding power indicates the complexity of power control involved in the mere handling of the entities and conditions present within the various countries of the hemisphere. Of equal importance are the sources of derived power that have increased through the growing interests of other nations. (A discussion of this derivative power is found in Chapter 15.) The total power is a resultant of changing components: some sources expanding, some new, some declining, some vanishing. The great hacienda, the latifundio, has unquestionably suffered in the process of power growth. Though merely a part of the general decline of agrarian mercantilism, the decline of the latifundio system should also be seen in terms of its effect upon the local scene. The landowner who appears in public with side arms is increasingly rare, though he may still be seen in some back-country areas and politically less nationalized regions. Economically, many of the older haciendas have proven so poor that their owners have turned to other, more urban, pursuits. The large farm still exists, however, and still exerts strong controls over the laborer in some areas. But the general trend has been to deal with labor on a more open market, to retreat from the former controls and thereby also to shed the earlier responsibilities.

The political history of the Catholic Church in Latin America has led to its severe restriction by the government in many areas. The church's insistence on a conservative position in the face of obvious changes has increased individual disinterest in the church. The parish priest, once quite powerful, now finds power something that must be worked for with increasing effort. Excommunication and fear of eternal perdition do not conjure up the results they did a hundred years ago.

The community, especially the peasant community, once exercised considerable local control because of its relative isolation from government and other power centers. Today, communication and transportation make most communities so much a part of the nation that much of the power they have for development tends to be derived from the outside. The communities that have been most active in the major peasant movements of recent years have been those under the severe control of latifundios or some other restrictive agent. Those communities that have made a special effort to develop themselves, however, have done so with outside aid and resources.

And finally, the household—never an organization of real power—may in some sense be said to be even less significant today. The growth of public education, the forced movement of agrarian laborers into the cities, and the demands for civil recognition of subsistence problems have made the household primarily an economic entity. And even in that capacity, its role is being challenged by the increasing number of public agencies and laws that must be observed. This shifting role of the family is also found in the upper sector, but to a lesser degree, since there the common interest in inheritance often holds households together with stronger bonds than those found in families where the common economic concern is absent.

The power bases within Latin America have grown in conjunction with the individual's ability to manipulate them. Power has declined in those areas in which the manipulation of power has not been the central issue in the pattern of life (as in the community), or where power has simply disappeared or is disappearing (as in the latifundios). In its place has emerged a new structure in which the government is playing a central role.

THE EFFECT OF POWER ON ECONOMIC DEVELOPMENT

This extraordinary growth in the amount of available power has naturally led to a concomitant expansion of the upper sector and to the continuing competition of power so characteristic of it. A thesis of this book is that this concern for power, while it may be contributing to the economic development of the upper sector, is manifestly acting as a severe inhibitor of development in the society as a whole. Economic development must suffer some retardation as long as power rests so completely with the upper sector of a society. The continued extreme inequality of income distribution reinforces the two distinctive sectors. The failure to achieve a wider distribution of wealth, thereby perpetuating the dual-sector system, also means that obtaining power will continue to be a central interest. So long as this process continues, wealth will be used to obtain power rather than to increase capital and achieve economic development.

It is quite clear that increased income per capita enhances or increases power in a society. There is, however, nothing in the process of economic development that determines how the increasing income per capita or national wealth is to be distributed. Initial increases in income are almost inevitably used for restricted ends, such as luxury expenditures on prestige items or, if directed by a rigidly socialistic government, for investment in heavy industry. However, the problem is not merely the distribution of income. Even if profits were widely distributed, it is equally reasonable to assume that they would not be reinvested and the income would soon shrink again to its former level. The limited segment of a society that controls the increased wealth uses it initially to enhance its power. Among the rationales cited are: that there really is not enough to go around anyway, so those who "earned" it should have it; or that since there is not enough to make everyone permanently better off, it ought to be invested in basic development items. No matter which is done, control over wealth gives additional power to the wealth holder.

While economic development automatically increases power, power does not necessarily foster economic development. Power may be said to be a necessary condition for economic development, but it is not sufficient nor are some of its forms applicable. Where there is an "open" environment—one unrestricted by claims of society—control over it (whether through invention or through borrowing of techniques) is necessary simply to extract greater wealth. Power in this sense is primarily a matter of control over adequate technology. In Latin America, however, it has always involved control over labor—either cheap labor, with easy turnover, or more expensive skilled labor that is in some manner tied to the enterprise. Such power may be sufficient to maintain a level of production to match a restricted market's needs, but it does not provide for the development of new markets nor for reinvestment to increase the capital holdings, Also, since power is basically a thing that is used tactically, it may well be that the particular power that is available is not in a form that can readily be used for development. For example, a military junta in Latin America may control an army of soldiers, but it is doubtful that it can make a peasant group of equal size increase its production. Power is effective if one has the right kind of power and the situation suitable for its application.

This much of the picture in Latin America is fairly well

understood. It is evident that the wealth produced by agrarian mercantilism was maintained at a level beneficial to the controllers of that wealth, and that one use to which they put their power was to see that it should not gain a wider distribution. Similarly, the increase in wealth that periodically occurs with the opening of a new market or the initiation of a new industry involves a decision about the use of the increased profit, and the decision, when in private hands, has usually been to satisfy those who controlled the investment. Efforts toward gaining wider distribution of wealth have usually been in terms of providing facilities for labor, hospitals, recreational areas, discount stores, and the like, rather than providing increased cash payments.

In the dual-sector society that predominates in Latin America, prestige symbols may be had with power, but wealth alone is not sufficient to gain them because a strong cultural separation exists between the upper and lower sectors. The lower sector is marked by illiteracy and simplicity of material culture. The upper sector is characterized, among other things, by skillful rhetoric and manners and strong habit differences that can be acquired only through formal learning, available solely to those who command certain resources in the society.

The central place of power in the Latin American upper sector can be better seen if contrasted with other societies. In societies that place special emphasis upon security and wealth— as in the case in the North American middle economic stratum— power is very important, but it is also regarded as somewhat undependable. Since power depends on its tactical use, greater emphasis is placed on obtaining conditions that seem to guarantee one's welfare. Power is a goal among North Americans primarily insofar as it provides a guaranty of security. While wealth is not sufficient to gain all the prestige symbols, the usual recourse is to attempt to get enough for some of the symbols and have some wealth left over, for security's sake.

Societies which place special emphasis on the so-called spiritual values may hold that the achievement of certain organic or mental sensations is the major goal in the society. Assurance that one is right with God, or that one has followed the correct steps or rules, or that one has performed the appropriate action is the desirable end. Where power is the means to the goal and the goal consists of prestige symbols, there is no strong motivation toward economic development. Such is the case among many Latin Americans of the upper sector. Consequently, it is surely of importance that so much of the power utilized in Latin America is derivative. When accumulation of independently controlled wealth or property is not the major basis of power, power derived from superior domains becomes extremely important. Since almost all the Latin American countries are relatively weak in terms of accumulated capital, the astute individual can play off one party against another and thereby gain much through the use of power derived from other countries. The position of Castro in Cuba is a prime example of such derivative power. While such power can be used in economic development, it can also interfere with rational decisions in economic matters.

The relation of power to economic development is, then, one wherein concern with power tends more to constrain economic development than to enhance it. How, then, may economic development be less inhibited by the concern with power? In answering this question, it must be clear that power will never be eliminated from the picture; it is really a question of how development may become a more important value.

So long as there is a dual-sector society, power will be the major means utilized by the upper sector. Furthermore, obtaining power will therefore continue to be a major motivation of individuals within that sector and of those moving into it. The dual-sector society is characterized by a severe differential in wealth and culture. Power is necessary to obtain the wealth, and it is equally necessary to remain in a position in which one may enjoy the prestige symbols of the upper sector. Many of these symbols are not achievable with wealth alone, because they require familiarity with the culture of the upper sector. Traits that are acquired only in certain company, that require learning and interaction with other people who do the same thing, can be acquired only by association with the society in question. These traits can be retained within the upper sector more easily if the wealth is unevenly distributed. To make power less important, it is necessary that other means be opened up for the acquisition of the prestige symbols. This change can be accomplished through a wider distribution of wealth, a more profound internal acculturation, a wider sharing of the culture, and a more penetrating system of education.

Greater distribution of wealth and greater commonality of culture would signal the dissolution of the dual society and thereby reduce the importance of the position that power now holds within Latin American society. While this conclusion may sound impractical, it does draw attention to the proposition that unless economic development produces an increase in per-capita income that is adequately distributed among the population, the importance of power will not diminish. It also seems inevitable that if greater income distribution is to be achieved through the use of power, it must be brought about by government.

In considering these propositions, it must be remembered that Latin America is an area of relatively low total wealth, of highly disparate incomes, and of great cultural extremes. There is no reason to assume that the society's motivations and preferences will parallel those elsewhere in the western world. Nor is it being suggested here—at least, not for the time being—that these propositions would necessarily apply in precisely their present form elsewhere, any more than they would in all corners of Latin America. Finally, it is obvious that broader income distribution will also generate further problems, one being that widespread distribution of income initially removes it from ready availability for further capital investment.

The basic argument of this chapter is that if economic development is not to be inhibited by the exaggerated importance of power in the entire system, it can only be achieved by providing other means of organizing the society.

Internal
and
External Power

〰〰〰〰〰〰〰〰〰〰〰〰〰〰〰〰〰〰〰〰〰〰

The basic problem of every nation today is to control the powers that operate internally and externally so as to achieve a better way of life for its growing population. Handling outside powers is largely a matter of balance; therefore, it is usually the case that little or no direct control can be exercised, especially when the nation concerned is weak. Consequently, for most of the nations of the world, the major area in which they can exercise control over development is within their own territories. It is for this reason—because development can be better controlled on the national than on the international scale—that the internal, or subnational, structure is important. The nation that has sufficient internal control to plan for growth is in a much better position to promote its own development than the one which must spend most of its time on internal reorganization.

POWER THROUGH SUBNATIONAL ORGANIZATIONS

Throughout nineteenth-century Latin America, the power structure within the countries was characterized by a multitude of strong regional and local organizations and by a central government generally able to exercise control over these entities only through marshaling the forces of others. The late nineteenth century saw the development of some nationally controlled police and military organizations that served to back up the control exercised regionally and, occasionally, to challenge it. In general, however, the national state continued to depend more upon regional strength than the regions depended on national control. By the same token, the state was an organization that specifically served special interests, both foreign and domestic.

The change that has occurred over the past one hundred years is the gradual strengthening of the central government—part of the process of the emergence of national governments—and the relative weakening of the regional and special-interest entities, such as haciendas, fundos, mining organizations, plantations, and the like. This process of change has two structural aspects. One aspect is the increasing strength of the government, as over and against the regional or special-interest bodies, reflected in the elaboration of statutes and codes setting forth government authority over all sectors of the national territory, and the strengthening of the enforcement arm of the government so that failure to observe these laws may bring about sanctions against the offenders.

The other, and more crucial, phase has been the gradual emergence of a whole new series of subnational power domains that have come into being through the combination of efforts of previously weak or nonexistent special-interest entities, on the one hand, and through their recognition by the government, on the other. Earlier, these special-interest entities had been counted among the new power bases and included a variety of political parties, peasant organizations, unions, and the like. The new power complexes form a series of multiple-power domains under the government, rather than the series of unique domains that previously existed.

The change is illustrated schematically in the accompanying diagrams. The first shows the traditional power relationship that has held between the government and any given hacienda, plantation, or cacique. Other such entities might include foreign enterprises such as Grace and Company or United Fruit Company. Each such subnational entity exercised a unique domain over the population in question; the government has had no direct control over the populations involved. Therefore, whenever the government may have wanted to institute some change with respect to these populations, or when the populations may have wanted access to the government to exercise judiciary protection for them against the controllers of the subnational entities, they had to work through these entities. Obviously, the hacienda, the community organizations, and the cacique would try to prevent anything that would be against their interests. Thus, for example, minimum-wage laws could be ignored.

The second diagram shows the introduction of new subnational organizations, which involve the same population segments as in Diagram 1. The diagram shows how such new organizations create a multiple domain, resulting in an inherent conflict of interests between the members of each pair. The labor union organizes against the hacienda, the peasant league tries to obtain preferences that crosscut those of the community organization, and the political party organizes the campesinos to obtain for them benefits that the regional boss has refused to allow. This diagram is, of course, simplified. In fact, the multiplicity becomes more than dual, as indicated in the third diagram. The laborers on a given plantation or hacienda may be organ-

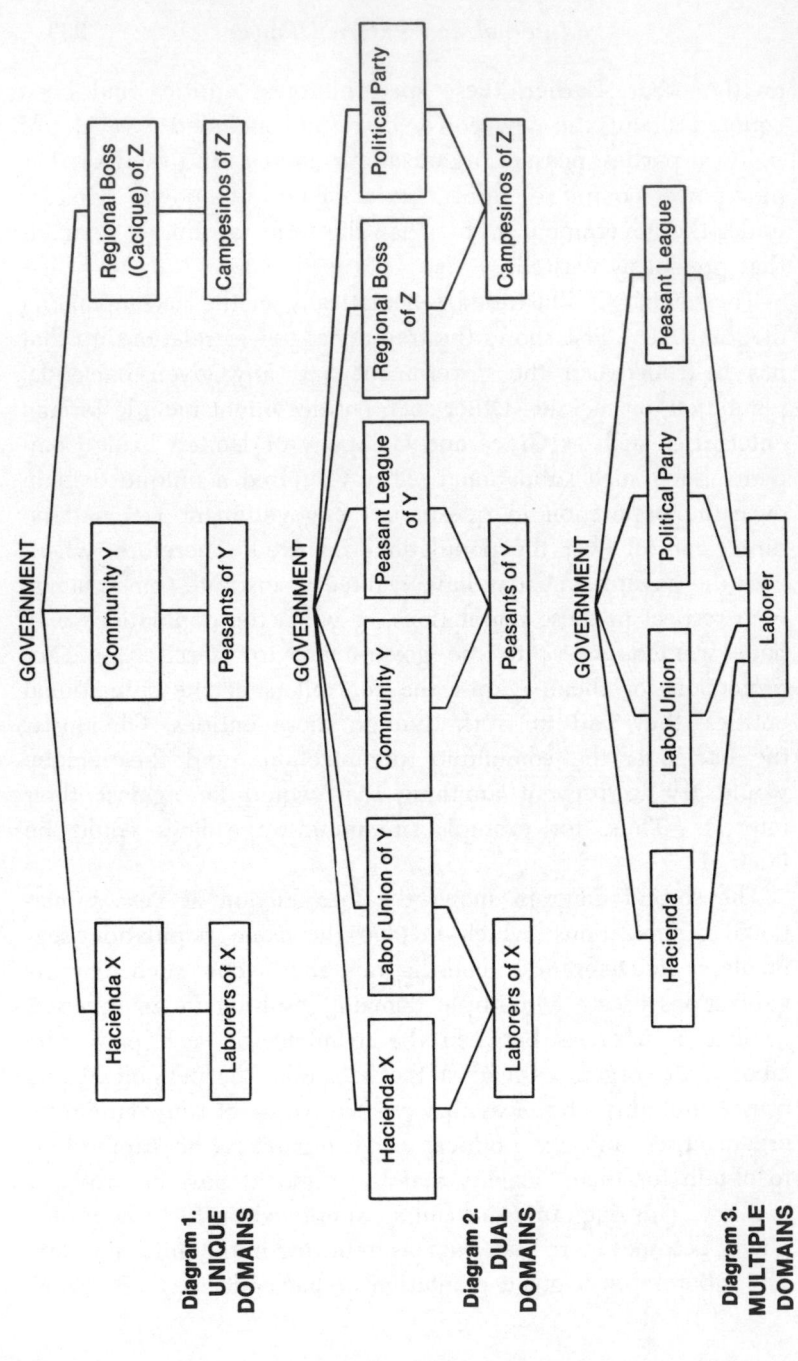

ized not only by the union, but also by the political party and by the peasant league. And since such organizations are seldom universal, a given laborer will belong to some but not others.

The crucial change that occurs, however, is that the laborer, *comunero,* peasant, or other individual now has a number of alternative channels of access to power. By holding positions in a series of domains, he has access to derivative power that lets him play one organization against another, each of which in turn operates with access to the power of the government. This aspect of derivative power is a major structural feature of multiple domains.

It should be noted in passing that the issue under discussion here should not be confused with the notion of "creating" a middle class for either political or economic reasons. The subnational organizations of which I am speaking are composed primarily of individuals from the society's lower sector, although some organizations have developed around the special problems and interests of upper-sector individuals, such as white-collar workers. The subnational organizations are formed by people who have common interests; and the membership includes not only those who share the particular interests, but also individuals who have organizing ability or special political interests in promoting the formation of such groups.

The manner in which these new subnational organizations have emerged reflects at least three different sets of interests: those of the government; those of the populations involved; and those of political entrepreneurs, individuals who see in the new organizations a way of achieving power for themselves. Most successful organizations involve all three kinds of interest. The interests of the populations have to be recognized, and such recognition must come either with the tacit support of the government or because the government is so weak that it cannot combat them. Moreover, there must be some individuals who believe they will achieve their own personal interests by supporting the organizations, and finally, the government must also be ready to support and back the organizations.

The fact that it is immaterial which kind of interest initiates organizations may be seen in the recent histories of Bolivia, Guatemala, and Cuba. In Bolivia, the organization of the peasant league that centered in the Cochabamba region was initiated by local peasants. Certain of them acted as the instigators and leaders of the development and retained leadership thereafter. In the early 1950's, the Bolivian revolutionary government found the action of the campesinos to be to their advantage. Since the campesinos had already undertaken an agrariaɲ reform on their own, the government simply ratified it by passing an agrarian-reform law, and provided its support to the action already taken. Had the government been against the campesinos in this instance, it is unlikely that it could have done much about it, since the peasants were armed and, in fact, were militarily probably better off than the government.

Prior to 1945, Guatemala was run as a private domain of Jorge Ubico. All important governmental decisions were made by him, and he was, as he himself allegedly said, "the politics" in Guatemala. Ubico ruled the country through a series of unique domains wherein the local populations found themselves effectively responsible to a single local government official who effectively supported the control that the large-scale farmers or Indian community elders or caciques had over the laboring population. The lower sector had no effective access to power to allow it to change its circumstances, except by recourse to the immediate superiors in the system. The period from 1945 to 1954 saw a severe change in this system. Under Arévalo and Arbenz, rural labor unions, rural mass organizations, and political parties were established. These organizations derived power from the government, which in turn both supported their development and utilized them as a way of trying to break the local power that had, until that time, been exercised by the larger farmers and local bosses. In the provincial areas, this system had irregular success; but by 1954 the southwestern coffee area and the south coast, together with the areas of the

United Fruit company, had in general been effectively organized so as to present the local upper class with effective political competition. The agrarian reform (through agrarian committees) and the law of forced rentals applied specific economic pressure to weaken the older controls. From the standpoint of the agrarian laborer, the system now provided him with a number of different avenues of access to power. If he were unsuccessful in getting what he wanted directly from the *finquero* (landlord) or from the cacique, he could approach the problem through his labor union, agrarian committee, political party, or the campesino league. Many municipal governments were also being controlled by individuals in strong sympathy with the political destruction of the finqueros and Indian elders and received special support from the central government.

This proliferation of lower-sector organizations was not immediately paralleled in the upper sector. There was an *Asociación General de Agricultores* (*AGA*), but it had little success when it tried to defend the interests of the large farmers in the face of the threat posed by the agrarian reform. The only effective response to the lower-sector threats was the support of the revolution of 1954 that threw out the incumbent government. This signaled a new period in the development of the power structure. An immediate consequence of the 1954 revolution was that all *sindicados*, campesino leagues, and existing political parties were eliminated. Thousands of campesinos and others were thrown in jail for varying periods. In effect, the entire organizational structure that had been developing within the lower sector during the 1945–1954 period was eliminated. A few sindicados, such as the railway-workers union, ultimately survived, but nothing survived within the agrarian sector.

The 1945–1954 period posed a severe threat to investors. Following the 1954 revolution, the government undertook the promotion of investment, both local and foreign. The experience of the previous years, however, led to the gradual emergence within the upper sector of a large number of interest-group organizations. By 1965, the AGA had declined in importance, but there was in its place a variety of independent and overlapping organizations of investors in the rural areas. The new organizations tended to be more specialized in their interests, both as to crop and product, and frequently also by region. Furthermore, they did not merely represent a structuring of existing interests, but also reflected the appearance of entirely new interests. Cotton, sugar, and cattle—which had been of minor significance before—grew in importance and provided new sources of incomes and new bases of power.

In broad terms, this period completely reversed the developments of the preceding one. Instead of a growth of lower-sector organizations accompanied by weak upper-sector organization, the upper sector grew and became increasingly complex. The lower sector, on the other hand, lost most of the organizations it had gained earlier. It was not until the 1960's that some new rural labor unions, a number of small campesino leagues, and cooperatives began to emerge in a very tentative way. Political parties came back into evidence, but since only those working immediately with the government had any access to power themselves, the needs and interests of the lower sector were little heeded.

The failure to organize the Guatemalan lower sector is instructive. One entity that was not successfully countered in the 1945–1954 period was the Guatemalan army. The military, as a group, was not committed either for or against the reforms and organizations that were developing. The Arbenz government tried to establish subnational organizations that would neutralize the military by arming the agrarian committees. The military forestalled the move by taking over an entire shipment of arms that Arbenz had brought in from Eastern Europe for this purpose. Shortly thereafter, when the country was invaded by a very small force bent on toppling the government, the army did essentially nothing. By not fighting, it effectively allowed the government to fall. In analyzing the more complex conditions, however, it is clear that the government had failed to obtain the full interest of the laborers and peasants, especially among Indians, and it had also failed to counter the opposing forces of the older regime. In the absence of the army, there was no organization with sufficient strength to defend the government.

In Cuba, the initiation of organizations may be ascribed to the efforts of a relatively small number of men—neither the government nor the poor. There were no organizations in Cuba to provide for a successful revolution, and Fidel Castro continued his guerrilla activities in the face of limited success for some time. The organization of the groups that represented the control of the land was extremely poorly formed. The heavy foreign ownership placed the government in a difficult position in respect to its own defense, and Castro could count on a strong antipathy toward the incumbent government, especially among the middle socioeconomic strata.

To return again to the general structure of the subnational organizations: a matter of considerable importance is the degree to which they are able to obtain for themselves some measure of independent power. The major difference between the Bolivian peasant league and the agrarian committees developed by Arbenz in Guatemala lay in the relative amount of independent power they could draw upon. No matter what the government did or what happened to it, the Bolivian peasants had their own organization and their own arms. The Guatemalan committees, on the other hand, depended entirely upon the government for their organization, and the failure of the government to obtain arms for them spelled the end of both the committees and the government. However, the organization that has only independent power and has nowhere to turn for derivative power to bring to bear on situations in which its own power is insufficient, is likely to be eliminated when counterforces become strong. The Guatemalan government did not, in the middle 1950's, have the derivative power from the communist countries that Cuba is currently able to command. Today, the long-range success of any guerrilla movement depends in some part on the amount of derivative power that it can elicit, unless the incumbent government is so weak that it can neither bring the guerrillas to an effective battle nor subvert the movement.

Some governments fear the establishment of subnational organizations, usually because they fear that the organizations will function independently. Mexico is the best example to date of a government that effectively controls a wide variety of subnational organizations through playing them against one another and at the same time allowing them to act in some manner for the betterment of their own interests. The Mexican government, through constituted authority and through the *Partido Revolucionario Institucional* (the major party because of its wide representation), has succeeded in countering almost every organization through some device: businesses with unions; the military through internal fractioning; foreign businesses with domestic ownership and legal controls; and so on. Perón's success in Argentina was, in great part, due to the manner in which he harnessed the major labor unions to stand behind him; effective subnational organizations that were able to work in spite of, and against, governmental action were few. When they were successful, it was through eliminating the government.

For the structural position of subnational organizations to be stable, it is necessary that they be based on both independent and derivative power, usually from the government. Independent power permits them to act in ways that may not be entirely in accord with the government's plan. Derivative power is necessary because they must be able to depend upon the extra power that the government (or some other source) can provide if they are to have over-all success.

The question naturally arises as to whether it is possible to anticipate the appearance of extensive, countrywide subnational organizations. A political party (as it operates in both the United States and Mexico) is an organization that cuts across many other organizations and provides the structure for such widespread multiple domains. One answer to the question depends upon the effectiveness of communication and transportation. Countrywide power structures, other than the government itself, depend upon effective communication. To the degree that the communications are controlled by the government, the organizations depend upon the government's favor. If the communication systems are multiple, that is, if the countrywide organization has its own communication system and can exercise control that is independent of the government, then it can act independently. It would seem, then, that at least at the outset the establishment of a countrywide organization at the subnational level is much easier with the assent, if not the positive assistance, of the government. As subnational organizations multiply and expand, their role becomes increasingly complex. The interlocking of interests among organizations can account for a temporary conjunction of controls that leads to a tremendous concentration of power, possibly larger than the government can counter. In countries that are still populated largely by illiterates and where communications and transportation are somewhat limited, the activities of most subnational organizations can generally be controlled if the government has sufficient knowledge and sufficient interest in doing so.

DERIVATIVE POWER FROM EXTERNAL SOURCES

When Fidel Castro was faced with the question of how to sustain a country that had been almost entirely within the economic system of the United States without resorting to any aid at all from the United States, he turned to Russia. That country, having failed to support Guatemala when she attempted the same thing in a much cruder and less organized way, had learned from experience and immediately provided the needed support for Cuba. Thus, Castro rejected one derivative power source (the United States) and then accepted another. Cuba moved from what was essentially an inferior position within the unique power domain of the United States to one in which she was under the multiple domains of Russia and the United States. The latter could, presumably, still exercise fairly severe economic, political, and military sanctions. Their effect, however, could be neutralized by aid from Russia; and at a later date, even the United States military threat was countered to some degree by counterthreats from Russia.

The missile crisis of 1962 provided the check with reality that permitted Cuba, Russia, the United States, and indeed the world at large to see precisely how much derivative power Cuba could elicit from Russia. No one could predict until that time how much power Cuba might expect the United States to exercise. Castro clearly found the presence of a hostile major power of some convenience both internally and externally. It permitted him to press home local reforms with greater vigor and to elicit greater aid from Russia and China to defend his developing communist regime.

While England, France, and the Netherlands retained political control of portions of the Western Hemisphere, the move by Cuba was the first major political break in what had since World War II been a fairly exclusive power domain exercised by the United States over much of Latin America. Since Latin America's period of independence in the early nineteenth century, when the United States was generally regarded as a model of constitutional democracy and freedom, the United States had been transformed by a profound industrial revolution and had changed greatly.

The constitutional form of government, as established by the United States, had proved to be amazingly well-designed and viable for a country that was to span a continent and rise from a backward set of colonies to a world power in the space of one hundred and fifty years. Urban populations exploded, the standard of living rose, a distinctive middle class emerged, through sheer abundance wealth became widespread, labor organizations gradually gained both legality and protection, and free enterprise emerged as something of a national symbol. The rapid economic development of the United States occurred in a period when the lands adjacent to the expanding western frontier were occupied principally by Indians, a population whose culture was so technologically inferior that it could be conquered militarily.

Economic development was a major process in this evolution, with the rapid development of technology being shared between the European powers and the United States. The success of the United States over this period gave rise to the notion that the way of life it had generated was particularly suited to the problems of development, and that democratic political processes, coupled with economic free enterprise, should also be good for other areas. By the end of the nineteenth century, the United States was willing to endorse this view and to terminate the Spanish colonial empire in the New World and the Far East. A few decades later, some of the smaller Latin American countries were unable to pay their debts and the United States intervened directly, with military force. From the standpoint of the United States population, these disorganized countries were being granted a favor, since the methods that had proved so effective in the United States were going to be transferred to them. By the time that the United States began to realize that this point of view was really extraordinarily one-sided and instituted the Good Neighbor policy, history had long since been written, and the general distrust of the United States, its methods, and its goals, was thoroughly implanted within Latin America.

Looked at in another way, the actions of the United States and the reactions increasingly elicited from Latin America simply reflected the gradual preeminence of North American power over the entire hemisphere. In the years between the

First and Second World Wars, this preeminence strengthened with increasing United States investments and United States concern for the interests of the investors. The expropriation of the oil installations in Mexico and the opposition to the Marines by Sandino in Nicaragua were among the first major signs that the nations of Latin America were beginning to challenge the right of the United States to exercise its power as loosely as it had. Mexico's action was the result of its conviction that it had developed sufficient independent power to control its own population, that the feeling of the hemisphere was against the traditional position of the United States, and that the Good Neighbor policy would have to be openly thrown out if the United States were to retaliate against its independent moves.

What tipped the scales in Mexico's favor was the threat of what would happen to United States leadership in the hemisphere should the United States react violently. It was the derivative power that Mexico gained from this circumstance that permitted it to depend upon its own insecure independent power to initiate its unprecedented action. It is the nature of derivative power that it cuts two ways. The United States stood, and afterwards continued to stand, in a position of gross military superiority to Mexico. The exercise of this superiority, however, would have destroyed the relationship the United States hoped to maintain with all the nations of the hemisphere. Mexico could, even in an inferior position of independent power, utilize her own situation among inferiors to act as spokesman, to provide a counterthreat, and to succeed in making it inadvisable for the United States to oppose the action.

Derivative power is usually called upon for one of three reasons: (1) to substitute for some needed goods or services that are being withheld by a superior power; (2) to obtain direct aid to counteract the force exercised or threatened by a superior power; and (3) to counter the action, or threat of action, by another power, either independent or derivative, within the same domain.

In Latin America today, strenuous efforts are being made to obtain substitutes for the various existing kinds of dependence upon the United States. The nature of the dependence differs from one instance to another, but a few illustrations will suffice. The welfare of a country with a single export-crop economy is heavily dependent upon the consumer nations and their manipulation of the market. It has been frequently pointed out that all the foreign aid given some countries by the United States can be wiped out by a drop in the price of the crop produced by that country, as happened with coffee in Guatemala. In Brazil, the threat of sudden price drops for coffee has led to a concerted effort to free the country from its former dependence on coffee alone. When the variety of exports—and therefore the variety of markets and consumers—is increased, the dependence of one country on any other country is reduced, and the relative power of the former country is enhanced with respect to the latter.

An important instance of seeking substitutes for dependence has been Cuba's change from almost complete dependence on the United States to a similar dependence upon a few of the communist countries. The kind of control that the United States formerly exercised over Cuba might be crudely categorized as economic, political, and military. Of the three, the economic dependence is all but entirely gone. The political dependence—that is, having the United States at its side in contests with other nations—is completely supplanted by the support provided by the communist countries, the underdeveloped countries of Africa and Asia, and the neighboring countries of Latin America. Militarily, the weapons and skills being provided by Russia and China—coupled with the warnings by Russia about a possible United States attack—are sufficient to neutralize possible action by the United States.

Direct foreign aid to counter the power exercised in a given place is illustrated by both the action of the United States against the government of Arbenz in Guatemala and by the aid being supplied by the communist countries, by way of Cuba, to the guerrilla groups operating in various parts of Latin America. Few countries in Latin America have been able to establish the rather useful position of receiving aid from both the communist and Western blocs so that they may play one off against the other. Asian and African countries are in a better position in this respect, since their colonial position was not within the sphere of the United States.

A very important aspect of the availability of derivative power is the effect it has on the internal power position of a government. Power coming from outside the system can be used inside the system. Thus the stability of the government of Bolivia has for some years depended upon the derived power of the United States aid. The power provided Castro by Russia has given Cuba a real chance to organize on a much more independent footing than was possible under the commercial control of the United States. The United States gives military aid to many Latin American countries so that they may have derivative power to counteract communist organization. The expropriation by Mexico of the oil establishment was based on both independent power and derived power, but the act provided Mexico with a significant strengthening of its independent power. In a sense, Mexico emerged as a full-scale nation during the presidency of Cárdenas, since it was during his term of office that it succeeded in challenging both the internal landowners and the external foreign interests. Perón's success in Argentina was dependent in considerable measure upon his coupling of a challenge to the landowners within the country with an outspoken challenge to the hegemony of the United States within the hemisphere. Chile's current (1965) effort to become part owner of the mining interests parallels this process, but in a much less belligerent way.

The relationship between the exercise of internal and external power is a crucial part of the general process of nationalization that characterizes Latin American countries today.

But what is often not admitted (perhaps simply for nationalistic reasons) is that the sovereignty of a developing nation is heavily dependent upon the kinds of external relations it maintains and the kinds of derivative power it can hope to manipulate. The success of nationalization, then, is in great part determined by a country's international position. The emergence of blocs of nations today provides the basis for obtaining derivative power for nations that otherwise would not have enough independent power to stand alone.

The role of international organizations in this picture varies. Essentially, they are of two kinds: those which are controlled by major powers and are thereby channels of derivative power stemming from those nations, and those which are constructs of the less developed nations and therefore may attempt to combine the independent power of weaker states to achieve jointly a degree of strength that they cannot hope to obtain alone.

In the first category are the United Nations and the Organization of American States. There is no question that these organizations are essentially controlled by the major powers. (This assertion does not deny other important qualities they have; however, here we are concerned principally with power.) For the most part, the United States has succeeded in controlling the OAS so that its political action is seldom at variance with United States policy. Within the hemisphere, the United Nations has proved to be politically less important, since the OAS exercises many of its functions.

In the second category of international organizations are the Latin American Free Trade Association and the Central American Common Market, both established under the sponsorship of the United Nations Economic Commission for Latin America. Since the United States is not a member of either of these organizations and since both were formed to provide better economic circumstances for the members, it is obvious that the policies developed by them need not in all respects be entirely beneficial to the United States. Since, however, it is to the benefit of the United States to have relatively strong sovereign powers within the hemisphere, these organizations receive various kinds of support from the United States. One feature of these associations is that their members are governments, not private investors. The power implications of this fact simply reflect what I have already said about the central position of Latin American governments.

The final, and most important, aspect of the derivation of power from external sources, both national and international, is that these sources provide power for entities other than governments. Thus, the subnational group or the population that seeks access to power to better its position may find it outside the country if it is not available inside. Potential guerrillas can now turn to Cuba for aid and training, and private individuals may turn to many agencies in the United States and elsewhere for a variety of aid. Among all the kinds of aid most broadly offered by the United States thus far, however, relatively little has been directed to subnational organizations that are or might be central to the interests of large masses of the lower sector of the population. The United States has thus far felt that its primary responsibility in Latin America is to the governments and to private investors. Lower-sector groups, failing to find derivative power offered them by their own governments, are finding it necessary to turn to the outside. Currently, they are finding the United States superficially willing, but usually tactically unable.

Society,
the Individual,
and Government

~~~~~~

A central thesis of this volume is that the evolution of culture in Latin America is producing a system in which the government plays an increasingly prominent and powerful role. It does not follow that this system is necessarily totalitarian, since governments can operate in response to the pressures and preferences of organized interest groups. The term "interest group" here refers to all of the many kinds of associations—no matter what their bases of organization—that foster collective or organized action by individuals who share some common or complementary interests. Government here is seen in the same light as Bendix sees it, in that "society and government are partly interdependent and partly autonomous spheres of social life." The secondary development that has evolved during the past two hundred years in Latin America is coupled with the now multiplying and expanding power bases within the countries and with the growing foreign power domains. Latin American governments thus face a limited number of alternatives. They may grow strong enough to hold their own against the competing internal powers, in which case, by definition, they are able to exercise more power than any of the particular power entities. They may succeed in this internal growth but also depend heavily on a single external source for derivative power and thereby become partially subverted to the interests of that power. Or they may simply go out of business, either through a coup or through a major revolution. Any government that follows, faces the same alternatives all over again.

The present situation is not merely one of change in the role of the government, but rather one that alters all the major relationships within the society, as also the entire structure of those relationships. To see how this change occurs, I shall focus on three phases: the society, the individual, and the government.

Society

The characteristic change in contemporary Latin American society is the breakdown of the internal structure of segments that have essentially constituted the entire body politic. Latin America of both the colonial and nineteenth-century republican eras was composed of segments of population. Although variously controlled, the segments were similar in that they were treated as separate units; the government treated with them through some recognized leader of an intermediate articulating entity. In the colonial period, the government, while reasonably strong, was distant from most populations; whereas in the first half of the republican period, governments were more numerous and therefore more accessible, but relatively weaker. The past seventy years have seen governmental strength increase. The structure of the emerging society can be seen more easily as a network of relationships between individuals and groups than as a series of segments, the network being held together by a government standing as a superior in a power domain.

The breakdown of the older, segmented social organization is being accompanied by the emergence of the individual as a major actor in some instances and by the introduction of new kinds of associations. In part, this emergence and this introduction are due to the increasing power of the government, since the growth of the government power domain makes derivative power increasingly available for both individuals and groups. Not only are there new interests, but the new interests are also expressed in new organizations, which can form because an increasing amount of strong derivative power is available.

If for analysis we set the individual aside as a separate problem, it may be said that these emerging groups—including the residual older groups and the network that relates them collectively—compose the society. A society of this composition obviously has an inherent and extreme disjunction of interests and is very aptly described by Kalman Silvert's term, the "conflict society." The old is competing with the new, and members of the new society are competing with one another. But the situation should not be oversimplified; nor should it be reduced to a simplistic Marxian class-conflict issue. The conflicts are manifest in the struggle of individuals and groups for power; but no part of Latin America has become so simple in structure that the society has developed into two competing class-conscious sectors.

The duality within Latin American society does not segment the whole into two active classes; it provides, essentially, two different views of life, two different systems of value priorities, and two different modes of obtaining these values. The dual sectors overlap in terms of economic status; there are individuals in the lower sector who are far wealthier than some in the upper sector. But the traditional ways of life, the subcultures of the two sectors, have different central foci. The overlap may also manifest itself when individuals who are comparatively poor take on the values of the upper sector and apply them to the situations in which they live. One result is a lack of interest in working more than is absolutely necessary to survive from day to day.

In addition to the general value dichotomy of the society, in every specific locale may be found a local view on how the society is composed. It is at the local level that the expression "middle class" may be found. Except in a few places like urban Argentina, the referent is often not a middle class but an arbitrarily sliced socioeconomic stratum characteristic of the specific locale. Hence in larger municipal capitals there are individuals or families that can, on the basis of some arbitrary criterion such as income or occupation, be set off as a middle stratum. The lack of a national or countrywide classification is reflected in the fact that almost everywhere it is possible to identify a local upper stratum which has its direct-kin and friendship connections with the urban middle stratum, not the urban upper one. Such provincial views are due, at least in part, to the absence of a national system of formal education that can succeed in inculcating a common folk view of the social order. The system therefore differs from that of the United States, but the two may be expected to become more alike as formal education spreads in Latin America.

THE INDIVIDUAL

The individual Latin American finds himself in a situation of apparent extreme social contrasts and contradictions. Because of the variety of socioeconomic strata, because of the dichotomy of value systems and of the means of achieving those values, and because of the multiplicity of specific groups and associations, the individual who enters the area of national activity is forced to participate in more than one such association and, in many instances, in a large number of them. In that they are not all coherent and have conflicting overt goals, the individual himself must find coherence in the pattern or seek it in some other available system of general meaning, in an ideology.

Unquestionably, the ideology most prevalent in Latin America today is a brand of nationalism in which the individual identifies himself with the nation but separates himself from the government. Patriotism to the average nationalistic Latin American is seen in somewhat the same light as the military sees it. One is patriotic to the nation but not to its government. To elicit loyalty, a government must be personally satisfying, no matter how lofty or low one's personal interests may be.

The multiplicity of associations in which the Latin American of today finds himself has, in one of its aspects, been referred to for years by sociologists and anthropologists as an increase in achieved roles. It especially involves individuals in the upper sector, and it is there that the question of identifying with an ideology has become most important. A number of ideologies are available, and, while they are substantively conflicting and exclusive, several of them may be pursued by the same individual. Leeds has observed how the ambitious politician in Brazil does not hesitate to use a far-left ideology as a means of obtaining political support early in his career, only to shed it for a more nationalistic garb as he becomes more successful and then, once he is in power, even to turn toward strong conservatism. Sometimes the change is in the other direction. Fidel Castro, in his guerrilla days, professed to be against extreme socialism; but after taking power, he reported that, in fact, he had always been a communist. Whether Castro's statement was true cannot be determined now, but there is certainly reason to acknowledge that he knew the usefulness of his earlier professed ideology at the time in his career when he needed support from sectors of the Western world. And Castro today shares with all Latin American leaders the disquieting thought that many of his officials, especially minor ones, would be as willing to support and work for someone else if it would gain them more personally.

There is no single ideology of nationalism in Latin America, but there is a variety of ideas and professions, and they can be called upon for a number of sometimes conflicting purposes. The nationalist instigates a revolution in the name of the nation, and the government defends itself in the same name. As an ideology, nationalism must be kept analytically distinct from the processes of change I am describing here. It may be said to be the predominant ideology today; it may even be, as has been claimed by some, the ideology of the mestizo, although such a claim seems to me to jumble further a series of already jumbled concepts. But is is certainly the only broadly accepted ideology over the entire continent. The extreme Eastern-bloc version of socialism or a United States version of capitalism are both generally unacceptable, unless set well within a nationalistic frame.

Also of particular importance in the upper sector is the behavior of individuals with respect to the power system. Power is seen by the individual to be the major means of obtaining the values and prestige symbols of the society, wherefore most of the time he is deeply involved in regulating, adjusting, and trying to improve his access to power and in utilizing any position he has in terms of its power content. An official in a small rural post office, a functionary in the third outer office of a government minister, or the conductor on a bus may decide that the person before him must be made to recognize the power that he as an official holds over him.

Mobility, too, is a characteristic principally of the upper sector. The individual achieves it by expanding his range of friends and acquaintances and by carefully utilizing them and any other immediately available individuals who can help him. However, this society is not, as it may sound, a society in which everyone is struggling to advance; one must agree with Benjamin Higgins that "Vertical mobility may be an important aspect of economic development and may have significant social repercussions, but it is not in any sense a cause of economic growth." Mobility occurs more commonly between generations than within them; and where it does occur within, it is often accompanied by geographical movement. The mobility of the individual depends upon his ability to obtain access to power, and when he does not already have some basis upon which to build, the government offers the largest single block of accessible power in sight.

GOVERNMENT

What is happening to the individual complements what is happening to the government. Basically, the government is centralizing the control of power and increasing the scope of its control over an increasing number of the nation's activities. This control obviously does not always involve actual ownership and operation but effective direction under the law. Because the individual may place his loyalty in the nation instead of in the government, the government must retain itself in power through the careful selection of officers and employees who will support the regime in power. The assertion that civil service is a "must" in Latin America may be a sensible one in terms of bureaucratic efficiency, but civil service means a severe political threat for some governments. Centralizing control always means internal control of the structure as well as control over the various parts of the nation.

The ability of a Latin American government to stay in power is usually calculated in terms of how well it satisfies the currently active organized interest groups and associations of individuals. The fact that the groups involved may represent but a very minor part of the total population of the country is, of course, the central problem in the long-range view. It will be remembered that a thesis of this volume is that power is so very important in Latin America specifically because it is not widely distributed. Were it more widely held, then the power of different individuals and groups could be balanced, one against another, each taking advantage of the tactical situation to better its own situation and each, over a period of time, being thus enabled to accomplish some improvement.

The government that operates primarily through subnational organizations is faced with problems peculiar to that system. In the first place, not all such organizations can be readily used by the government; some are even a severe embarrassment to it. Second, it is often very difficult to form an organization in a locale where a unique domain has long been in power. The initiation of a labor union on a large plantation whose owner resists it and is also strong in the government obviously presents problems. Third, there is no way to be absolutely sure that the organizations that are formed or so incorporated will remain responsive solely to the needs of their members. It is possible and common that they will find some other power domain besides the government to which they may turn—for example, some foreign power. It is thus that associations become "subverted" and sometimes inadvertently act as fronts for groups that do not want to work through the incumbent government but are trying to eliminate it. The problem of subversion arises when the system of multiple channels is working imperfectly. If the organization has access to governmental power to satisfy its needs and if it is sufficiently dependent upon the government for its purposes, then it will not very likely turn elsewhere. The question of establishing such organizations, however, and of using ones that have been established for other purposes, is a tactical matter that cannot be treated here. The major problem lies in whether or not the government has both the skill and the commitment to use such a method.

North American political analyses of governments often emphasize the number of political parties and the degree to which the individual has access to regular voting procedures. Even in the United States, however, where voting generally provides an expression of the voice of the people in government, the vote has lost some of its effectiveness in almost every state in the union through disproportionate representation of urban and rural populations or through the constraints placed on Negro voting in the South. There seems to be no question that the validity of voting depends on a number of circumstances: a relatively high degree of politicization, effective communication, and recognition of the legitimacy of the instituted governmental procedures. Above all, however—as is so well illustrated in both North American and Latin American countries—the government must accept and protect voting as a means of expression and not merely as a political ritual. Where the government does not provide this protection, voting takes on other functions. In Mexico, voting is less a way for voters to express their preferences than it is a way in which the government may change regularly without resorting to violence.

The Mexican system, however, has a degree and kind of representation that is not necessarily achieved in the North American two-party system. The Mexican political party is composed of sectors that include all the major occupational elements of the population. The strength of each sector is not necessarily proportional to the number of members. Although frequently certain sectors may not be heard, on many occasions the government will take action in behalf of some group that seems to warrant it. The decision of the Mexican president on the distribution of additional agricultural land is not determined primarily by how loudly the campesino is yelling. This situation may be contrasted to that in the United States, where Negroes have had to resort to public demonstrations in order to be heard by the government.

The sector system of the Mexican political party makes it possible for organizations of people to have their interests constantly represented by both a party and an internal group. The system provides one way for subnational organizations to channel power both up and down. The individual is not heard as an individual, but his interest will be heard as an expression of the organization to which he pertains. This representation is, in many respects, equivalent to the voice of the people as expressed through American political parties. One difference is that when division on an issue occurs in the two-party system, almost half the population will go away dissatisfied. The one-party system, insofar as it is viable and its sectors representative (and insofar as it actively recognizes the problems of development), may over the long run provide more extensive satisfaction for a majority of the people.

Another important distinction between the two kinds of systems lies in the differing responsibilities of the governments. In the United States, development is still very much in the hands of private interests, although the government does steer it to some degree by the allocation of contracts for different kinds of specific problems. Latin American governments, for the reasons discussed earlier, must take a greater responsibility in the development of the nation than has been the case historically in the United States.

Besides the one-party and two-party systems, there is also the system now operating in Cuba under which the government eliminates all competitive subnational organizations through revolution and establishes in their place an entirely new structure by which the government controls all the power. While this kind of situation can be achieved, there is serious question as to whether economic development can be carried out in it unless external competition in the international environment is greatly reduced, as was the case to some degree following the Russian Revolution. Lacking this contingency, the country in question must have access to an enormous amount of derivative power in order to guarantee its protection during the years necessary to make the shift to internal consolidation. Cuba's current progress is clearly dependent on the extraordinary derivative power provided by the communist countries. Bolivia's survival has been in great part due to massive amounts of United States economic aid. Guatemala's government under Arévalo and Arbenz failed, partly because it was unable to get this kind of help from any source. However, such aid is now becoming increasingly available to Latin American countries.

Whatever the system of government, the only real alternative that a government has under the conditions of secondary development is to become as strong as it can, to take advantage of all accessible derivative power, and to push economic development as rapidly as possible in order to increase the amount of its independent power. Given this kind of goal, the particular political philosophy chosen for the task may be a matter of ideological persuasion or of tactical convenience.

POSTSCRIPT

A Policy for Social Change

〰〰〰〰〰〰〰〰〰〰〰〰〰〰〰〰〰〰〰〰〰〰〰

The major purpose of this book has been to set forth some observations and their analyses, and thereby to suggest some features important in understanding Latin America today. It has not, until now, been my purpose to consider recommendations, since these, quite naturally, depend upon one's preference for the shape of the world. There is, however, a wide gap between understanding as a mental exercise and understanding as a basis for overt behavior. There is much in the model of Latin America that leads to pessimism, and it is easy to conclude that little can be done for improvement. It is my preference, however, to attempt to bridge the gap between the two types of understanding and in a modest way to advance a policy for social change. My discussion is based on the assumption that the United States has manifest ambiguities in its foreign and domestic policies and that these ambiguities reflect the fact that our ideals are themselves conflicting. The United States is at once a capitalist nation of primary development and a conveyer of notions about the condition of man. It is a concern for the condition of man that generates this postscript.

A crucial deficiency in the development of Latin America has been the failure to develop the lower sector. In this secondary-development area where much of the countryside continues to be an economic hinterland, the entire concern for development has been in the upper sector. Aside from receiving charity and enjoying public works, the lower sector continues to have almost no access to the fruits of development. The nature of both public works and charity is the product of choices made by the upper sector as to what is good for people. While the decisions may be well made, it is also true that much that the lower sector most needs goes unrecognized. The reason that the lower sector has so little access to power is implicit in the system: It is the lower sector because it has no power; it cannot effectively compete with the upper sector because the power lies primarily at the top. Power is allowed the lower sector only when it is seen to be to the advantage of the upper sector to permit it.

It has been the overt policy of the United States to leave it to the discretion of the Latin American upper sector to decide what is good for the lower sector. Pressure has been applied to encourage distribution of land, but not to reform the tenure system. Similarly, emphasis has been placed on the ample collection of taxes, but not upon representation. The United States has failed to see that it is to her advantage to encourage the lower sector to reach for power so that it can directly compete for the fruits of development. If left to the upper sector, development itself will be inhibited and the lower sector will continue to share but little in the process.

The socialist nations have taken the lead in encouraging the lower sector to take things into its own hands if it is to participate in development. Violent revolution is encouraged because it is the easiest way to reverse the components in the power system and to completely alter it. The socialist revolution, however, institutes a power system that again places the lower-sector individual in a position of no power. The dictatorship of the proletariat is nonetheless a dictatorship. The United States has tended to confuse the process of widening power distribution with a revolution that inverts it, and has therefore feared to leave it up to the lower sector to make some decisions in its own behalf. But the problem of power distribution should be viewed realistically: encouraging people to reach for power means placing it within their grasp and enabling them to use it, whether skillfully or not. Once they have it, they will naturally use it to their own advantage.

Development in Latin America has generally meant the expansion of the upper sector and an elaboration of its structure. Upper-sector interest groups have multiplied, whereas there has been very little successful and continuing organizing in the lower sector. Mexico, Bolivia, Perón's Argentina, and the Guatemala of Arévalo and Arbenz have been the major areas of lower-sector organization, but the organizations in the last two, if not three, have been failures.[1] Few governments have had sufficient power, independent of upper-sector interests, to take a firm stand in promoting lower-sector organization. The consequence is that few organizations have emerged.

Fundamentally, the lower sector needs to gain power. The fact that most power is concentrated in the upper sector means that the only way the situation can be reversed is through the mobilization of the power latent in the lower sector. It will be remembered that one facet of any power structure is that some power always exists in both sides of the relationship. While the upper sector clearly has dominant control, it is also the case that the lower sector has within its grasp power that could only be exercised if it were organized. It lies within the control of the lower sector to withhold certain factors of production, to deny

---

[1] See Bibliographic Notes, p. 273.

certain services central to the way of life of the upper sector. But this control can be applied only if the lower sector is organized. It can be applied without some kind of violence only if the lower sector is provided with the organization, the skills, and sufficient resources to permit survival through the inevitable period of conflict that would accompany the effort. Organization in this sense implies training and development of leadership. Resources are necessary since individuals participating in the effort would be placed under special constraints.

Most important, however, is the fact that there must be a source of derivative power that will permit the lower sector to achieve a position from which it can bargain for its interests and make gains without having to resort to violent revolution. As it stands, a government is the only possible source of such power and the only possible sovereign entity that can play the role with continuity.

The argument used by the upper sector against the promotion of such lower-sector organizations is that they would endanger capitalistic economic development. The answer to this argument is simply that if such organizations are not able to introduce serious competition for power, there will be repeated and continuing attempts—some of which must be successful— to eliminate capitalism entirely. Violent revolution is the way in which this elimination will be ultimately accomplished, just as it is currently being used in various parts of the world.

Why not recommend violent revolution? I hesitate to recommend it not merely because of my own cultural prejudices, but because inherent in it is uncertain success and the need to gamble with forces that are extremely dangerous to human survival. Violent revolution is a social invention, and as is the case with any invention, it is possible to invent countermeasures. The effectiveness of revolutions is uncertain because the capitalist nations are probably inventing countermeasures more rapidly than inventions for revolution are being made in the socialist sector. An even greater disadvantage is that violence, whether through organized war or otherwise, always means loss of control. One or both parties lose power, and when this loss occurs, the most natural reaction is to resort to extreme measures. The case against violent revolution today is not merely a consideration of the incalculable loss implicit in the unnecessary death of even a single human being, but also the realization that it is a constant gamble with the possibilities of massive nuclear warfare. Neither the West nor the East can afford to play this game continuously. It is crucial that other means for achieving power be developed.

Obviously the successful organization of interest groups within the lower sector of Latin America cannot be achieved solely by an alteration in the foreign policy of the United States. Currently, however, lower-sector development is being hindered through the lack of a relevant United States policy. While lower-sector development must ultimately and substantially rely on the national governments concerned, the direction and quality of United States economic, military, and political policy can have material influence. The most serious question on which this recommendation hangs is whether the United States is capable of a policy favorable to the Latin American lower sector. Put in simplest terms, the lower sector of Latin America has no lobby in Washington. This fact might be of little consequence were it not true that the upper sector has an extremely strong lobby, both because its economic interests coincide with those of United States entrepreneurs and because its political and military preferences coincide with the extraordinary fear of communism that pervades so much of the United States thinking. Irrespective of the historic traditions of the United States, its foreign interests, as currently interpreted, closely parallel those of the contemporary Latin American upper sector.

Only recently has poverty become an open issue for policy makers in Washington, and it has not yet dominated their thinking about Latin America. Insofar as the United States can do anything to help the Latin American lower sector, the decision for action must rest with Latin American governments. Providing rights for southern Negroes is certainly congruent with seeking similar representation for millions of campesinos in their own countries. Nothing in the historic ideology of the United States holds that the benefit of foreign investment to the investors should outweigh its benefits to the total population. The United States, however, in an extension of nineteenth-century hinterland liberalism, has shown little interest in whether its investors were seeing to these benefits or not. Certain commercial companies have promoted efforts within their specific area of interest, but the fact that the Latin American lower sector has not been within the United States domain has meant that it could not react to the same authorities to which the United States foreign interests had to respond. Management in Latin America could resort to United States derivative power; labor and campesinos could not. In recent years, the inaction of the United States has been further rationalized through the argument that campesino support would lead to strengthening the position of China or Russia in the hemisphere. The United States government, under existing pressure from upper-sector interest groups, finds it difficult to promote openly a position such as is suggested here. But presumably the issue is not whether it is the easy thing to do, but rather whether it is the wise and necessary thing to do.

If a government as strong as that of the United States finds itself unable to make wise decisions independently of the pressures of some of its citizens, then it can hardly criticize the governments of Latin America for the same failure. If the United States is to have a policy in Latin America, it must be a policy that is illustrated by the behavior of the United States itself. So long as predominantly upper-sector interests determine the foreign policy of the United States, the lower sector of Latin America will find increasingly attractive the alternative of violent revolution.

BIBLIOGRAPHIC NOTES

~~~~~~

The following comments are not intended to be a thorough reading list on the subjects touched on in this volume, but are intended instead to indicate some sources of the ideas propounded, and to provide references to the principal works that have, so far as I am aware, played a role in their development. For a general reading list on Latin America, the bibliography and the topical lists in the recent collection edited by Dwight Heath and myself, *Contemporary Cultures and Societies of Latin America* (New York: Random House), 1965, together with the annual volume of the *Handbook of Latin American Studies* (Gainesville: University of Florida Press) will provide a base. To these books may be added the new periodical *Latin American Research Review* (currently issued at the Institute of Latin American Studies, University of Texas).

FOREWORD (pp. xi–xiv). The essay on Guatemala appeared in the volume *Social Change in Latin America Today* (New York: Council on Foreign Relations), 1960, and is in paperback (Vintage Books), 1960.

CHAPTER 1. SECONDARY DEVELOPMENT AND CULTURAL EVOLUTION (pp. 1–29). On the nature of cultural evolution, the best brief statement is that by Marshall Sahlins in Marshall Sahlins and Elman Service, editors, *Evolution and Culture* (Ann Arbor: University of Michigan Press), 1960. The essays by Leslie A. White in *The Science of Culture* (New York: Grove Press), 1949, and by Julian Steward in *Theory of Culture Change* (Urbana: University of Illinois Press),

1955, are both central to the subject. For an expression of the general evolutionary position that I am trying to avoid, see the various works of Robert Redfield, especially *The Folk Culture of Yucatan* (Chicago: University of Chicago Press), 1939, and *The Primitive World and Its Transformations* (Ithaca: Cornell University Press), 1953. On the evolution of culture in Latin America, the material on pre-Columbian patterns is taken from various works by Wendell Bennett, Pedro Armillas, Angel Palerm, Eric Wolf, and many others. George Foster's notion of "conquest culture" appears in his *Culture and Conquest: America's Spanish Heritage* (New York: Viking Fund Publications in Anthropology No. 27), 1960. On the concept of "Nuclear America," see Gordon R. Willey, "The Prehistoric Civilizations of Nuclear America," *American Anthropologist*, 57(3):571–593, 1955. For general reviews, see the papers in Robert Wauchope, editor, *Handbook of Middle American Indians*, Vol. 1 (Austin: University of Texas Press), 1965. On imperial patterns in Latin America, see the papers by George Kubler and John Rowe in Julian Steward, editor, *The Andean Civilizations*, Vol. 2 of *Handbook of South American Indians* (Washington, D.C.: Bureau of American Ethnology, Bulletin 143, 1946, and the general summary by Julian Steward and Louis Faron, *Native Peoples of South America* (New York: McGraw-Hill), 1959. Kalervo Oberg's paper, "Types of Social Structure among the Lowland Tribes of South and Central America," *American Anthropologist*, 57(3):472–487, 1955, and Elman Service, *Primitive Social Organization* (New York: Random House), 1962, are also relevant.

On the concept of secondary development there is no particular background material aside from the growing literature on economic development and its sociological problems in underdeveloped regions. For comparison, consult Pablo González Casanova's paper "Sociedad Plural, Colonialismo Interno y Desarrollo," *América Latina*, 6(3):15–32, July–September 1963, and a volume by Andrew Gundar Frank on the economic history of Latin America currently in press with the Monthly Review Press (New York). Fairly crucial as background material is Homer Barnett's *Innovation* (New York: McGraw-Hill), 1953, which takes the position sustained here that the difference between invention and diffusion, between an idea that appears from within a society and one that comes in from the outside is for many purposes not a significant difference.

CHAPTER 2. POWER (pp. 31–46). The concept of power that dominates most of the political-science and sociological literature is that of Max Weber, which may be found in his *The Theory of Social and Economic Organization* (New York: Oxford University Press), 1947. The concept of power used in the present book is derived principally from the fields of ecology and evolution. On the sequence of change that occurs when power increases in an otherwise steady-state society, see Charles Erasmus, *Man Takes Control* (Minneapolis: University of Minnesota Press), 1961, Richard Salisbury, *From Stone to Steel, Economic Consequences of a Technological Change in New Guinea* (Cambridge: Cambridge University Press), 1962, and possibly Cyril Northcote Parkinson, *Parkinson's Law* (Boston: Houghton Mifflin), 1957. Somewhat more detailed papers on the subject are my own "Power and Power Domains," *América Latina*, in press, and "Rural Labor in Latin America," in J. J. Johnson, editor, *Continuity and Change in Latin America* (Stanford: Stanford University Press), 1964.

CHAPTER 3. DUAL SECTORS (pp. 47–69). Concern with the "middle sector" marks J. J. Johnson's *Political Change in Latin America* (Stanford: Stanford University Press), 1958. John Gillin in various of his perceptive papers, and Charles Wagley, with particular reference to Brazil, have also devoted some time to exploring the emerging middle culture. Ralph Beals, "Social Stratification in Latin America," *The American Journal of Sociology*, 58(4):327–339, January 1953, is still a good review of basic material of that time. Lowry Nelson, *Rural Cuba* (Minneapolis), 1950, is one of the few who clearly recognized the continuing dual sectors. Andrew Whiteford's study that is cited a number of times is *Two Cities of Latin America* (New York: Doubleday), 1964. The Melvin Tumin and Arnold Feldman study is *Social Class and Social Change in Puerto Rico* (Princeton: Princeton University Press), 1961, and the quotation is from p. 324. Bertram Hutchinson discusses subjective allocation of individuals into classes in "Class Self-assessment in a Rio de Janeiro population," *América Latina*, 6(1):53–64, 1963. The kind of middle-class allocation made by Whiteford, Tumin, and Feldman is also made by Eugene Hammel in *Wealth, Authority, and Prestige in the Ica Valley, Peru* (Albuquerque: University of New Mexico Publications in Anthropology No. 10), 1962. Oscar Lewis's important paper is "Urbanization Without Breakdown," *Scientific Monthly,* 57: 31–41, July 1952. The quotation is from "The culture of the vecindad in Mexico City: Two Case Studies," *Actas del XXXIII Congreso Internacional de Americanistas,* 1:387–402. Among the papers on the question of rural-urban migrants, see Douglas S. Butterworth, "A study of the urbanization process among Mixtec migrants from Tilantongo in Mexico City," *América Indígena,* 22(3):254–274, 1962; William Mangin, "Cultural and psychological characteristics of mountain migrants to Lima, Peru," *Sociologus,* 14(1):81–88; the many papers in Philip M. Hauser, editor, *Urbanization in Latin America* (New York: International Documents Service, Columbia University Press), 1961; and Arnold Strickon, "Class and Kinship in Argentina," *Ethnology,* 1(4):500–515. For the effect of nearby urban centers on villages, see Ralph Beals, "Acculturation, economics and social change in an Ecuadorian Village" (Proceedings and Selected Papers of the 29th International Congress of Americanists) in Sol Tax, editor, *Acculturation in the Americas* (Chicago: University of Chicago Press), 1952; and Rubén Reina, *Chinautla, A Guatemalan Indian Community* (New Orleans: Tulane University, the Middle American Research Institute), 1960. Albert O. Hirschman's observations are in his *The Strategy of Economic Development* (New Haven: Yale University Press), 1958. The Whiteford quotation is from *op. cit.,* p. 166. Eric Wolf used the expression "power seekers" in *Sons of the Shaking Earth* (Chicago: University of Chicago Press), 1959. Anthony Leeds's paper is "Brazilian Careers and Social Structure: An Evolutionary Model and Case History," *American Anthropologist,* 66(6):1321–1347, 1964, and is also in Heath and Adams, *Contemporary Cultures and Societies of Latin America.* The di Tella study is that of Thomas C. Cochran and Rubén Reina, *Entrepreneurship in Argentine Culture* (Philadelphia: University of Pennsylvania Press), 1962. The W. Paul Strassmann quotation is from "The Industrialist" in J. J. Johnson, editor, *Continuity and Change in Latin America* (Stanford: Stanford University Press), 1964, pp. 161–185. The Kerr quotation is also cited in Johnson. The material from Gino Germani is from his "Inquiry into the Social Effects of Urbanization in a Working-class Sector of Greater Buenos Aires," in *Urbanization in Latin America,* edited by Philip M. Hauser (New York: International Documents Service, Columbia University Press), 1961. The reference to Raymond Vernon is to his *The Dilemma of Mexico's Development* (Cambridge: Harvard University Press), 1963.

CHAPTER 4. TECHNOLOGY AND THE LAND (pp. 73–89). The Middle American symposium was edited by Sol Tax as *Heritage of Conquest* (Glencoe: The Free Press), 1962. The A. O. Hirschman quotation comes from *The Strategy of Economic Development* (New Haven: Yale University Press), 1958, p. 129. Oscar Lewis's hoe-plow comparison appeared in *Life in a Mexican Village* (Urbana: University of Illinois Press), 1951, p. 154–157. The Venezuelan implement comparison appears in George W. Hill, et al., *La vida rural en Venezuela* (Caracas: Ministerio de Agricultura y Cría), 1960. The term "speculative agriculture" was first discussed by Frances Le Beau in "Economía Indígena," in *Integración Social en Guatemala* (Seminario de Integración Social Guatemalteca Publication No. 3), 1956. The Latin American view on agrarian reform referred to here is illustrated in Oscar Delgado's paper "Revolución, reforma, y conservatismo como tipos de políticas agrarias en Latinoamérica," *Universidad Libre* (Bogotá), IV(15):3–41, 1963.

CHAPTER 5. BASIC AGRARIAN ADAPTATION (pp. 91–108). Certain material in this chapter has been taken from the author's "Rural Labor," in J. J. Johnson, editor, *Continuity and Change in Latin America* (Stanford: Stanford University Press), 1964. The material on Bolivian Indians and campesinos is from Richard Patch, "Bolivia: United States Assistance in a Revolutionary Setting" in *Social Change in Latin America Today* (New York: Published for the Council on Foreign Relations by Harper and Brothers), 1960. The Santander sharecropping description is from Roberto Pineda Giraldo, *Seguridad Social Campesina* (Bogotá: Ministerio del Trabajo), 1955. On exchange labor see Charles Erasmus in Heath and Adams, *Contemporary Cultures and Societies of Latin America,* pp. 173–199. The crop information comes from Elman and Helen Service, *Tobatí: Paraguayan Town* (Chicago: University of Chicago Press), 1954; Orlando

Fals-Borda, *Peasant Society in the Colombian Andes: A Sociological Study of Saucío*, (Gainesville: University of Florida Press), 1955; Donald Pierson, *Cruz das Almas: A Brazilian Village* (Washington, D.C.: Smithsonian Institution, Institute of Social Anthropology Publication #12), 1951; and Isabel Kelly and Angel Palerm, *The Tajin Totonac, Part I: History, Subsistence, Shelter and Technology* (Washington, D.C.: Smithsonian Institution, Institute of Social Anthropology Publication #13), 1952. The Vicos hacienda case has been widely described; the most recent appeared in a series of articles in *American Behavioral Scientist*, VIII (7), March 1965. The work of Ofelia Hooper in Panama, from which the term "interior frontiers" is taken, has not, so far as I know, been published. On the peasant leagues in Brazil, see Benno Galjart's "Class and Following in Rural Brazil," *América Latina* VII(3):3–24, 1964.

CHAPTER 6. WORKSHOPS AND INDUSTRIALIZATION (pp. 109–122). Marvin Harris's study is *Town and Country in Brazil* (New York: Columbia University Press), 1956. The regional market systems are described in Luis Valcarcel's "Indian Markets and Fairs in Perú," in Vol. II (*The Andean Civilizations*) of the *Handbook of South American Indians* (Washington, D.C.: Smithsonian Institution), 1947, and in Webster McBryde, *Cultural and Historical Geography of Southwest Guatemala* (Washington, D.C.: Smithsonian Institution, Institute of Social Anthropology Publication #4), 1945. The study of the larger Latin American businesses (in Argentina, Brazil, Chile, Colombia, Mexico, and Venezuela) was Frank Brandenburg's *The Development of Latin American Private Enterprise* (Washington, D.C.: National Planning Association, Planning Pamphlet No. 121), 1964. The Cantel textile factory and the neighboring community was studied by Manning Nash, *Machine Age Maya* (Memoir of the American Anthropological Association, No. 87), 1958. Studies of sugar plantations include those by Sidney Mintz and Elena Padilla that appear in the volume edited by Julian Steward, *The People of Puerto Rico* (Urbana: University of Illinois Press), 1956; Harry Hutchinson, *Village and Plantation Life in Northeastern Brazil* (Seattle: American Ethnological Society, University of Washington Press), 1957; and George W. Hill, et al., *La vida rural en Venezuela*. The study of the Antioquian plant is Charles Savage, *Social*

Reorganization in a Factory in the Andes (Society of Applied Anthropology, Monograph No. 7), 1964. Raymond Vernon's study is *The Dilemma of Mexico's Development* (Cambridge: Harvard University Press), 1963. For a generally valid statement on union development see Bruce H. Millen, *The Political Role of Labor in Developing Countries* (Washington, D.C.: The Brookings Institution), 1963. See also Wilbert Moore's pioneering work, *Industrialization and Labor* (Ithaca: Published for the Institute of World Affairs, New School of Social Research, by Cornell University Press), 1951. Some of the basic problems are taken up in Celso Furtado's paper "Political Obstacles to the Economic Development of Brazil," *Obstacles to Change in Latin America* (London: Published for the Royal Institute of International Relations by Oxford University Press), 1965.

CHAPTER 7. ENTREPRENEURS, ECONOMISTS, AND CAPITAL (pp. 123–134). Much of the thinking in this section has been derived from various works of Daniel Cosio Villegas, Victor Urquidi, Raymond Vernon, W. Paul Strassmann, Celso Furtado, Oswaldo Sunkel, as well as the already cited works of Frank Brandenburg, Reina and Cochran, and Charles Erasmus.

CHAPTER 8. SCIENTIFIC REVOLUTION AND EDUCATION (pp. 135–148). The material that provided much of the basis for this section stems from the study by Charles Cumberland and myself, *United States University Cooperation in Latin America* (East Lansing: Institute of Overseas Research), 1960. John Harrison, "The Role of the Intellectual in Fomenting Change: The University," in John J. TePaske and Sydney Nettleton Fisher, editors, *Explosive Forces in Latin America* (Columbus: Ohio State University), 1964, and various papers by Kalman Silvert in the *American Universities Field Staff Reports* have been particularly relevant.

CHAPTER 9. FAMILY, HOUSEHOLD, AND KINSHIP (pp. 149–160). Much of the basic orientation in this chapter stems from a set of studies carried out by the author's students among Texas Mexican families in Austin and San Marcos, Texas, and in Monterrey, Mexico. George Foster's paper on "The Dyadic Contract," *American Anthropologist*, 63(6):1173–1192, 1961, is relevant and helpful. The family in Brazil has perhaps received more attention than families elsewhere: Thales de Azavedo, "Familia, Casamiento, e Divorcio no Brasil," *Journal of Inter-American Studies*, III(2), April 1961, Gilberto Freyre, *The Masters and the Slaves* (New York: Alfred A. Knopf) 1956; Charles Wagley, *An Introduction to Brazil* (New York: Columbia University Press), 1963. Also relevant are the already cited works of Whiteford, Reina and Cochran, and Strickon.

CHAPTER 10. COMMUNITY, REGION, AND NATION (pp. 161–176). Some of the material in this chapter, either in spirit or in fact, is derived from my two earlier essays: "The Community in Latin America: A Changing Myth," *Centennial Review*, VI(3):409–434, 1962, and "The Latin American Community in Revolution and Development," in *The Community in Revolutionary Latin America* (University of Kansas Center of Latin American Studies Occasional Publications #3), 1964, pp. 5–10. The basic paper by Eric Wolf is "Types of Latin American Peasantry," *American Anthropologist*, 57:452–471, 1955. Also of importance is Wolf's "La Formación de la Nación," *Ciencias Sociales*, 4:50–62, 98–111, 146–171, 1953. Robert Redfield's contributions to the understanding of the community provide something of a backdrop for the present interpretation. Consult his *The Little Community* (Chicago: University of Chicago Press), 1960, and two works on Chan Kom—Robert Redfield and Alfonso Villa Rojas, *Chan Kom: A Maya Village* (Washington, D.C.: Carnegie Institution of Washington Publication #448), 1934; and Robert Redfield, *A Village That Chose Progress: Chan Kom Revisited* (Chicago: University of Chicago Press), 1950.

CHAPTER 11. GOVERNMENT (pp. 177–191). No notes for this chapter.

CHAPTER 12. VIOLENCE AND THE MILITARY (pp. 193–206). This topic has received increasing attention in recent years. The important pioneer work by Edwin Lieuwen, *Arms and Politics in Latin America*, Rev. ed. (New York: Published for the Council on Foreign Relations by Frederick A. Praeger), 1961, is still of value, although theoretically unsound. J. J. Johnson, *The Military and Society in Latin America* (Stanford: Stanford University Press), 1964, contains much good material. Most perceptive has been the work of Lyle McAllister, "The Military," in J. J. Johnson, editor, *Continuity and Change in Latin America* (Stanford: Stanford University Press), 1964. For the reference to Mexican unrest, see Neale J. Pearson, "Latin American Pressure Groups and the Modernization Process," *Journal of International Affairs*, XX (2):312. On the middle class, see the notes to Chapter 3 of this volume.

CHAPTER 13. RELIGIOUS INSTITUTIONS (pp. 207–222). For a general introduction J. Lloyd Mecham's *Church and State in Latin America*, Rev. ed. (Chapel Hill: University of North Carolina Press), 1966, is still the standard work. For a summary of the condition of the church, see François Houtart and Emile Pin, *The Church and the Latin American Revolution* (New York: Sheed and Ward), 1965. In Chapter 14 therein will be found a brief summary of data on religious participation. Although they contribute little to my chapter, I would recommend William D'Antonio and Frederick Pike, editors, *Religion, Revolution and Reform: New Forces for Change in Latin America* (New York: Frederick A. Praeger), 1964, and Ivan Vallier's "Religious Elites in Latin America: Catholicism, Leadership and Social Change," *América Latina* VII(4):93–115, 1965. The estimate of the number of clergy is for 1960; see Houtart and Pin, *op. cit.*, pp. 156–57. Sociological work on this subject is singularly unenlightening.

PART III. No notes for this section.

POSTSCRIPT: A POLICY FOR SOCIAL CHANGE (pp. 267–272). The situation in Cuba requires serious examination. There is clear evidence that Cubans continue to act in matters of self-promotion much as their older upper-sector predecessors did. However, there has been an extensive organization of the lower sector, and both this internal organization and its power relations with the rulers of the country are of special interest to students of secondary development.

INDEX

~~~~~~